Corvette

America's Sports Car

Randy Leffingwell

MOTORBOOKS
INTERNATIONAL

This is for Jim C. Perkins, General Motors vice president and general manager for Chevrolet Motor Division, from 1989 until his retirement in April 1996. The 1997 Corvette was developed under his leadership. No one deserves the dedication of a Corvette history more than Jim Perkins.

This edition first published in 2002 by Motorbooks International, an imprint of MBI Publishing Company, Galtier Plaza, Suite 200, 380 Jackson Street, St. Paul, MN 55101-3885 USA

© Randy Leffingwell, 1997, 2002

Motorbooks International titles are also available at discounts in bulk quantity for industrial or sales-promotional use. For details write to Special Sales Manager at Motorbooks International Wholesalers & Distributors, Galtier Plaza, Suite 200, 380 Jackson Street, St. Paul, MN 55101-3885 USA.

On the front cover: The split rear-window Sting Ray was introduced in 1963 and made a strong design statement. Some thought it was the most beautiful body style ever—others hated it. *David Newhardt*

On the frontispiece: 1988 was a milestone year in Corvette history, representing 35 years of production. A commemorative coupe package, Z01, was offered at a $4,795 price premium. *David Newhardt*

On the title page: On the 1962 production model, side coves were no longer two-tone paint schemes. Even chrome trim was eliminated. These coves subtly disappeared into the car sides, set off only by a single louver. *David Newhardt*

On the back cover: Introduced in 1997, the C5 is Chevrolet's latest incarnation of the immortal American sports car, the Corvette. *David Newhardt*

Library of Congress Cataloging-in-Publication Data Available
ISBN 0-7603-1352-0

Printed in Hong Kong

Contents

Acknowledgments

Very early in the production of this book, Jerry Burton, executive editor, *Corvette Quarterly*, offered wise and solid advice.

I am most grateful to Gary and Eric Mortimer, National Corvette Restorers' Society, Cincinnati, Ohio, for their advice and suggestions. My sincere thanks goes also to *NCRS* editor John Amgwert, Sedona, Arizona, for his exceptional help at the 23rd hour.

Thanks go to many people within Chevrolet Communications. I particularly appreciate generous help and cooperation from Suzanne Kane and Carl Sheffer.

I thank Peter Brock for his recollections and for the loan of his extraordinary drawings produced while he was working in GM Styling. My further thanks go to Gene Garfinkle, similarly, for his recollections and for the use of his most interesting drawings of a variety of Corvette projects during the late 1950s.

I am indebted to the late Zora Arkus-Duntov, Grosse Pointe Woods, Michigan; Reeves Callaway, Old Lyme, Connecticut; Robert Cumberford, Paris, France; Ralph Kramer, vice president of communications, Indianapolis Motor Speedway, Indianapolis, Indiana; Tony Lapine, Baden-Baden, Germany; Gary Laughlin, Dallas, Texas; Strother MacMinn, Pasadena, California; Robert S. Morrison, Ashtabula, Ohio; Bob D'Olivo, Burbank, California; and Carroll Shelby, Los Angeles, California, Larry Shinoda, Livonia, Michigan, for sharing their recollections and reminiscences with me.

I am very grateful to Mark Patrick at the National Automotive History Collection at the Detroit Public Library for his extraordinary cooperation and his wry wit.

I want to thank Maggie Moore, the Dave Friedman Photo Collection, Tustin, California; Byron Olson, Minneapolis, Minnesota; Mike Mueller, Lakeland, Florida; Dale von Trebra, Santa Paula, California; and Bob Tronolone, Burbank, California; for wonderful historical photos that have added greatly to the story of the Corvette.

Many enthusiastic owners and historians provided me access to their cars or introductions to others with automobiles to photograph for this book. Thanks to Chanda Abbott, Ramona, California; Chuck Austin, San Diego, California; Ron Austin, La Mesa, California; Wayne Austin, San Diego, California; Raoul Balcaen, Los Angeles, California; Ron Burgandine, California; Glenn and Deni Bator, Ojai, California; Bob Brown, Bonanza Corvette, San Diego, California; Otis and Bettina Chandler, Ojai, California; Tom Crockatt, California; Charles DeBisschop, La Mesa, California; Darcy Dimuzio, Jamul, California; Steven and Debbie Earle, Monterey Historic Automobile Races, Santa Barbara, California; Mike Ernst, Hales Corner, Wisconsin; Ron Fingerman, San Diego, California; David Finkelstein, San Diego, California; Lisa Foland, Spring Valley, California; Skip Frenzel, San Jose, California; George Goldberg, Inglewood, California; Joseph Heidrick Jr., Woodland, California; Helen V. Hutchings, Thousand Oaks, California; Bruce Jacobson, San Diego, California; Tim and Roni Keiser, Escondido, California; Steve Kotanan, San Diego, California; Jim Lerud, LaMesa, California; Charles Lillard, Woodland, California; Mona and Steve Lucero, San Diego, California; Steve LuVisi, California; Jamey Mazzotta, Redding, California; Mike McCafferty, Borrego Springs, California; Tim McKeon, Canyon Country, California; Rich Mason, Carson City, Nevada; Jim Medina, El Cajon, California; Bruce Meyer, Beverly Hills, California; Ed Mueller, Hawthorne, New Jersey; Charlie Mullins, San Diego, California; Bob Paterson, Woodside, California; Steve Perrin, California; Jeff Reade, Santa Monica, California; Steve Sailors, Huntington Beach, California; Sharon Sceper, Lemon Grove, California; Gene Schiavone, Essex, Connecticut; Dorothy Shirley, McAllister, Oklahoma; Vickie Stanley, El Cajon, California; Detlef Stevenson, Culver City, California; Mike Vietro, "Corvette Mike," Anaheim, California; Carlos and Sherry Vivas, Torrance, California; John Waters, Alpine, California; and Ian Wotherspoon, San Diego, California.

In addition I owe a great debt of gratitude to the enthusiastic and hardworking members of the Corvette Owners Club of San Diego. Under sometimes adverse conditions, they helped and helped. I offer to all of them my sincere appreciation.

Last but far from least, I am most grateful to my friend, photographer David Newhardt, Poway, California. David took over a work in progress and blended his photographic style with what was already started. Many of the best pictures in this book are his.

Randy Leffingwell

Though not an instant favorite when first produced in 1963, the split-window coupe is now arguably the most beautiful Corvette body ever produced.

chapter 1

Abrupt Beginnings: 1953

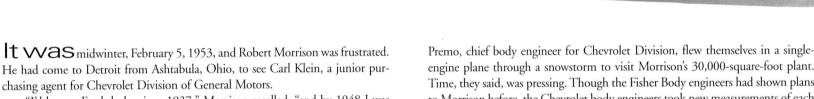

It was midwinter, February 5, 1953, and Robert Morrison was frustrated. He had come to Detroit from Ashtabula, Ohio, to see Carl Klein, a junior purchasing agent for Chevrolet Division of General Motors.

"I'd been a Ford dealer since 1937," Morrison recalled, "and by 1948 I was unhappy with the allocation of cars, so I decided to get out of the Ford business." He thought he was out of the automobile business for good. "With some other investors," he continued, "we developed the Ashtabula Industrial Corporation to provide land and buildings for companies for manufacturing."

When one of the corporation's first tenants failed, Morrison and his partners inherited an undercapitalized ailing operation that produced items made of molded glass, reinforced plastic (GRP). Within a year, Morrison turned things around. He was providing thousands of molded fiberglass bread palettes for Wonder Bread's Continental Baking division. He spun off that business into a tray division. With 12 presses in Ashtabula and 10 more in a satellite operation in nearby Linesville, across the Pennsylvania state line, he was busy.

He and his partners talked about getting into the auto industry, but they concluded, without much sadness, that it was too big and they were too small. Then in late fall 1952, some body engineers came to visit from General Motors' Fisher Body fabrication and assembly division. They had with them drawings of slightly more than 100 parts. Could Morrison's Molded Fiber Glass Company (MFG) produce them? How long would it take? What about cost? What kind of quantities?

"'Yes, we could make them,'" Morrison told them. "But after the Fisher Body engineers went away, we heard nothing. When we called them several weeks later, they told us the project had been dropped."

Months later, just after New Year's Day 1953, a supplier sent him a telegram: "Go to the Waldorf Astoria Hotel in New York City this coming weekend," it said. "Go see the display."

"We didn't go. Money was too tight. And none of us knew what was there," Morrison said.

"In that ballroom was Chevrolet's new fiberglass two-seat sports car. GM had planted the car with microphones, to eavesdrop on the guests they had invited in to see it and some other prototypes. They heard, 'It's lovely. It's cute.' They heard people say they wished they had one.

"And on Monday, we heard from Chevrolet. Could some men come down to see the plant the next day?" Project engineer Carl Jakust and his boss, E. J. "Jim"

Premo, chief body engineer for Chevrolet Division, flew themselves in a single-engine plane through a snowstorm to visit Morrison's 30,000-square-foot plant. Time, they said, was pressing. Though the Fisher Body engineers had shown plans to Morrison before, the Chevrolet body engineers took new measurements of each fiberglass press. They would redesign their parts to fit Morrison's machinery.

"That makes no sense," Morrison told them. "These presses were busy anyway. We'd buy new presses, the right presses."

Morrison offered to help redesign the parts himself so that they would not only mold well but so they would also be strong. Yet Jakust and Premo were a little nervous. Did MFG have the capacity to meet Chevrolet's demand? This was a huge question. Chevrolet had lost the youth market to Ford. Ford's postwar cars had V-8 engines, while Chevrolet still had only its cast-iron "stove bolt" six. Ford had a convertible. Chevrolet needed to get this two-seat sports car out into public hands as fast as possible. It wanted to produce 50 of these cars each day.

So, on Tuesday, February 5, less than a month after Jakust and Premo's visit, Morrison drove from Ashtabula to meet with Klein at 9:00 A.M., to discuss plans to produce 12,300 sets of the 103 body parts that made up the car they called Corvette. General Motors needed delivery spread over 18 months.

Signals got crossed. At 9 in the morning, Klein was gone for the day. Morrison asked to see his boss, Ed Furbacher, Chevrolet's senior purchasing agent. Furbacher, too, was gone for the day. Morrison felt that he'd been stood up.

"'Well, great,' I said. 'How the devil are they supposed to meet with me?' I was hot," said Morrison.

He punched the elevator button angrily. When the door opened, out stepped Elmer Gormsen, chief purchasing agent for Chevrolet Division and boss of the two missing buyers. Gormsen had met Morrison on his previous visits to the GM building. He quickly asked if Morrison had a moment.

Morrison had a lunchtime appointment across town with Kaiser-Frazer. MFG provided 10 parts for the Kaiser-Darrin sports car. For someone like Gormsen, Morrison had all morning.

Gormsen was straightforward. "We've decided to make the body of the Corvette out of steel," he explained.

"The hell you say . . . ," Morrison said.

"Look, there's nobody in the industry with the capacity big enough to make 50 Corvettes a day."

But Morrison hadn't had his say. Harold Boeschenstein, chairman of Owens-Corning, was a friend and an ardent supporter of Morrison and of MFG.

"I had already received oral confirmation that if I needed," Morrison explained, "Owens-Corning would help me. I told Gormsen about a large building over in Meadville, Pennsylvania, that was available. We could get it right away!"

Gormsen was noncommittal. Walking Morrison to the door, he told him that if anything changed, he'd get in touch.

"I walked out the door," Morrison said, "and thought to myself, 'What the hell. That's gone.'"

Morrison's afternoon stretched into evening with Kaiser's engineers, checking fits and finish of each piece. He took them to dinner. That long session with Kaiser was scarcely fruitful, however. Kaiser had ordered 500 sets, but Morrison warned his people "to go easy on this, make a hundred parts and then stub your toe. Don't make anymore. I had a feeling they weren't too solid by that time."

Disappointed, he left Detroit around 8:30 P.M. He didn't push the pace, driving easily south toward Toledo and then east around the shore of Lake Erie through every small and large town nearly all the way across the state, back to Ashtabula.

"I got home about 1:30 the next morning. My wife got up and told me, 'There's a man calling you from Detroit. Wants you to call him no matter how late you get in.'

"So I called the number and it's Elmer Gormsen. He kind of laughed and said I didn't need to call him so late. But since I did, he said to go ahead and get that building because we've decided we're going to do the Corvette with a fiberglass body."

Robert S. Morrison was back in the automobile business. MFG had just received a $4 million contract. Chevrolet wanted the first of the 300 complete sets of body panels before June 1. It was a night Morrison's children would remember all their lives.

His son, Robert Jr., recalled that the early morning of February 6, 1953, was the first time that he and his sister had ever tasted champagne.

Few Motorama show cars were much more than push-around models. But the Corvette, already tentatively approved for production before the January 1953 Waldorf Astoria debut in New York, was a fully driveable prototype.

chapter 2

History B.C. (Before Corvette): 1900–1952

It was inveterate tinkerer David Dunbar Buick's Flint, Michigan-built runabouts that first seduced Billy Durant. Durant, the silver-tongued, almost-movie-star-good-looking founder, knew more about people—especially individual investors instead of bankers—than he understood about internal combustion and buggy-chassis engineering.

Durant may have existed to marry people with money and vision to what he thought was America's preeminent growth industry in the early 1900s. Automobiles had been around since Charles and Frank Duryea first clattered up the streets of hometown Springfield, Massachusetts, in 1895. But Durant caught the bug late.

He proselytized the glories of Buick's motor cars to the skeptics and the already converted alike. He pumped up sales to nearly 8,500 cars in 1908. His goals were grand, preposterous even. He wanted to merge Buick with Ransom E. Olds, Henry Ford, and Ben and Frank Briscoe (who produced Maxwell and Briscoe automobiles). The further talks progressed, the less Ford liked the idea. Durant's concept of United Motors, incorporated July 1, 1908, (with Maxwell-Briscoe and Oldsmobile) would dissolve shortly after. Like an ill-fated phoenix, United Motors rose and quickly fell as the International Motor Car Company. From this residue, Durant incorporated General Motors on September 16, 1908. Within a year, while holding onto Oldsmobile, he brought in Oakland and Cadillac. He continued acquiring ailing car companies and strong, essential suppliers of axles, tires, seats, brakes, springs, and electrical parts. He wanted to own and control every element that went into the production of his automobiles. Vertical integration was a term that hadn't been imagined yet, but Durant was one of its pioneers.

His Buicks raced and won (at first) against Frenchmen Louis and Arthur Chevrolet. Durant hired Arthur as his chauffeur, while Louis began producing his own cars by 1914. In 1916, Durant reorganized General Motors into a corporation capitalized at $100 million and acquired Chevrolet as well.

An economic recession in 1921 hit hard in the United States, brought on because Europe finally could stand on its own after the damage of World War I. A philosophical difference between Durant and Ford dropped General Motors to second place for the next several decades.

Durant cut production and laid off workers. Ford cut prices. Durant consolidated spending; its ripple effect consolidated the earnings and spending of his workers and suppliers and their workers, and its effects trickled down the economic chain. Ford saw it differently. His goal was to let every adult who wanted to purchase a Model T meet that aspiration no matter how tight the economy. He cut his profit margin. Ford's fortune, from sales of his basic car and his stone-simple tractor, absorbed the losses as he kept wages and Tin Lizzies flowing out the doors.

Durant's wealth had come from the idea of providing an automobile for every pocketbook in the marketplace. By 1921, GM offered cars from $700 Chevrolets to $6,000 Cadillacs. This philosophy totally eluded competitor Henry Ford, even as it inspired Durant's successor, Alfred P. Sloan.

Sloan, who as early as 1921 elucidated the General Motors philosophy, almost as a slogan: "a car for every purse and purpose." By 1925, GM held major interests in Vauxhall Automobiles in the United Kingdom and Adam Opel A.G. in Germany. Its most significant idea in the United States was financing the purchases of its automobiles rather than watching that interest income go elsewhere. By the end of 1925, GM's many divisions produced one of every five automobiles sold in the United States, while it kept $1 in every $3 of profit the industry reaped.

Sloan's business acumen affected the automobile business in other, profound ways. He was among the first to recognize that a product's appearance influenced sales. Car buyers knew they could go virtually anywhere and get back.

The gigantic Y-Job was perhaps Harley Earl's most famous single design. It was his personal car, built in 1938. He used it for tens of thousands of miles, commuting to downtown Detroit from Grosse Pointe. With its hidden headlights and its nearly 20-foot-long flowing body, it broke new automotive design ground and allowed Earl a rolling test bed for his ideas. *Detroit Public Library-National Automotive History Collection*

Sloan wrote Henry Bassett, general manager of Buick, in July 1926 hinting at the industry's next direction. The letter was reprinted in Sloan's autobiography, *My Years With General Motors:* "Are we as advanced from the standpoint of beauty of design, harmony of lines, attractiveness of color schemes and general contour of the whole piece of apparatus as we are in the soundness of workmanship and the other elements of a more mechanical nature . . . ?"

Lawrence P. Fisher, general manager of Cadillac Division and a founding brother of Fisher Body, agreed with Sloan that auto makers must pay more attention to the way cars looked. His Los Angeles dealer, Don Lee, acquired a custom-coach building firm. Lee's customers included Hollywood stars made fabulously wealthy by sound movies. They wanted cars more personal than the standard fare and something different from those of their peers.

The J. W. Earl Automobile Works first built custom car and truck bodies in 1911 as service vehicles and props for the new talking-film industry. By 1918 Earl occupied its own three-story block-long building just south of downtown Los Angeles. It displayed its first complete automobiles at the L.A. Auto Show. The car bodies were designed by Earl's Stanford University–educated son, Harley.

Born in 1893, Harley Earl grew up in the business. J. W. Earl founded a carriage-building company in 1899, and when Harley left college in 1918 to take over his father's

business, J. W. Earl also had done airplane fuselages for the Glen L. Martin Company, a southern California aircraft pioneer. The contours of airplanes were part of Harley Earl's vernacular.

Fisher came to visit Lee and Earl in the early 1920s. In Earl's workshop he watched the 30-year-old designer form scale models of the cars in clay. These allowed Harley to make mistakes, experiment with lines, shapes, and reflections of light before committing to full-scale wood bucks. Earl's fender lines blended into running boards. His hoods flowed into windshields. Sheet metal surrounding engine compartments swept into car side panels. Fisher knew car assembly; at GM, Chassis Engineering designed and delivered to the body divisions the frame, wheels, tires, fenders, engine, radiator, and hood. The body division then bolted on its separately conceived passenger compartment afterward. Yet Earl's work was integrated; its appearance was molded from one piece and cast from one mind.

Fisher returned to Detroit with photographs and reported to Sloan what he saw and thought. The Cadillac Division manager and the General Motors chairman conspired to bring the *work* of "Hollywood Harley" Earl, if not the man himself, to GM. They would introduce the LaSalle, a new car line, in early 1927. It was an entry-level Cadillac product. Fisher and Sloan hired Earl as a consultant to design a car as beautiful as any of his customs. Earl came and molded clay.

The 1929 Buick Model 29-51 soon earned the unfortunate nickname of "The Pregnant Buick." While designed by GM's rising star Harley Earl, this car was redesigned by Buick Division's production engineers who could not make Earl's shapes and sizes fit their existing car. Earl, preoccupied with subsequent projects, never saw the car once it left his studios. Here, at the Waldorf Astoria during one of GM's Investor Luncheons, it didn't succeed. It was withdrawn from production after only a year. *Detroit Public Library-National Automotive History Collection*

Fisher showed Earl drawings of the 1927 Cadillac that was too far along in production to be changed. It would be overshadowed by Earl's LaSalle. Earl called the cars drab but suggested that wire wheels would lower them, changing the appearance somewhat. Bright paint, he said, would surprise everyone.

The LaSalle turned heads and brought buyers into showrooms. Favorable reaction and improved Cadillac sales brought Earl to General Motors on July 27, 1927, to head the newly created Art and Colour Section. Answering only to Sloan, Earl would have 10 designers and 40 shop, clerical, and administrative staff members to design general production car bodies and do research and development work by creating special car designs. For someone whose title was "manager," MistErl, as he was known to his staff, soon had as much clout as a division vice president.

Not until September 1940 would his promotion to vice president of styling, his renamed section, give him title to match his impact. This recognition occurred after a highly visible stumble, a car he designed that was changed by Engineering to fit their chassis. This 1929 Buick tapered at the middle below the window glass by Earl's design. It was squeezed at the bottom, along the running boards, by engineers who also raised the roofline 5 inches. Earl was preoccupied by work following the Buick, and he was not trusted by Engineering. He never saw the car after its designs left his studio, until it got to the streets.

Earl's design was a grand, if not radical, leap from previous models. Engineering's revisions made it a disaster. Stretched and pulled out of shape, it quickly was nicknamed the "pregnant Buick." It was literally laughed out of showrooms and was pulled from production after only one year.

Earl was unscathed. It taught conservative Sloan about car styling that solidified over the years into another General Motors policy: the annual model change. In the early days of automobiling, successful car builders updated their cars as improvements happened, shutting down the assembly line, such as it was, to make changes. Shrewd car makers observed that heralding these changes through advertising or signs in the showrooms brought in owners of older models as well as passersby to see what was new. Sloan's sales department capitalized on this phenomenon. The entire corporation waited until year end to introduce next year's new, improved models. Car design and production sequence required nearly two

Once World War II ended, GM's top priority was to redesign the entire Cadillac line. As its premier make, it would set the style for all the other divisions. War planes and civilian aircraft alike sported twin tails and Earl was taken with the sleekness they suggested. When the Cadillacs appeared for 1948, the cars had tail fins. The trend it started lasted more than a decade. *Detroit Public Library-National Automotive History Collection*

years in the early 1930s. Designers had to measure the pulse of America even longer in advance. Sloan and Earl learned from the pregnant Buick that they couldn't lead the customers too far too fast.

When Earl's 1933 Chevrolets were introduced, the public, already startled by the curves and uneasy proportions of the earlier Buick, looked upon the Chevrolets with enthusiastic acceptance. Earl, whose approach was always to make a car appear longer and lower, covered all the unattractive, individual components of the car—the radiator, the gas tank, the trunk, the panel between the frame and car body—on the Chevrolet in a consistently conceived bodywork. Even the fenders got skirts to hide the interruptions of the tires and any mud or dirt that might be kicked up. Its appearance was "stylish," its style was unified, and its perpetrators were thereafter known as "stylists."

Earl's cars sold, so his influence grew. Those who first derided his department as "the beauty parlor," came around when year-end reports summed up each division's performance. Sloan was an enthusiast from the start, writing about Earl's contribution to the corporation in his autobiography, *My Years With General Motors.* "For a long while," he wrote,

"the Art and Colour Section occupied quarters in the General Motors Building Annex in Detroit. The focal point of the work area was the blackboard room. To this room came executives from Fisher Body and every car division. . . . We were all window-shoppers in the Art and Colour 'sales' rooms," Sloan continued. "Art and Colour was proposing new designs, presenting new idea sketches, selling progress. And as time went by more and more of these ideas appeared to be feasible. New divisional customers materialized as more and more people in the corporation bought the ideas."

Earl and other division vice presidents traveled throughout the United States and Europe. Differences between cars built there and those manufactured in the United States were clear. Gasoline, in short supply after the war, was very expensive in Europe. Autoroutes in France, autobahns in Germany, and autostradas in Italy existed, yet most goods and people traveled by bicycle or public transit in the cities and on long-distance trains between them. What worked in one part of the world would not be appropriate in another. It might be adapted and modified, however.

In 1952, as Dwight David Eisenhower resigned as supreme commander of the Allied Forces in Europe and

headed to the presidency, the United States detonated its first hydrogen bomb, vaporizing Eniwetok Atoll in the South Pacific in a blinding flash and a millionth of a second. As president, Ike watched the red menace, the threat of communism, taking over the world. To help combat that threat, he authorized an interstate highway system—similar to the autoroutes, -bahns, and -stradas of Europe—for the quick, efficient deployment of America's armed forces. These long, smooth roads fueled a new hunger for automobiles. The country's economy, at peace but ready for imminent war, grew. Personal income increased. A middle class developed, and members of that class had extra money. Vacation travel, once strictly the reserve of the very wealthy, was now within reach of many Americans, but for the want of their own automobile.

By the early 1950s, even the popular magazines had recognized what sold American cars. *FORTUNE* magazine reported in September 1953 that "the car industry has found itself selling more car per car—more accessories, luxuries, improvements and innovations. Now it has to plan it that way."

Air conditioning, radios, and automatic transmissions were primary options that GM wanted to become standard equipment on all but the lowest priced products. These were what Americans wanted most in their cars.

With some 80 models in their portfolio by the early 1950s, the Central Office came close to meeting Alfred Sloan's promise of a car for every purse and purpose. On MistErl's blackboards there appeared yet another new idea, a new car meant for a purpose as yet barely considered in America.

Harley Earl called his next personal car Le Sabre. It was initially designated the XP-8. This Buick-based car took inspiration for the nose and rear end of this car from the F86 Sabre jet. He even referred to it as his jet for the road. First modeled in clay in 1949, Earl had his running version two years later and he eventually drove some 45,000 miles in the car. *Detroit Public Library-National Automotive History Collection*

15

chapter 3

And Then There Were 300: 1953

By the early 1950s Alfred Sloan's confidence in Harley Earl allowed Earl to expand his role far beyond designer into the as yet unknown realm of product planner. Earl used carefully controlled environments to gauge customers' reactions to his ideas.

These previews began during the late 1930s with the "Industrialist's Luncheons," held in the main ballroom of the Waldorf Astoria Hotel in New York City. These gave East Coast financial and business leaders an insider's look at GM's upcoming policies, real products, and fanciful ideas for the future. Sloan and Earl learned what these usually conservative individuals thought and what appealed to them. It was clever psychology; GM showed the future to these men (and it was men only, their wives were not invited). It accomplished Sloan's directive of preparing the consumers, by measured steps, for more radical changes in styling. When these men left the luncheons, they felt comfortable with where the company was headed, and so they advised their clients to invest in GM. The company left the luncheons knowing better what kind of automobile might sell to these most influential—and wealthy—customers.

One vehicle raised little interest among any American customers—the sports car. In 1952, while more than 4,000,000 new automobiles were registered, only 11,199 of them were sports cars. Some of this lopsided interest was due to America's demand for the family cars that had been put on hold during World War II. Still, by 1950 many young people, among them Earl's own sons, Jerry and Jim, were attracted to sports cars. (Earl himself enjoyed racing; he had entered and won a car race in 1911 when he was 18, driving his father's Mercer roadster.) The moderate-priced choices were few, tiny Crosleys or curvaceous Kurtis-Krafts built in

the United States. The Cunningham or the Anglo-American Nash-Healey were far too costly for a college student's budget. England produced the sensuous Jaguar XK-120, the spindly MG-TC, the Austin-Healeys, or the Triumphs.

As GM's vice president of styling, Earl's budget was nearly unlimited; it was certainly unquestioned. Each year, Earl and his Styling Department produced automobiles for the major European shows. He took cars to Paris, Geneva, London, and Milan, and he often stayed on for weeks, visiting other car makers and even attending international races. He appreciated the cars he saw overseas, and he admired the Jaguars even if he recognized that the European sports cars might not translate directly to GM's audiences.

Earl was well acquainted with international sportsman Briggs Cunningham who had raced yachts for the America's Cup. In 1950 Cunningham took Cadillac coupes to LeMans to compete in the 24-hour race. Later that year, at an endurance race at Watkins Glen, New York, where

Individual seats were contoured into the interior. There were only two options offered, a heater for $91.40 and the signal-seeking AM radio at $145.15. However, these were included on each car produced. The radio's antenna was a wire mesh that was embedded into the inside of the fiberglass trunk lid.

Only 300 Corvettes were produced during 1953. This is number 283. The whereabouts of roughly 225 of the cars are known these days. The first two cars appear to have been intentionally destroyed by Chevrolet at the proving grounds.

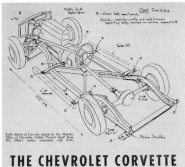

THE CHEVROLET CORVETTE

Road & Track technical editor and publisher John R. Bond wrote the cover story on the sports car, leading off with a reproduction of chassis engineer Maurice Olley's June 1952 "Project Opel" chassis sketch.

The Flint assembly line, photographed on July 27, 1953, was a tidy, uncluttered operation. Here the frame, designed by former Rolls-Royce engineer Maurice Olley, remained inverted prior to fitting the rear axle assembly. The center point of the X was low enough that the drive shaft rode above it to the differential. The front suspension was already attached. *Mike Mueller archives*

Despite the existence of Corvettes by the fall of 1953, enthusiast magazines such as *Road & Track* couldn't get a thorough test reported before the following summer, for their June 1954 issue.

The end of the assembly line was not always so formal. But completion of each of the early cars was a significant occasion. First year production was set at 300 cars but supply exceeded demand for a car that leaked rain and had primitive side curtains instead of roll-up windows. By year end, 183 had been delivered. This may be the second, third, and fourth car produced. *Mike Mueller archives*

Cunningham was competing, Earl arrived in his 20-foot-long two-seat Buick Y-job. Cunningham teased him, asking him why GM couldn't build a "proper" sports car, something that he could race. A year later Earl arrived in his new, smaller Buick LeSabre, but still this was no sports car from General Motors. So Cunningham built his own, using Chrysler V-8s. His cars set racing standards in the United States and brought attention to the modest American efforts at sports car production wherever they competed overseas. But Cunningham continued to chide his friend Harley.

A true niche market developed. A number of English-American hybrids appeared, using Cadillac engines in Frank Allard's crude, brutish hot rods, or using Nash engines in Donald Healey's Pininfarina-bodied coupes and roadsters. Frank Kurtis produced 36 of his Sports before television super-salesman, Earl "Mad Man" Muntz acquired the rights. Muntz renamed the car the Muntz Jet and eventually built 394 of them.

Henry J. Kaiser entered the small market for compact, sporty cars with his Henry J in late 1950 after he'd collaborated with Joseph W. Frazer, a former Chrysler vice president of sales, to form Kaiser-Frazer. They hired two exceptional designers, Howard "Dutch" Darrin and Bill Stout. Darrin had done stunning bodies for Packards, Lincolns, and others;

one of Stout's more significant designs had been his own Scarabs, design-study vehicles, some produced in fiberglass.

In Milwaukee, industrial designer Brooks Stevens adopted a Henry J 100-inch wheelbase chassis and a Willys 2.8-liter in-line six-cylinder engine. He wrapped them in bodywork somewhat reminiscent of the grand Mercedes-Benz racing two-seaters of the 1930s. Stevens called his car the Excalibur J and built three prototypes. His goal was for Kaiser-Frazer to put into production a road-going version of the Excalibur. Instead, the three cars performed very successfully in D-modified classes in SCCA racing. Kaiser wasn't yet convinced that America was ready for a sports car.

Dutch Darrin worked for Kaiser out of his own studio in California. During his off hours, and funded from his own pocket, Darrin created a low, sleek-looking two-seater, hoping Kaiser would produce it. Like Steven's car, Darrin based his roadster on the Henry J chassis, using the 161-cubic-inch-displacement Willys in-line six. He fabricated its body out of fiberglass. In August, he showed the car to Kaiser, who didn't like it until his new young wife fell in love with it. When Kaiser asked Darrin why he'd done it, the designer told him that he'd heard rumors that Chevrolet and Ford were already working on similar projects. This car, Darrin explained, would be the Kaiser-Frazer answer to the others' challenges.

The "Blue Flame Special" was Chevrolet's passenger-car six-cylinder engine slightly modified to produce 150 horsepower instead of the sedan's sedate 115 horsepower. General Motors aggressively pushed the Powerglide automatic transmission for the Chevrolet line and no manual three-speed was available nor could one be modified quickly enough for production.

GM's challenge was a not-so-well-kept secret by mid-1952. In Styling's back rooms, designers worked hard to meet Harley Earl's deadline for next January in the Waldorf Astoria. The "Investor's Luncheons" had long ago caught the attention of corporate accountants who balanced cost per attendee against possible sales revenues and came up short. Harlow Curtice, who would become president of GM in 1953 and was heir-apparent to Sloan, had a business background. Under his influence, the luncheons evolved into something broader and more public. Renamed *Transportation Unlimited,* these automobile shows would last several days. Wives were invited. These programs in 1949 and 1950 met with so much success that the sales staff considered taking the show beyond New York. For financial reasons and product offerings, there were no exhibitions in 1951 or 1952. (Earl introduced his LeSabre dream car at the Paris show in 1952.) But for 1953, GM added Miami, Dallas, Kansas City, Los Angeles, and San Francisco. The event was renamed *Motorama.* For 1953, Harley Earl's crew introduced dream cars from Cadillac, Oldsmobile, Pontiac, and two from Buick. During the 1949 and 1950 shows, Chevrolet had been excluded from the glamour; GM management reasoned that the division producing cars for the masses didn't have the right image for dream cars. Thomas Keating, Chevrolet Division general manager, disagreed. Between 1950 and 1952, Chevrolet Division sales dropped almost 40 percent. Keating needed something novel to excite customers, to draw them into the showrooms. He made it clear that the next Motorama would have at least one car from his division. Chevrolet, he argued, would show the small,

plastic-bodied two-seat open car; it was perfect for the youth market his division sought.

Earl's first idea for this GM sports car was refined from the same mold that Sydney Allard, Donald Healey, and the others had used: fit a unique, stylish two-seat body around a production frame and engine. His beloved Buick-based Y-Job was basically that. After driving the Y-Job for 10 years, Earl replaced it with the smaller, two-seater, the LeSabre. This car, and its sister, the XP-300 Buick-based convertible for GM's chief engineer, Charles Chayne, provoked widespread public interest when articles about the cars began to appear. Nationwide consumer hunger fed GM's decision to expand the Motoramas. But Harley Earl heard the same discussions about his LeSabre and XP-300 at home at his dinner table. He listened again and again to his sons' talk about sports cars.

Earl first proposed that this type of car from GM could sell for about $1,800, close to Triumphs or MGs and about half the price of Jaguar's $3,345 XK-120. He had a Jaguar moved into the body development studio as a design target. He assigned Bob McLean, a young California Institute of Technology graduate in both engineering and industrial design, to create a car. He tagged a recent hire, Duane "Sparky" Bohnstedt, to style the body for the project.

Earl wanted to use a V-8 engine, but only Cadillac, Buick, and Oldsmobile produced them. Earl's other parameters, including using the Jaguar as a model, set McLean's direction. In those days, virtually every sports car followed the long hood/short rear deck characteristics of classic 1930s sports cars. McLean and Bohnstedt were faithful to convention. McLean used Chevrolet's in-line six-cylinder engine set far back in a newly designed Chevy frame whose wheelbase he set at 102 inches, to match exactly the Jaguar target. His car had nearly equal weight on the front and rear axles when it was loaded. McLean's car was drawn with 57 inches front track and 59 inches rear, some 6 inches wider at front and 9 inches wider at the rear than the Jaguar. This followed Earl's standards of making cars appear lower, longer, and wider. To accomplish all of this, McLean adopted an unorthodox practice of beginning his design work at the rear axle. He fit in the passenger/driver compartment and worked forward. This let him keep the weight as far to the rear as he did. Time passed rapidly. Harley Earl still wanted a V-8 in his little sports car. On June 2, 1952, he first showed Bohnstedt's full-size clay model to a small group that included GM chairman Harlow Curtice (Earl had shown it to him privately already). Along with Curtice were Tom Keating, Chevrolet Division general manager, and division Chief Engineer Edward N. Cole. Cole and Keating were enthralled. Cole's staff started improving the performance of the standard "Blue Flame Six" to something closer to sports car proportions and engineering the chassis to meet GM auto production procedures.

Building the First Corvettes

Body assembly took place in Chevrolet Division's converted Customer Delivery Garage on Van Slyke Road and Atherton, near Flint. Start up was slow, grueling, exhausting. It took work crews three 16-hour days to assemble the first car, which was completed on June 30, 1953. Through July, they were satisfied to finish a car a day. Thereafter, three cars a day rolled off the line.

By fall, Chevrolet had the plant running smoothly enough to open for tours, to show off not only its completely fiberglass car, but also its somewhat unusual assembly system. Throughout October and November, members of the Michigan Education Association visited the plant, and among those teachers were John and Jean Anderson, now retired in Cresco, Pennsylvania.

"The pace was frantic," Jean Anderson remembered. "The workers really appeared to be under great pressure. They were working like crazy."

Their tour lasted four hours, long enough that Chevrolet fed them a box lunch. "We saw everything; I mean *everything*," John recalled. "We were on a kind of trolley. They showed us where the cylinder blocks were being bored. They had what may have been the first robots in the auto industry, and these things would just pick the block up and turn it every which way. From there to transmission assembly, to body assembly. The tour guide stressed that the assembly-line procedure at this plant brought all the parts together for various subassemblies and then all of those to final assembly."

"Everything was done at that factory," Jean added. "I think the only thing they said that came in from the outside was just the tires. They wanted us to see every last element to understand how the car went together, so we could tell our students about a modern assembly line." (In fact, the engines from the Tonowanda, New York, plant and the bare frames were assembled by A. O. Smith in Granite City, Illinois.)

"But that pace. Things were flying around overhead, and below us, too! The line would speed up and slow down and speed up again."

On December 24, 1953, production ended at Flint. Four days later, production started at St. Louis, Missouri. This plant was the old millwork building for buggies and early automobiles.

In late November 1953, assembly had slowed again to a crawl. Division General Manager Tom Keating authorized production of only 300 cars for 1953. These were allocated to high-visibility customers, Hollywood stars and sports figures. Here an assembler fits the rear axle to the inverted frame prior to engine installation. *Mike Mueller archives*

Both Styling and Engineering wanted glass covers over the headlights, like many of the European show cars at that time. But this was illegal in the United States so the fencing mask became an acceptable alternative.

Ed Cole had graduated from the GM Institute in 1933, and he promptly joined Cadillac Division as an engineer. He worked with Briggs Cunningham preparing his Cadillacs for the LeMans effort. When Cole was promoted to chief engineer at Chevrolet Division, he brought along chassis expert Maurice Olley as well. Early in his career, Olley had worked for Rolls-Royce in England and in America. Olley had definite opinions about the difference between European, English, and American cars, having lived and worked on both sides of the Atlantic. He directed a new research and development section within Cole's offices, to produce both the definition of a sports car for Chevrolet and the chassis for Chevrolet's sports car.

The sports car was code named Project Opel to mislead curious insiders. The Styling Department did work for GM's German subsidiary. Within days of the Cole showing, most engineers saw the plaster model. Cole authorized one car to be completed to show standards for the 1953 Motorama event and, provided it didn't bomb, production would begin the following summer for presentation as a 1954 model.

Olley had his work cut out for him, even with Cole's full support. Fitting existing passenger car technology beneath McLean's slim lines was a challenge. The front suspension was slightly revised from a 1949 sedan configuration; however, the final drive gear was a Hotchkiss rear end, anchored in place by four-leaf springs that sloped upward at the rear and were attached to the frame by tension shackles. This spring angle induced understeer, the kind of plowing steering that engineers felt was safest for sedans. The regular Chevrolet worm-and-sector steering system was quickened to provide a more sports car-like response. Brakes were regular production units, but front-to-rear bias gave slightly more to the rear, and the master cylinder was enlarged.

The low rearward engine placement that McLean duplicated from the Jaguar caused Olley to design a unique, new frame on which to hang the collection of suspension, brakes, and steering parts. This was made up of side members of boxed steel sections, tied together by a central crossing X-member. The frame swooped low enough that the engine drive shaft fit above it without drilling holes for it, which was the more conventional technique. The principal drawback was a weakening of the torsional strength of the chassis; however, any frame represented a huge expense in the development of a car. While Olley saved money by using a number of stock, or mostly stock, pieces elsewhere, the new frame cost couldn't entirely be made up without other economies. Further compromises were necessary.

Using Chevrolet's existing six-cylinder engine was all right, finally, with both Earl and Cole. Cole's assistant Harry Barr increased power output from the 235-cubic-inch-displacement engine, basically an evolved Chevrolet truck powerplant first seen in 1941. In stock trim in the sedans, this engine produced only 115 horsepower. Adding mechanical lifters, a new aluminum intake manifold for three Carter carburetors, a kind of split exhaust manifold leading to separate exhaust mufflers, and pipes on each side at the rear, and increasing compression ratio from the stock 7.5:1 up to 8.0:1 raised output to 150 horsepower. Olley examined the mufflers and later wrote, "A requirement in the minds of sports car enthusiasts is that the exhaust should have the right note. They don't agree what this is. Some prefer 'foo-blap' while others go for 'foo-gobble.' It is impossible to please them all." Olley chose the latter.

The Corvette engine's output came up short, not close to the Jaguar's 210-cubic-inch-displacement six-cylinder's 180 horsepower, but it was much better than anything else quickly available. (Ironically, the whole point of Jaguar's sports car was to provide a vehicle to surround its new high-performance six-cylinder engine. Jaguar conceived a four-cylinder XK-100 as well, so uncertain was it about future direction. Had steel not been so tightly rationed in postwar Britain, the XK engine was meant to appear in a new sport sedan from Jaguar. The company would have left sports cars to others.)

Earl and Cole wanted a manual transmission for their sports car, just like the Jaguar, MG, and others. But no four-speed existed in America. Again, it was a matter of time and cost. The dedicated, well-developed two-speed Powerglide automatic transmission was perfectly mated to the engine that fit the Olley-McLean package. Olley defended the decision, citing reasons sounding more like Alfred Sloan than Ed Cole when he presented a paper to the Society of Automotive Engineers (SAE) in January 1953. Americans, Olley concluded, were less willing to trade the luxury that was increasingly available in American sedans for the austerity common to any sports cars.

The cost and time constraints that led to Chevrolet sedan-running gear and the in-line six with its automatic also caused the decision to build the Motorama show car out of fiberglass. If the car went into production, Chevrolet would build the car body in steel, formed first with Kirksite die tooling. Production could be as many as 10,000 cars in its first year, still considered at that point to be 1954.

Appearing in brilliant white fiberglass in the Waldorf ballroom, it already bore the name Corvette, "named after the trim, fleet naval vessel that performed heroic escort and patrol duties in World War II," by Myron Scott, Campbell-Ewald ad agency's chief photographer. Handout material explained that the Corvette, its name written in a simple script across the nose of the car, was 6 to 12 months away from production. Most of the 55,000 visitors to the 1953 Motorama had no idea how car production really happened. They took this target date at face value.

Motorama show cars were usually powered by human sweat pushing them around show floors. This Corvette

Each of the first 300 cars was essentially handmade both in the molding of its fiberglass panels and the assembly of its mechanicals. The car was available only in Polo White with a black convertible top, red wheels and red interiors.

was a preproduction prototype; nearly all of its development and testing was complete. The short lead time was possible only because Cole and Keating had already decided to go ahead with it.

On February 6, several hours after

Elmer Gormsen gave Robert Morrison the news about Chevrolet's decision, (and as the prototype car was being prepared for the opening of the Miami Motorama), Morrison and his partners drove to Meadville, Pennsylvania. They knew that Chevrolet was still concerned about Molded Fiber Glass's capacity to meet its needs. In Meadville, they found an old railroad building still laced with tracks and totally unusable. When they returned, Morrison called Harold Boeschenstein at Owens-Corning to accept his offer of help. Then he called Gormsen to tell him that they'd be constructing a new building just for the Corvette.

When MFG got the order, the whole young fiberglass industry knew about it. Morrison had only four of his key people left after spinning off his tray operation for Continental Baking's palettes. When the new 167,000-square-foot Corvette building was complete, his organization was stretched thin.

"Chevrolet was quite cooperative with manpower," Morrison recalled. "And resin suppliers and Owens-Corning sent people in. Paid their expenses. Didn't cost us a penny. You'd see a salesman from one company and a salesman from another working on the same press. Competitors working alongside each other helping us to get the work out."

Chevrolet told Morrison it rejected steel, in the end, because tooling costs would have been four or five times

higher for steel than for fiberglass. They had learned from Morrison that they could consolidate parts, which meant fewer dies. What's more, it would have taken much longer to produce steel stamping dies than MFG needed to make its forms. Still, Chevrolet had concerns.

"There *was* a sort of betting going on up in Detroit that we wouldn't be able to make the underbody," Morrison recalled with a gentle smile. "There was some trouble. In early June 1953, the foreman in charge of repairing the underbodies said he needed 40 more people.

"The underbody was breaking right at the junction of the drive shaft tube and the kick-up right before the rear axle. There were two sharp angles and no way for it to give at all. Every damned one of them was breaking."

Morrison, who graduated from college with a bachelor of arts degree in economics and a minor in chemistry, learned engineering the hard way, by doing it. MFG's Corvette presses were huge compared to the 42-by-48-inch platens Fisher Body saw when it first came to Ashtabula. The underbody piece for the 1953 car was 120 inches long, 72 inches wide, and 26 inches deep from the lowest spot to the highest.

"I took a look at the break and I knew what to do," Morrison said.

"'Get a big bucket of water and get some cloths,' I said. 'When the press opens, put the cool wet cloths right over that spot that breaks. And leave it there for a few seconds.'

"It eliminated all the breakage. Most any resin is weak when it's hot. Cooling it down with the wet cloth, we got it strong enough quickly so we could lift it out without breaking."

chapter 4

The Sound of Few Hands Clapping: 1953–1955

When the new Corvette hit the streets in September 1953, it landed with a big splash that resonated more like a dull thud. Its price came in at $3,513, not Earl's $1,800.

The Blue Flame Special six-cylinder engine and Powerglide transmission moved the car from 0 to 60 miles per hour in 11 seconds and gave it a top speed of 105 miles per hour. This wasn't bad. Except Jaguar reduced the price of its 1954 XK-120 to $3,345, and it hit 60 miles per hour a second quicker and went 25 miles per hour faster. While Jaguar, MG, and the fiberglass Kaiser-Darrin with its odd, slide-open doors, were available in a variety of colors, Corvettes were offered only in Polo White. Tops were black only. Build quality was inconsistent. Assembly line workers struggled to get machine-made bits to fit handmade bodies. The car suffered teething problems.

Corvette's biggest obstacle was basic economics: supply versus demand. Chevrolet General Manager Tom Keating hedged his bets when he authorized first-year production of only 300 cars. He wanted to rekindle the momentum developed at the Motorama shows. He needed to gauge customer reaction, monitor factory production glitches, and watch assembly costs. Cars manufactured in June and July were still prototypes in many ways, with hand-formed stainless steel trim and cast bronze pieces fitted where cars built in August had pot metal. A. O. Smith Corporation, the outside contractor making Corvette's frames, fabricated hand-formed gussets to reinforce rear spring mounts. These were often revised between one frame and the next until Cole and Olley settled on a final design. (Once these inconsistencies were fixed, Cole wanted production to reach 6,000 cars in 1954 and again in 1955.)

The press introduction was September 29; 50 journalists shared eight cars; each drove a 7-mile course at GM's Milford Proving Ground. Before October 1, a few dozen cars were delivered. Some of these stayed within GM, issued to engineers for further development, or they were provided to executives. Dealers learned in early July that they should not accept orders promising delivery in 1953. Another 50 cars were delivered through Chevrolet's highest-volume dealers to an A-list of handpicked, carefully selected, highly visible entertainers, prominent athletes, and executives from other major companies. Normal customers found that a few Corvettes circulated from one dealer to the next, staying two or three days as display models. The 55,000 Motorama visitors who had spoken unwittingly into Styling's concealed microphones, said if General Motors would build it, they would come. Some 20,000 went to their local dealers and repeated the same words. They never had a chance. It got worse. While there were about 250 cars available, there weren't another 250 celebrities, authorities, and athletes anxious to pay a high price for a crude car. Corvettes had side curtains like the inexpensive MG-TC, and owners had to reach through them to find door latches. The car leaked water at the windshield and the top. It wasn't a cheap car, but it looked like one.

The car sent mixed signals. Tom Keating, sensitive to public perceptions, attempted to direct the public's view. In a statement released after the introduction, he said, "In the Corvette, we have built a sports car in the American tradition. It is not a racing car in the accepted sense that a European sports car is a race car. It is intended rather to satisfy the American public's conception of beauty, comfort, convenience plus performance."

Corvette's target in every way had been Jaguar's XK120. Chassis engineer Maurice Olley configured the car's layout based on Jaguar's 102-inch wheelbase and Harley Earl's handpicked chief stylist and engineer Bob McLean designed the car from the rear axle forward, emulating Jaguar's long hood. But the Corvette was American in every other way.

In May 1953, a month before production began, Chevrolet hired an ambitious, inventive engineer who first saw the Corvette at New York's Motorama. Zora Arkus-Duntov came with good credentials. He was born Zachary Arkuss on Christmas Day 1909 in Brussels. Writer George Damon Levy, interviewing Duntov in 1988 for *Corvette Quarterly*, learned his story. When he was in his teens, his mother, a Russian physician, divorced her engineer husband. She remarried Josef Duntov, another engineer, and "Zora," the Russian nickname for Zachary, began hyphenating his name. He was educated in Germany, and with considerable European racing and engineering experience behind him, he joined Cole's staff when we was 44 and went straight to work for Olley. He quickly got into the first engineering prototype Corvette. Pressing it to its limit, he found Chevrolet "had a car in which the two ends were fighting each other." While the rear end's canted springs did induce understeer, the front end configuration caused oversteer from which it was difficult to recover.

While it was too late to help the 1953 production cars, Duntov performed the first of countless surgeries he would undertake over the next 22 years, and he brought some manners to the 1956 cars. Duntov's first "fix" was an exhaust modification for 1954; buyers complained that the exhaust stained the trunks. Duntov learned that inefficient aerodynamics actually sucked the exhaust forward and into the cockpit. In midyear 1954, Duntov opened a slot in the bottom of the exhaust extension with a baffle to project the fumes down. This continued through 1955 production and led to the conclusion that placing the exhaust at the fender tips eliminated the problem completely. What started as a simple appearance matter became a much greater safety issue.

Sales did better in 1954, aided by the start of major advertising for the car. (A Detroit-area newspaper ad first appeared in late May 1953 announcing a chance to see "America's Sensational Sports Car!" at the Michigan Motor Show in early June.) One 1954 series was image-oriented. It ran several times in the *New Yorker*, each time using the tagline, "First of the dream cars to come true." These ads emphasized Corvette's styling, handling, and its unique appeal. Ads in other magazines with sedans, station wagons, and trucks made it clear the car was part of the giant, popular, Chevrolet family.

Engineering modified the camshaft, which added 5 horsepower and raised the total to 155. Two paint colors were added, Black and Sportsman Red, all with red interiors, and toward the end of the year cars began to appear in Pennant Blue with beige interiors. The black top for 1953 became tan in 1954. While St. Louis had the capacity to produce 10,000 Corvettes a year, only 3,640 came off the line, and of those, only 2,780 sold. Between 1953 and 1954 sales, Chevrolet found itself with a surplus of nearly 1,100 unsold cars on January 1, 1955.

Designer Howard Darrin created this fiberglass-bodied car in 1952 using a Willys 2.6-liter inline six-cylinder engine for his employer Henry Kaiser. Darrin designed a three-position cloth top (up, down, or partial coverage, like a formal town car). Innovative sliding doors disappeared into the front fenders. Production ended with only 435 cars built when Kaiser Motors Corporation relocated to Toledo, Ohio, in 1953, to merge with Willys.

While its exclusivity was directed toward the country club set, it was too unsophisticated and uncivilized for them. On the other hand, sports car enthusiasts wanted more power and a transmission that they shifted themselves. In all, only 183 cars were sold in 1953.

The Flint assembly plant was small; its line was long enough for only six chassis. This converted garage on Van Slyke Avenue gave engineers and manufacturing personnel the chance to get the bugs out of the system while the line in St. Louis was being converted to Corvette's permanent home. Before the end of 1953, the first 14 St. Louis factory cars were produced. By June 1954, when the first magazine reviews appeared, production was up to 50 per day in St. Louis (it was 50 a month in Flint).

Ed Cole reflected on the dilemma surrounding the Corvette in an interview at the time. Quoted 18 years afterward in Karl Ludvigsen's 1973 book, *Corvette: America's Star Spangled Sports Car*, Cole explained that Chevrolet "had no real feeling for the market. Was the Corvette for the boulevard driver or the sports-car tiger? We weren't quite sure." The inability to define their customer—*Road & Track* readers or *New Yorker* subscribers?—caused a great deal of soul searching. St. Louis production was throttled back to 16 cars a day.

While management wrestled with the Corvette's future, Harley Earl's stylists and Ed Cole's engineers pressed ahead with revisions and updates. Styling wanted to use an egg-crate grille design similar to the 1955 Bel-Air, and it

proposed a functional hood air scoop and several dummy louvers along the body panel behind the front wheels. They wanted to rid the rear end of its troublesome taillight bullets. These required extensive hand work from the beginning because matched metal molds had difficulty with the abruptness of the curves and the complexity of shapes projected out into space. But there was no money. So for 1955, colors could be changed; Harvest Gold replaced Pennant Blue and Sportsman Red went away for Gypsy Red. The body could be only barely modified. Harley Earl began to hear that the car's future was in doubt.

Throughout 1954 the car still suffered from what reviewers and enthusiasts alike thought was insufficient

Two paint colors were added for the 1954 model year, Black and Sportsman Red, all with red interiors. Toward the end of the year cars began to appear in Pennant Blue with beige interiors. The black top for 1953 became tan in 1954.

Records indicate that 95 percent of all 1954s were either blue or white. Chevrolet cut the retail price down to $2,774.00 from $3,498.00 at introduction, partially by listing the standard automatic transmission as a $178.35 option.

Chevrolet General Manager Tom Keating optimistically projected 1954 sales at 6,000 cars. Production ended at 3,640, with the car's reputation slightly damaged by the difficulty ordinary buyers experienced even ordering a car in 1953.

horsepower. When Ed Cole arrived at Chevrolet Division, its own new 231-cubic-inch V-8 engine was being developed. This was a legacy from Ed Kelley, the previous chief engineer, and one of Cole's first moves was to increase its displacement to 265 cubic inches. Engineers were anxious to see how it would affect the performance of the Corvette, so they refitted 1953 car 002 with a prototype V-8. It ran flawlessly for 25,000 miles out at Milford, convincing Keating and Cole to offer it not only with the Powerglide but eventually with a three-speed manual gearbox for 1955.

The new engine brought life to the Corvette. Performance jumped, with 0-to-60-mile-per-hour times cut three full seconds to 8.0 in the late 1955 cars fitted with the three-speed. Top speed climbed to 120 miles per hour, and fuel economy rose from 17 to 20 miles per gallon. Engineering used a single Carter four-barrel carburetor with an automatic choke replacing the triple carburetors with their temperamental manual chokes. The new engine brought with it a 12-volt electrical system.

Chevrolet's timing was nearly miraculous. In early 1954, Ford announced its V-8 Thunderbird with roll-up windows to sell for $2,695. Production began in September.

Motor Trend's Don MacDonald compared and contrasted the two in an insightful story in the June 1955 issue. "The basic difference between the Corvette and Thunderbird is not so much the body material, but a conflicting analysis of the American market. The Corvette was patterned closely after the European concept of a competition car. *Conversely,*

By year end, only 2,780 Corvettes had sold and Chevrolet found itself with a surplus of nearly 1,100 unsold cars. Division and corporate executives searched their souls and scratched their heads, trying to figure out what the car was and who might buy it. Engineering knew that the car needed a V-8.

Some of the magazine reviewers commented on the slender bumpers fitted to the Corvettes. They were, however, no more or less fragile than Jaguar, Porsche, Ferrari, or Mercedes-Benz models at the time, each equipped with bumpers as styling trim, not impact protection. Early 1954 Corvettes had short exhaust extensions, but after Zora Duntov's tests to discover the cause of stains on the back of the car, the extensions were lengthened.

the designers of the Thunderbird aimed at and achieved a California custom flavor [italics MacDonald's]. This is why Corvette presently has an *almost* purist indifference to the problem of weather protection. It was easy for the come-lately Thunderbird to offer adequate coverage. . . ." Mac-Donald couldn't know that it was economics, not purism that affected weather protection.

By the end of 1955, Ford sold 16,155 copies of its T'bird, ironically based on the same Jaguar XK-120 that had defined the Corvette) while Chevrolet produced only 700 more Corvettes and sold just 675 (a few dozen of which were fitted with the manual gearbox).

These kinds of numbers sent ordinary men to the showers, defeated and humiliated. But neither Earl nor Cole, Keating nor Curtice were ordinary men. In 1953 General Motors sold 45 percent of the new automobiles and trucks in the United States. Chevrolet knew it had scored a home run with its V-8. Sales of passenger cars fitted with the new engine topped 1.83 million and another 393,000 buyers ordered V-8 trucks. The Corvette just had not yet caught the buyers' imaginations.

After this, few people were confident that the engine and gearbox alone could save the car. "By the looks of it, the Corvette is on its way out," Duntov wrote privately to Cole and Olley in mid-October 1954. "Dropping the car now will have adverse effect internally and externally. It is admission of failure. Failure of aggressive thinking in the eyes of the organization, failure to develop a salable product in the

eyes of the outside world. The Corvette failed," he continued "because it did not meet GM standards of a product. It did not have the value for the money. If the value of a car consists of practical values and emotional appeal, the sports car has very little of the first and consequently has to have an exaggerated amount of the second." Thunderbird's "success" did nothing for the folks at GM but sharpen their senses and tempt them with the smell of fresh blood, even if it was their own. Chevrolet research reported that 17 percent of American households were two-car families. Ford had found 16,155 buyers where Chevrolet had not; GM had to recapture those individuals. It had no idea Ford was about to help.

chapter 5

Making the Real McCoy a National Champion: 1956

When the paper wraps came off the 1956 Corvette in the Waldorf ballroom that year, Harley Earl's stylists and Ed Cole's engineers had transformed the car. When Tom Keating approved production through 1957, the designers and engineers had little time to make changes to attract any of the buyers lost to the Thunderbird.

Chevrolet's planners had found a new target. Mercedes-Benz 300SL racing coupes first appeared in 1952, featuring modestly raked headlights like the first Corvettes. When the road-going SLs appeared for 1954, Mercedes' designer Paul Braiq moved the lights out and mounted them vertically in the fenders. Its inline six-cylinder engine was tilted slightly, but still the hood had two gentle bulges for clearance. These hinted at power, the image Earl's stylists wanted for Chevy's new V-8s. When stylist Bob Cadaret finished the front of the 1956 Corvette, it resembled the 300SL. (Stylistic plagiarism was common. Jaguar's own designers admitted to duplicating a 1940 BMW Mille Miglia race car when they designed the XK-120.)

Another design element was adopted from a 1955 Motorama Cadillac dream car. The LaSalle II introduced a long horizontal scallop cut into the body side, like great sweeping front fender curves from the late 1930s. This imparted a classic elegance to the Corvette side view, creating visual appeal, yet breaking up the side panel.

Cadaret cleaned up the rear end of the car, removing the projecting taillights and scalloping them into the fenders. For 1956 Corvette achieved an economy of line and clarity of design by removing the excesses. Even the scallop, while an addition, seemed intentional, not merely decorative.

Bringing the Corvette creature comforts that *New Yorker* readers expected, the car got roll-up windows (with

power window lifts available), outside door handles, and an optional power system for the convertible top. These things couldn't be done between Motorama and production start in 1953. Windows required forming curved glass and fabricating lift mechanisms and support rails. The show car was supposed to remind everyone of sunny days. Purists who bought MG-TCs and Jaguar XK-120 roadsters endured side curtains, so Harley Earl's expectations seemed less scandalous at the time.

Styling changes were finally approved in February 1955. The Motorama unveiling was made possible only by using fiberglass. (Had dies been necessary for steel stamping rather than for fiberglass molding, the 1956 car would have arrived closer to 1957.) Fiberglass even allowed Styling to position a chrome strip around the side scallop and to add the twin decorative scoops just ahead of the windshield that had appeared on the Motorama prototype.

The 265-ci V-8 was introduced in 1955; however, buyers that year could still order the Blue Flame Special inline six-cylinder engine. For 1956, three V-8s were offered. The base was 210 horsepower. Regular production option (RPO) 469, with two four-barrel Carter carburetors, offered 225 horsepower. A limited issue RPO 449, the Duntov Cam, provided 240 horsepower and was strictly "for racing purposes only."

Coves, the scalloped insets on the body sides, first appeared on the 1956 production cars although they originated with the 1953 Motorama Buick Wildcat II and they reappeared on the 1955 LaSalle II show cars. Motorama shows allowed Styling to give buyers hints of designs in the works.

Dr. Dick Thompson squints from the cockpit of Racer Brown and Bob D'Olivo's 1956 Corvette before the start of the Palm Springs season ender. Racer Brown, *Hot Rod* magazine's technical editor, walks away in the background. Thompson raced this car and another he kept on the East Coast to win Corvette's first national SCCA racing championship. *Bob D'Olivo*

Road & Track put the 1956 redesigned Corvette on its March 1956 cover.

In mid-December 1953, Zora Duntov wrote a memo to his boss that became a wake-up call to Chevrolet Division. He expressed his concern that car enthusiast magazines were filled with stories about Ford. He felt this kind of exposure would encourage the readers to stick with Ford as their financial status improved.

"It is reasonable to assume," Duntov wrote, "that when the hot-rodders . . . buy transportation, they buy Fords. As they progress in age and income, they graduate from jalopies to second-hand Fords, then to new Fords."

He suggested there was room for Chevrolet in this market, but it would take time to get in.

"Like all people, hot-rodders are attracted by novelty," he continued. "However, bitter experience taught them that new development is costly, long and therefore they are extremely conservative. From my observation, it takes an advanced hot-rodder some three years to stumble towards the successful development of a new design."

Duntov suggested that Chevrolet produce special engine and chassis performance parts and market them to the public.

"The association of Chevrolet with hot rods, speed and such is probably inadmissible, but possibly the existence of the Corvette provides the loophole. If the speed parts are carried as RPO [regular production option] items for the Corvette, they undoubtedly will be recognized by the hot-rodders as the very parts they were looking for to hop up the Chevy.

"If it is desirable or not to associate the Corvette [with] speed, I am not qualified to say but I do know that in 1954 sports car enthusiasts will get hold of the Corvette and whether we like it or not, will race it. [The] most frequent statement from this group is 'we will put a Cadillac in it [in order to get V-8 power to be competitive]. They are going to and I think this is not good! Most likely they will meet with Allard trouble—that is, breaking, sooner or later, mostly sooner, everything between [the] flywheel and [the] road wheels. Since we cannot prevent people from racing Corvettes, maybe it is better to help them to do a good job at it.

"To make good in this field, the RPO parts must pertain not only to the engine but to the chassis components as well. Engineering-wise, development of these RPO items, as far as the chassis [is] concerned, does not fall out of line with some of the planned activity of our group. Use of light alloys, brake development—composite drums, disc and such—are on the agenda of the Research and Development group already."

Duntov knew the value of creating a sense of loyalty in Chevrolet buyers and a belief that the company would produce what they wanted. He still had to prove himself, however, before his ideas took on credibility.

The Real McCoy ran in *Hot Rod* and *Road & Track* in July 1956. Its *Life Magazine* style photojournalistic image—grainy black-and-white against a scorched sky—of a car that obviously had run hard, did as much as any competition victory to establish the car as a real racer. *Campbell-Ewald*

By the time of the Palm Springs race, Petersen Publishing's photographic director, Bob D'Olivo and *Hot Rod* magazine technical editor Racer Brown had dialed in the production car as a race car. During midseason, SCCA rules allowed entrants to replace the stock windshield with lower windscreens. That and the roll bar were among the few obvious improvements. The rest was beneath the skin. *Bob D'Olivo*

His work on camshafts and cylinder heads with his brother Yura, prior to joining Chevrolet, earned them respect as creative development engineers. Duntov's work taming the handling of the 1956 V-8 production model established his credentials within Chevrolet. The mark of Zora meant something on his adopted car.

Corvettes came closer to realizing Duntov's handling goals with the new 265-cubic-inch V-8, which weighed 41 pounds less than the old Blue Flame Special. The V-8 was shorter and lower as well, so the *center* of its weight was better placed within the automobile. The engine, with its single Carter four-barrel carburetor, produced 210 horsepower. An optional second four-barrel, improved the output to 225 horsepower.

The Corvette arrived with new skin, new colors, and even an optional plastic hardtop and heater to keep out New York winters. Chevrolet hoped to tantalize those *New Yorker* readers. Its improved V-8 and transmission got attention in magazines such as *Road and Track*.

Duntov drove a preproduction 1956 full-sized passenger car camouflaged-prototype and set a new class record on the 12.5-mile climb to the top of Pike's Peak in September 1955. He reached the summit in 17 minutes, 24 seconds. This performance meant little to average customers. Timed speed on a track, however, was what caught peoples' attention. The Jaguar XK-120 in hottest trim was capable of 130

miles per hour. Mercedes' gull-wing 300SL coupe was reported to do 136 to 146 miles per hour in standard trim. What if the engineers could coax 150 miles per hour out of the Corvette?

Cole gave Duntov clearance, and the Daytona Beach project moved to GM's Phoenix test track to determine how Duntov could reach this speed. He needed another 30 horsepower, which he could get with a special cam. Several were cast and shipped to Duntov in Phoenix. He found the engine would pull to 6,300 rpm, and it had enough power to reach, theoretically, 163 miles per hour.

At Daytona, the right combination of sand conditions, low tides, and minimal winds eluded Duntov and his fellow engineers. December slipped into early January before managing a two-way certified run averaging 150.58 miles per hour. He had met his goal, using an engine that produced 240 horsepower from parts soon to be available over the counter. The crew went back for the official Daytona Speed Weeks in February with three cars, each with an engine with modified heads producing a 10.3:1 compression ratio and developing 255 horsepower. Betty Skelton and John Fitch, experienced racing drivers, each had a car to run and Duntov kept the third for himself.

Ford showed up with several Thunderbirds. Competition was fierce. Times were measured not only for top speed runs but also for standing-start mile runs. At the end of the

week, suffering traction problems not solved even by running snow tires on the sand, John Fitch finished third (at 86.87 miles per hour) behind two Thunderbirds at the completion of the standing-start mile runs. Duntov averaged 147.3 miles per hour for the flying mile, zipping back and forth over the beach, to beat all the Thunderbird challengers but also Fitch and Skelton as well.

Cole and Duntov understood competition; however, short runs, time trials, and hill climbs were one thing. Races that required brakes and handling were another. While Duntov and company waited Daytona's weather, they took a car with softer springs to Sebring to test the car and the course. A few laps hinted that Sebring might be a good track for Corvette. Before the final runs at Daytona with Duntov, Fitch, and Skelton were completed, Cole started engineers preparing four cars for the 12-hour race six weeks later.

Bill Pollack ran the car in Cal Club events through the entire season. For the first half of the season in both Cal Club events and in SCCA races (with Dick Thompson driving), the D'Olivo/Brown prepared car ran with its full windshield and side-mounted exhaust pipes. D'Olivo shot in those days with a 4x5 Graphic Press camera. Its shutter mechanism made the car appear to be reaching forward while the spectators fell away. *Bob D'Olivo*

While driver Bill Pollack gestures, Bob D'Olivo in white coveralls, runs up to tell Pollack where to go for a tire change between sessions. Early in the season at Palm Springs, the car still carried its front bumper protector, full chrome-trimmed windshield and wiper blades. Midseason, SCCA rules permitted lower racing windscreens. *Bob D'Olivo collection*

Chevrolet initiated a racing strategy it used for decades, entering factory-prepared cars by private individuals, dealerships, or teams. For Sebring, it was Dick Doane of Dundee, Illinois, and his Raceway Enterprises operation, though Duntov's friend John Fitch managed and directed it. This operation initiated Duntov's memo suggesting that parts developed for racing be listed as regular production options. Now hot-rodders and other competitors could have access; it also meant that Corvettes ran in regular production categories, against Mercedes-Benz 300SLs and Jaguar 120s and 140s rather than in prototype classes against pure racing machines. Duntov, Maurice "Rosey" Rosenberger, an engine and transmission problems trouble-shooter, and Russell Sanders, chief of passenger-car chassis design, had plenty to do in about 90 days. They invented and tested parts so they could catalog each one for eventual over-the-counter sales.

They fitted the engines with dual carburetors and Duntov's cam. They enlarged intake and exhaust ports to allow better engine breathing, and they even bored and stroked one engine out to 307-cubic-inch displacement. That car ran with an imported ZF four-speed transmission.

For a first-time effort the four cars may have let down Chevrolet's engineers, but they won respect from the crowd. Two of the cars quit early. The third entry finished 15th overall, running with only top gear for hours. A virtually dealership-stock entry finished next to last, but it finished. Best of all, the big-engine car, limping through the race on a slipping clutch, placed ninth overall. For a major corporation, it was a less than satisfying result, but for anyone who knew racing, it was a very impressive debut.

Chevrolet's advertising agency, Campbell-Ewald, used the opportunity to steer Corvette promotion into new terrain. An ad in the April 1956, New York Auto Show program prepared by agency writer and racing director Arthur "Barney" Clark, invited viewers to "Bring on the hay bales!" Campbell-Ewald pressed harder in the July issues of *Road & Track* and *Hot Rod*. The ad showed a gritty black-and-white photo of a grilleless 1956 Corvette, headlights on, driving lights mounted below the grille while a figure in a driving suit ran around the back of the car. It had the visual effect of a *Life* magazine photo story. In the bleached white sky above the runner, Clark burned in the words, "The Real McCoy." The text reminded readers of the "glove soft upholstery, roll-up windows, ample luggage space and a velvety ride." But it went on: "Other people make a luxury car," Clark wrote, "that has much the same dimensions as this. That's not so tough. And the Europeans make some real rugged competition sports cars—and that's considerably tougher. But nobody but Chevrolet makes a luxury car that *also* is a genuine 100-proof sports car."

Engineering learned from its race cars. Braking had plagued the Corvettes at Sebring. Production brakes ran out quickly even under the speeds allowed by the earliest

six-cylinder engines with automatic transmissions. For competition, with a 255-horsepower V-8, Engineering tried everything that was available. As Karl Ludvigsen reported, Corvette engineers experimented with massively finned brake drums and Halibrand wheels. "The only combination that proved it could stay the distance," Ludvigsen wrote, "was that of Bendix Cerametallix linings inside heavily finned iron drums, liberally supplied with cooling air through screened scoops. . . . But [these brakes] were heavy, and they forced the Corvette to become heavier too."

Selecting the brakes was a decision with ramifications that went far beyond race day, March 26, 1956. It set the stage for future decisions where weight was balanced against safety or performance or comfort. Zora Duntov told Ludvigsen these brakes represented "a watershed decision that took the Corvette irrevocably in the direction of a larger, heavier car, barring any possible return to a lightweight design concept."

One month after Sebring, two Californians drove up to Pebble Beach to see another kind of racing. Bob D'Olivo was Petersen Publishing's staff photographer. W. G. "Racer" Brown, was technical editor at Petersen's *Hot Rod*

Petersen Publishing advertising salesman Bill Pollack proved a worthy pilot in Cal Club events on odd weekends when Dick Thompson was not driving the car in SCCA West Coast events. Under both drivers, the 1956 car won championships in both SCCA and Cal Club. Here Pollack sweeps through esses at the Pomona Fair Grounds. *Bob D'Olivo*

Harley Earl's son Jerry purchased a Ferrari to race in SCCA events. Earl felt his son should drive an American car, so he had Styling's mechanical assembly shops prepare a Corvette. Zora Duntov added Sebring-type Cerametallic brakes and other improvements to otherwise stock running gear. After its first race, some 300 pounds of weight was removed. The rear wing headrest came later in the season.

magazine, based in Los Angeles. Brown owned a 1955 V-8 Corvette that he'd modified with an Edelbrock triple-carburetor manifold. D'Olivo and Brown were anxious for the April 22, 1956, SCCA season opener and its 15-lap Cypress Point Handicap for production cars over 1,500 cc.

The race offered a field of Jaguars kept honest by three highly competitive Mercedes-Benz 300SLs. Mixing it up within the 38-car field were two Corvettes. One of these was to be driven by a dentist from Washington, D.C., R. K. "Dick" Thompson Jr., who posted times fast enough in practice to worry his competition. When the race began, Thompson in his Aztec Copper number 46 hardtop, roared away. He held onto the lead until lap 5 when his hard-braking driving style took its toll on the car. On the seventh lap Tony Settember in a 300SL passed Thompson. They finished in that order, but Thompson's brakes smoked long after he shut off the engine in the pits.

Brown and D'Olivo went to the hotel where Chevy people were staying. Duntov was there with Campbell-Ewald personnel and some engineers. Brown and D'Olivo knew Duntov, and they were invited in. They got to talking. Some 40 years later D'Olivo recalled the night: "One of us just said to Duntov, 'Give us a car, we'll make the thing run.'

"They didn't respond. Or look terribly excited. But two, three weeks later, we got a phone call. Where did we want the Corvette?

"Racer had an apartment. I had a little three-bedroom house. Kicked my Buick out of the garage and that was the shop for the car. The car came on a Wednesday and that weekend was a Pomona SCCA race."

This was not Thompson's car from Monterey. This was red, painted with number 106 on it. The convertible top and radio were still in it, but it had no roll bar. With barely a day before practice, D'Olivo yanked the radio, the top mechanism, and anything else that race cars don't need. Brown adjusted the two four-barrel carburetors.

"It came with Firestone 170 Super Sports tires, as hard as a table as far as compounds went," D'Olivo continued. "Pomona being a parking lot course with smooth blacktop, these tires didn't fare too well.

"We took the car out to Pomona, put it in the race. Dick Thompson flew out here, drove it and we got beaten pretty badly."

Through personal experience and effective arguments, Duntov convinced management that race wins attracted buyers. Chevrolet, however, continued to race through private entries; these two Corvettes were registered outside the company. Thompson was contracted to drive both cars, number 46 on the East Coast, registered to him, and number 106, the Brown/D'Olivo car that was registered to Dick Jess (who at the time worked for Campbell-Ewald.) With this arrangement, neither Chevrolet nor Thompson had to haul a car back and forth across the country.

In its first appearance at Road America, the SR2 was a handful. Jerry Earl turned over the driver's seat to veteran Corvette racer Dick Thompson. Because of Harley Earl's body styling changes, the car competed in a modified class. By the end of the race, Thompson had a list of real modifications in mind to make the car successful.

"They told us they didn't want any factory acknowledgment or recognition, even though they supplied the car and all the parts, spare engines, and whatever. It all came from Engineering," D'Olivo explained. "I think they saw the [1957 Automobile Manufacturers Association] racing ban coming and decided, 'Let's not get into racing now and then have to get out of it.'

"After our first race, we had some work to do on the car. We added an extra leaf in the rear springs. Glendale Spring Shop made up three different front stabilizer bars, in different increments each up a 16th of an inch in diameter. We put them on and went out behind my house on a little road. When we lifted the rear inside tire a little bit, we'd go back down to the next bar. It was the only way we had in those days of telling whether the thing was doing it right.

"We played around with shocks, put larger rebound bumpers on the rear to limit the travel on the suspension. The car had canvas limit straps for the rear axle, and I shortened those, to snug the car down a little bit. I went all over looking for rubber bumpers in the length I wanted. I finally found them at a Chrysler dealer. We drilled two holes in the front A-arms, and we put these big bumpers between the lower A-arm and the cross-member to limit their travel. We took the steering wheel off and shortened the column about 4 inches, pushed it in so it wasn't in Thompson's chest anymore. We put in a roll bar and a Jones Direct Drive tachometer.

"From that time on, we never lost an SCCA race. It won every one that Dick drove." D'Olivo paused a moment, his mind briefly gone 40 years back and a thousand miles away.

"Mercedes 300SLs dominated C production, blowing everything off the race track. We went up to [the] Seattle [Seafarer Race], flat-towed the car behind our Chevy. It had a new motor and somewhere up in Oregon we disconnected it from the tow car. Racer drove it on the highway at night for maybe 100 miles to break it in. We got there and it just blew off all the Mercedes.

"It was the first time any of those Mercedes racers had ever been beaten. We noticed in the very first race at Pomona where there were a couple of slow turns, that with a three-speed gearbox, you're not gonna compete with these Mercedes. We were limited to the three-speed box because of production class rules. We asked Chevrolet to give us a higher first gear. That really helped. We could get it into first gear and really accelerate out of the slow turns. I think that's what made the difference against the Mercedes.

"Halfway through the season, SCCA allowed racers to take the windshield off production cars. So I took it off, had Harry Mann Chevrolet fill in the trough that was left; it looked good and it was very smooth. Chevrolet Engineering sent us a little windscreen to bolt on in its place.

"It came down to the Palm Springs race in November, the final SCCA race. We needed a win to take the title. Dick did a hell of a job, went out there and beat the Mercedes—not by much—the timers said by one second, maybe 100 feet—but he won the race and that gave a Corvette the national championship."

D'Olivo called Engineering on Mondays following the races to tell them how they'd done and *what* they'd done. Chevrolet Engineering provided assistance and equipment for the car; however, they seldom asked questions. D'Olivo and Brown submitted all their receipts, including travel, and Campbell-Ewald paid the expenses.

"Sometime in there we asked Chevrolet about running in Cal Club races. Bill Pollack worked as an ad salesman at Petersen for *Auto* magazine. He was a *driver*. He drove Tom Carsten's J2 Cad-Allard very well. We asked him and he said, 'Hell, yeah!' and Chevrolet said fine.

"We started running Cal Club races in B production with Pollack driving in between the SCCA events that Thompson ran. Pollack won every Cal Club race with that car except the very last one, which was Paramount Ranch. The only mechanical problem we ever had with that car came when the throttle stuck. He came out from underneath the overpass before a left hander. He couldn't make the turn, and he ended up down in the ditch, and it dinged up the left front corner of the car.

"It was the last race and the car had already won the SCCA championship. We were through with SCCA and that was our commitment to Chevrolet," D'Olivo said.

"You know, in those days, you just go to the races and find your own pit. Somebody moves next to you, fine. Sometimes other Corvettes would pit next to us and we felt so sorry for those guys. They didn't have a chance, didn't come close to this car. They'd come over and look at the car. Same as theirs. They never counted the leafs in the rear spring. I don't know what else visually you could see because everything else was pretty well disguised or hidden.

"They'd just shake their heads. They didn't understand why ours was so fast and theirs wasn't. They'd look at the tires, what tire pressures were we running. We'd tell them. But their motor wasn't blueprinted at Edelbrock's. Vic Sr. did it. I'm sure it was blueprinted out to max displacement. He weighed all the valves and springs and every piece so they were all the same. We never asked, just took the motor down there, and picked it up a week later, put it in the car and went off to the races.

"We did our stuff by seat-of-the-pants reasoning. Look at it and say, 'Hey, maybe it needs this, maybe that.' Racer was awfully good on tuning. He knew those four-barrel carburetors inside and out, and he would twinkle and twitch with those things. He'd get them running; he did it himself because he was an old hot-rodder. We got some decent tires after that Pomona race, some Engleberts, a German-made tire that Ferrari used at the time. It had a softer compound, and so between the Engleberts and the Firestones, we suited the tire to the course.

"It all just worked into a really good, reliable car. It was the first car to beat the Mercedes. It went right down to the last race at Palm Springs that gave Dick Thompson the championship. Gave Corvette its first national championship.

"I could have bought it, after we smacked it up at Paramount. It sat in my garage, dusty and dirty, with the left front fender cracked. It sat there for three months, and I wanted to put my Buick back in the garage. I had tires stacked to the roof, spare engines, spare transmissions. I called Chevrolet and said I'd like my garage back. They said they'd get back to me. They called back about two weeks later and asked me if I wanted to buy it.

"How much? They said $1,400. I could have everything.

"Hell, I was just starting out with my family. I didn't have $1,400 to spend on a race car. If I bought it, I'd have to race it because when I took that windshield off, it had fiberglass over the trough where the stock windshield fit into it. So you'd never be able to put it back to a street machine again. . . .

"So I said, no. Come and get it.

"Somebody, I think the Chevy dealer, Lou Williams Chevrolet, across from our office came with a flatbed and hauled it away, all the spares and the car."

Before 1956 was over, Ed Cole succeeded
Tom Keating as Chevrolet Division general manager. Harlow Curtice and his board members saw that Cole's efforts with the Corvette had simply not had enough time to prove themselves. If Cole, Harley Earl, and Zora Duntov needed more reassurance that the Corvette was safe, it could not have been announced more clearly.

Curiously, even the combined brilliance of Earl, Duntov, and Cole again failed to light the spark within American car buyers in 1956. Chevrolet Division produced only 3,467 Corvettes, while Ford *sold* more than 15,000 of its Thunderbirds.

Ford knew from the start that Harley Earl and Ed Cole planned to keep the Corvette a sports car. Chase Morsey, a Ford product planner, set the Thunderbird's direction. Frank Hershey, a very talented and influential former Cadillac division stylist and longtime friend of Harley Earl (whom Earl fired), had gone to Ford. He concurred with Morsey's vision. Ford Thunderbird was to be a "personal car," something that buyers knew fit between a sports car and a family passenger car. Chevrolet could keep its sports car.

chapter 6

Provoking Management: 1957

Robert Cumberford knew he wanted to design cars. Two classmates from his alma mater, Franklin High School in Los Angeles, won the Fisher Body Craftsman national senior (Ron Cadaret) and junior (Ron Hill) awards in 1950. Others who would make careers in GM styling also attended Franklin, Stan Mott and Larry Shinoda.

Their desire to be automotive designers led them to the nearby Art Center College of Design. Cumberford himself did three terms there before his funding ran out and he had to face a future doing something else. An older friend who had done a short stint designing at Ford, however, told Cumberford if he wanted to work at GM he should draw against an alarm clock. When Cumberford got comfortable making 10-minute drawings, his friend set the clock for 5 minutes, and after a couple of weeks, he shortened the time to 3 minutes. When he had done these quick sketches for a while, the friend said it was time to send the best ones off to Harley Earl. It was July 1954 and Cumberford was a month shy of 19.

One day, Cumberford's mother suggested to him that perhaps automotive design was not for him. As if on cue, the mailman arrived with Cumberford's portfolio and a $455-a-month job offer from Earl himself. Six weeks later to the day, Cumberford started at the Argonaut Building, General Motors Research Annex B, in downtown Detroit. Cumberford worked in a body studio with Herb Cadeau on the 1956 Motorama Cadillac Eldorado Brougham town car. When that was done, Cumberford was sent to the Chevrolet studio, his longtime goal.

During mid-September 1955, the same time as the Watkins Glen Sports Car races, all 1,200 of the Styling staff, as well as researchers and engineers, had a three-day weekend. Everyone left work Thursday from downtown Detroit and reported to work Monday at the brand-new Eero Saarinen–designed Technical Center. Begun in 1949, the $125 million, 990-acre, 25-building campus was located in suburban Warren, Michigan, about 10 miles north of the General Motors building.

In 1949, as ground was broken for the Tech Center, Cadillac promoted its V-8 engine. Ed Cole was the chief engineer, and he directed development of this new 331-cubic-inch powerplant. Ed Kelley was Chevrolet's chief engineer when Chevy began its own 231-cubic-inch V-8 in 1951. In 1950, Kelley retired and Cole took his job, bringing along his assistant chief engineer, Harry F. Barr, to Chevrolet. They quickly abandoned the 231 displacement idea for a larger capacity engine based on the Cadillac.

Assistant staff engineer Al Kolbe, Barr, and Cole first considered an engine of 245 cubic inches, but as Anthony Young reported in his 1992 *Chevrolet Small-Block V-8*, later they pushed bore and stroke dimensions to 265 cubic inches overall. This engine, with its 3.765-inch bore and 3.00-inch stroke, was soon known as the "small-block" V-8.

Prototype engines were running in Chevrolet's engine testing lab in suburban Hamtramck by the spring of 1953. Road testing solved oil smoke problems and countless other little things that vexed Cole, a perfectionist who had come from General Motors' quietest car division. Chevy engineers came to understand a statement Cole made early in his career at Chevrolet. Anthony Young reported the quote: "Instead of Chevrolet engineers driving Cadillacs, Cadillac engineers are going to be driving Chevrolets." It meant that, good as Cadillac's engines were, Chevrolet's were going to be much better. It didn't matter to Cole that his division

The 1957 body was unchanged from its 1956 version. Base price rose slightly to $3,176.32. Most popular options included a heater (5,373 sold, not yet standard equipment), white wall tires (5,019), the auxiliary hardtop (4,055), the signal-seeking AM radio (3,635), and two-tone paint (2,797).

The major developments were under the hood. Engineering introduced a new 283ci V-8, developed from the previous 265. Base power rating was 220 horsepower. At the other end of the range was the new Rochester fuel injected 283 horsepower engine. This was good for 5.7 second 0-to-60 miles per hour times, while still in first gear.

Sports Cars Illustrated's August 1957 cover announced SCI technical editor Karl Ludvigsen's analysis of the Corvette SS on its inside pages.

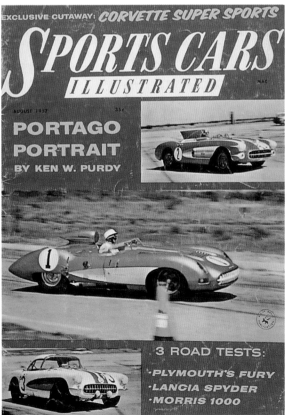

produced cars for the masses where he had earlier produced engines for the elite. It only mattered that *his* people produced the *best* engines. When the 265 V-8 was introduced, it weighed 531 pounds—41 less than the Blue Flame Six. This weight loss allowed chassis engineers such as Russ Sanders and performance-envelope-stretchers such as Zora Duntov to improve the 1956 Corvette's handling.

For 1956, a new camshaft increased output to 210 horsepower from the previous year engine. Regular Production Option (RPO) 469 loaded two four-barrel carburetors on top of a new manifold, resulting in 225 horsepower. This could be coupled with the three-speed manual transmission. *Road & Track* magazine tested an RPO 469 Corvette fitted with the 3.27:1 rear axle. With the manual transmission, *R&T*'s car hit a top speed of 129 miles per hour and, using a 3.55:1 axle, ran 0 to 60 miles per hour in 7.3 seconds.

The Chevrolet Engineering Center opened in December 1956. One of the first projects completed was one started downtown in the old, drafty bank building that was Engineering's former home. Set on improving intake/exhaust flow on the 265, Engineering enlarged the cylinder bore by 0.125 inches to 3.875 inches, creating an engine with a 283-cubic-inch displacement. Corvette for 1957 offered the engine with two Carter four-barrel carburetors and 245 horsepower. A still-hotter version cranked out 270 horsepower, while the wildest tune developed 283

Inca Silver was the least common paint color delivered in 1957. Records indicate that just 65 of the 6,339 cars produced in St. Louis wore this distinctive color. More common by far was its 283-horsepower fuel-injected V-8 and four-speed transmission. This car, originally sold at Three-Way Chevrolet, Bakersfield, California, went for $3,875.75 with tax and license.

Part of the *Sports Cars Illustrated* August 1957 technical story on the Corvette SS was artist C. O. LaTourette's center spread cutaway drawing and technical specifications.

horsepower. This was the first General Motors production engine to reach 1 horsepower per cubic inch of displacement. It did it with Ramjet Fuel Injection, the production successor to Rochester's system that Zora Duntov ran at Sebring in 1956 in the prototype. While the Ramjet system was publicly announced in October 1956, cars fitted with the "Fuelie" system didn't appear until spring 1957 (before the May 1 four-speed introduction). Of the 6,338 Corvettes produced for 1957, a total of 1,040 were built with the Rochester Ramjet injection. *Road & Track* recorded 0-to-60-mile-per-hour times of 5.7 seconds in a test car with a 4.11:1 rear axle.

Ed Cole knew that Chrysler and Ford had new bodies on much of their 1957 line-up; however, Engineering delays held up GM introductions. To keep enthusiast interest in Chevrolet, Cole approved the Ramjet injection for 1957 models. Development began early in the 1950s, directed by John Dolza of GM's Engineering staff, who was inspired by Mercedes-Benz's success with constant-flow injection for its 300SL in 1954. Measuring, metering, and maintaining the airflow into the system through the engine was challenging, yet this was necessary to make injection work. Duntov recalled a Holley carburetor with various air pressure taps in it. Dolza went back to the drawing board and, with help from GM's Rochester Carburetor Division, solved a problem using a circular venturi; this injected gasoline into the

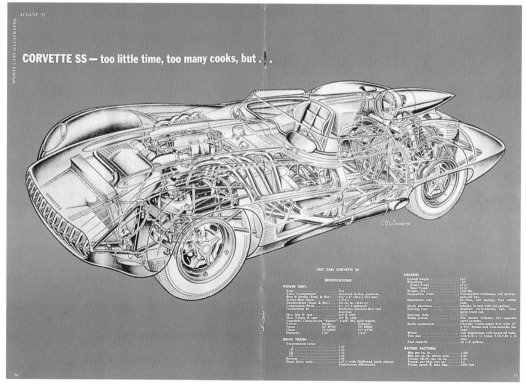

CORVETTE SS — too little time, too many cooks, but . . .

June and July 1957 advertising in *Road & Track, Sports Cars Illustrated,* and *Sports Illustrated* went on to say, "Well, that's what it feels like." Campbell-Ewald

Peter Brock's August 22, 1957, sketch launched the idea of the Sting Ray for Bill Mitchell. It is easy to trace from this drawing the eventual lines of the 1963 coupes, although at the time Brock was told it was for a car that would go into production much sooner.

metered, measured air through nozzles imbedded in the intake manifold. This resulted in no change in power output compared to carburetor systems, but it got their test cars to 60 miles per hour faster than carbureted versions. It also provided quicker, throttle response through the entire range while eliminating flat spots, the lags in acceleration common to carbureted engines at certain speeds. The final advantage appeared in high-speed maneuverability tests where the fuel sloshing that often emptied gas from carburetor float bowls in high-speed turns would starve the engine. None of this occurred with the Rochester fuel injection.

By this time, Harley Earl was nearing the end of his long career; however, he heard his young designers talking about the thin edges of Chrysler rooflines, about slender shapes that seemed extruded from the metal, not pasted on. These were lines designed by former Pontiac stylist Virgil Exner who now led Chrysler. Alfred Sloan wanted a body restyle every other year, but this was difficult because each

division was adding to the number of cars it offered. GM's product lead time was about three years in those days. The Corvette had not sold well during its first two years, yet by 1954 stylists were finishing up the new body for the 1956 car. Chassis and powertrain engineers had steady mechanical improvements arrayed before them, not only for Corvette but also for the entire truck and passenger car lineup. Substantial engineering and body styling changes were in the works for the 1957 Corvette. Engineering would introduce fuel injection and the four-speed transmissions in this heavily revised body.

"We were in the studio," Cumberford explained, "working on the '57 Corvette. It just got behind. The regular car line had too many new things and they couldn't handle it. It had a new engine, gearbox, chassis, suspension, body, and interior. The new pickup truck had a hood with Corvette-style hood speed bumps. That took body engineers away who would have made my four-headlight,

San Francisco's Lombard Street was the location for this August 1957 ad introducing readers to the lessons of "the sports car world—the world of precision driving. . ., a world in which every mile is a reward not a chore. . . ." This lesson was made available to readers of the August issues of *Road & Track*, *Sports Car*, and *Sports Cars Illustrated*. Campbell-Ewald

three-grille 1957 Corvette. This is the car that everyone knows as the 1958." After the dismal production and sales of 1955, however, a quick nip and tuck was all that was possible for the 1957 model year.

"I wanted to design Chevrolets," Cumberford explained, "because they were making a sports car. When I got to Tech Center, they let me do Corvette-type things. Probably because I was the youngest and the least well paid. Corvette was not a plum assignment. There was nothing really desirable about it at all. When I got the Corvette to do, it was the year they sold 700 cars. Chevrolet dealers didn't like them. How rich a plum can that be?"

Cumberford settled down in Chuck Jordan's Studio 5, doing drawings for Earl for the proposed 1958 Corvette. The young designer came up with ideas for a car for which he'd been given no direction and no parameters.

Earl's seeming indecisiveness was not unintended. In fact, it was a key element of his management style and

design strategy, according to Dave Holls, former GM director of corporate design. Holls worked for Earl from 1952 through Earl's retirement in 1958 and he understood his boss' procedures.

Holls collaborated with Michael Lamm on a history of car design, *A Century of Automotive Style*, published in 1996. In it, Holls wrote about working with the inventor of styling:

"Earl developed ways for getting the most from his designers. For example, he rarely dictated and never gave clear, precise instruction. He purposely kept his suggestions vague. . . . By remaining vague and ambivalent, though, and by changing direction often and unexpectedly, Earl gave his designers the greatest possible latitude to use their imaginations. He realized that by committing himself, he ran the risk of stifling creativity."

In those days, studio etiquette dictated that designers took direction from the studio managers. Jordan spent his days circulating the halls; the bulk of his design work got

Peter Brock returned to the Sting Ray shape with its smooth humps over the wheels. Mitchell encouraged him to sketch anything that came to his mind. Brock devised an open car with an integral roll bar, removable top panel and a zip-out rear plastic window. This Porsche Targa-type roof treatment appeared in GM Styling on November 21, 1957, on a car meant for production perhaps beginning 1959.

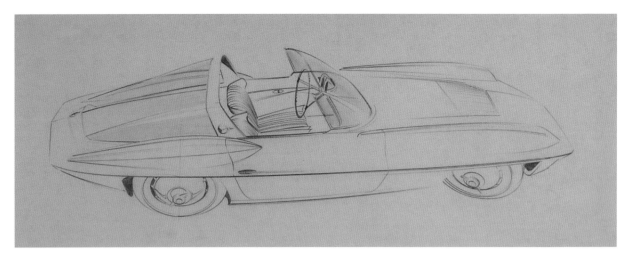

This side view, also drawn November 21, 1957, shows more clearly the integral roll bar that Peter Brock envisioned for the Sting Ray. All of these exercises were meant for a car that could be introduced for model year 1960. Peter Brock's coupe and a convertible designed by friend and fellow stylist Chuck Pohlman, went into production as the 1963 Sting Ray. Their overall appearance and styling details were completed by Larry Shinoda.

done at home at night. These designs appeared the next morning when Cumberford came down.

"This was common practice," Cumberford explained 40 years later. "The studio boss says 'We're not going to show this or this.' I'd go over to the wall to look at these new drawings to try to figure out what he was working on. And they looked familiar.

"I sat in this studio by myself drawing a Corvette the way I thought it ought to be and I would draw a Corvette the way the drawings were going on the wall. I'd been around long enough to know what Harley Earl and his design committee didn't like.

"And then one day, in comes Harley Earl. Chuck started explaining that he was so excited about the project that he'd even worked on it at home.

"Harley Earl had this high, squeaky voice. And he stuttered. Well, he really talked that way to fill time so that nobody else could talk. It was his way to keep everybody else silent.

"'Now, Chuck. . . .' You could see he was appalled. 'Didn't we . . .' Earl knew this project was not to go in the direction that the wall showed.

"I reached over and pulled out one of my drawings. 'Like this, Mr. Earl?' Cumberford emptied the drawer onto his table, and Earl asked him why these weren't on the wall as well. Cumberford said that while he liked his own ideas, he followed the studio direction. Cumberford's own designs didn't have the trademark Corvette grille. To Earl, this was part of the identity of the car, just like its name.

"'Now, why not, Bob? You wouldn't change your name just if you changed your job, would you?'

'That sort of depends what kind of job I did at the other place, Mr. Earl.'

"And there was this little twitch at the corner of his mouth and everybody left."

The next morning, Security told Cumberford to report to Clare MacKichan, Chevrolet studio manager.

"You and a kid from drafting are doing the Corvette around the corner," MacKichan told Cumberford.

Every studio in the building had a name or a number. The room Cumberford and the "kid" would use was Harley Earl's temporary office before his own was being completed in Styling's administration building. It was a windowless 20-by-40-foot space. Tony Lapine was "the kid from drafting." He and Cumberford named the room Studio X.

"We had no direction from anybody. Zora would come in and he and Tony would tell stories back and forth," Cumberford said. Lapine had raced in Europe, as had Duntov, and Cumberford had designed race cars in California before taking his job at GM. This gave the three of them a common bond. Some tasks, especially racing related, just walked in the door.

Jerry Earl, Harley's sports car-enthusiast son, purchased a Ferrari to race in SCCA events in 1956. Earl didn't want his son driving anything foreign made. So he had Chevrolet designers and engineers build his son a race car. Cumberford did the styling.

"That car was done in four or five weeks. They just brought in a car in early May, took the body off, did molds,

The space frame of the 1957 Corvette SS went together as a delicate-looking lattice work. While the overall appearance of the car was strongly influenced by Jaguar's racing D-type, the chassis was more than loosely based on Mercedes-Benz's 300SL. In fact, Duntov purchased a 300SL, had it delivered to Styling, had the body removed, and from it the engineers developed their own version of the framework.
Mike Mueller archives

and sent it off," Cumberford explained. "The windshield panel was the same as the Sebring car. There was no headrest on the SR at the beginning, and the fin came later too. Other than the extended front, out 10 inches to make a better aerodynamic line over the hood, there were very few changes. It was just a stock car, [it] had a radio."

The "stock" SR-2 went down to the Styling mechanical assembly shops where it received Sebring-type Cerametallic brakes and a few other components under Duntov's direction. At the June Sprints at Elkhart Lake, Wisconsin, Jerry Earl entered the car, but national championship contender Dick Thompson drove.

"Harley Earl wanted his son to race an American car," Robert Cumberford recalled, "but what Earl didn't know was by making the car prettier, it was 'modified,' even though the chassis was a stock Corvette. At the end of the [modified class] race, Thompson came back and said that it needed a lot of weight out of it." When the car came back to Detroit, Cumberford and his colleagues removed about 300 pounds from the SR-2 without doing anything obvious.

Later Earl suggested molding a headrest into the SR's rear deck, similar to what had been done for the Daytona cars. But by this time, Cumberford was back doing drawings for Earl for the proposed 1958. "Then he got a wild hair about doing the SS," Cumberford said with a broad smile.

"The original idea was to provoke management. Harley Earl wanted to provoke management." The speaker here is Anatole C. Lapine, the kid from drafting, a former GM stylist who went on to work at Opel in Russelsheim, Germany, and then to Porsche in Stuttgart where he was responsible for the appearance of the 928, among other things. But Tony Lapine was speaking of the past, of 1955, in that small room.

"When we got there one day, there was a dirty white D-type Jaguar sitting there, waiting for us," Lapine continued. "Belonged to an Indy racer Jack Ensley, who had driven it at Sebring."

Zora Duntov looked on while engineers weighed the front half of the Corvette SS to determine weight distribution. Its total was barely 1,850 pounds without gas, oil, or coolant. It was built on a 92-inch wheelbase, and work was begun in mid-1956 so as to compete at Sebring in early 1957. The engine was a fuel-injected 283-ci V-8 producing 307 horsepower.
Mike Mueller archives

Zora Duntov inspected several of the parts for the SS race project. Brakes, as in the drum he was holding, represented a significant part of the Super Sport's problems in competition. Duntov devised a kind of early-day antilock rear brake system, but it was erratic during the race. In addition, the magnesium car body trapped engine heat, roasting the driver.
Mike Mueller archives

"'If nothing else,' Harley Earl said, 'let's use the D-type. Change the body and drop a Chevy into it.' He had a supporter in this plan, his heir-apparent, Bill Mitchell.

"'And let's go to Sebring and beat everybody,' said MistErl. That was how we called him, like one word: MistErl. That was his plan when Ed Cole and Harry Barr walked into the room. Harry Barr had followed Cole up the ladder, and he was now Chevrolet Division's chief engineer.

"Harley and Bill Mitchell outlined what they had in mind. Cole and Barr just stood there and smiled. Then Zora Duntov came over, in the company of Jim Premo, the assistant chief engineer. Then Zora began to tell them what they'd really do.

"We already knew," Lapine continued, "that you couldn't change the body of a D-Jaguar without putting tin snips to structure. It didn't matter that MistErl didn't know this. Or that Ed Cole and Harry Barr *did*. Or that when Zora came in with Jim Premo, they also knew. None of it mattered because Harley had accomplished what he set out to do." Earl wanted a Styling exercise to go racing.

"And soon, very soon, Stan Mott, Bob Cumberford, an engineer called Del Probst, and I, as the kind of draftsman of the day, were set to work on a car that became the SS Corvette.

"Zora purchased a Mercedes 300SL. They took the body off and underneath was its tubular space frame."

Bob Cumberford picked up the narrative: "Once Zora had the body off the 300SL chassis, he put the chassis up on steel stands. Then he put a Chevrolet engine, transmission, and differential beside it. He made a tube frame out of wooden dowels, copying the Mercedes around Chevrolet running gear.

"It was really not possible to get a Corvette engine to fit the space of the Jaguar engine in the D-type. You'd have

In retrospect, Harley Earl's Corvette Super Sport was a styling exercise. It was clearly meant more to look good than to perform well on the track. Its appearance, influenced by the Jaguar D-type, was the work of Clare MacKichan in the Chevrolet studio. Also known as the XP-64, it was built of sheet magnesium, not fiberglass; it was a beautiful car from any perspective. *Mike Mueller archives*

to redo a lot of stuff and Zora didn't want to do that. He wanted his own car. Of course, so did Harley Earl; so the SS came out of that."

Internally the car was referred to as the XP-64, the letters standing for Experimental Pursuit, an abbreviation Earl adopted from the military during World War II. It represented jet fighter planes still in the development stage. Ed Cole approved the funding for one car to be built. Zora Duntov, through creative accounting methods, succeeded in having enough spare pieces fabricated to assemble a second car, a vehicle dubbed "the mule." This test car, partially skinned in rough fiberglass, was built to evaluate any number of innovations that he incorporated into the XP-64. The mule had a number of critical differences. Its engine developed much less horsepower than the aluminum head 283-cubic-inch V-8 with special fuel injection that was being prepared for the XP-64. The body of the actual race car was formed of magnesium sheets; the mule was thick fiberglass and weighed some 150 pounds more. Yet it served its purpose well. The weight showed up flaws in cooling and in the brakes.

Duntov and his engineers had developed a remarkable braking system. Delco-Moraine were working on disc brakes, but Duntov felt there was not enough testing time before the March 1957 Sebring to rely on unproven equipment. The front-wheel two-leading-shoe center-plane brakes came off a 1956 Chrysler. He put those inside 12-inch-diameter, 2.5-inch-wide cast-iron face, finned aluminum drums and used them on all four corners. He also created a kind of early-day antilock braking system that used two separate Kelsey-Hayes vacuum servos; one operated the front brakes, modulated by pedal pressure. The second servo was connected by a pressurized air system, and it reacted to the amount of pedal pressure and front brake force, adjusting the rear braking to that pressure. The goal was a 70/30 front/rear brake bias. There was an in-line mercury switch actuated by the car's angle during hard braking. When the switch closed, it sealed off the air pipe, effectively holding the rear brakes at the last pressure that was applied. Without this clever system, as front braking pressure increased, there was a strong tendency for the rears to lock, jeopardizing directional stability. With the mercury switch, rear lock-up was impossible, no matter how hard the driver hit the pedal. The switch could even be reoriented during a race as weather or track conditions required. In competition, Duntov learned that the lines to the rear brakes were too small, causing a delay in system reaction that brought about spectacular brake lockups, almost always at the worst possible moment. Duntov eventually replaced the lines with larger diameter tubing.

In Friday practice at Sebring, both Juan Manuel Fangio, the Argentinian grand prix world champion, and English racer Stirling Moss drove the mule and turned exceptionally fast times. Chevrolet had a contract with Fangio to drive during the race, but when the actual car arrived late, it missed Fangio's cut-off date. He was released to drive a Maserati. Moss also was under contract to Maserati. So John Fitch, the production Corvette racing team manager, was invited. He reached Piero Taruffi, Italian grand prix and endurance champion, who flew overnight from Rome to co-drive.

The mule qualified on the front row. Race morning presented the actual race car in its Harley Earl–specified blue finish, completed to Motorama show standards. It suffered inconsistent brake balance problems and fearsome cockpit heat. As Karl Ludvigsen reported in *Corvette: America's Star Spangled Sports Car*, the magnesium body panels trapped the heat that the fiberglass had insulated away from the drivers. Tin snips quickly modified the sleek body, but that did not remedy the braking bias problems that alternately locked up the front tires or the rears.

Crowds swarmed the SS, happy to see an American-built car on the track. Fitch started the race. He quickly found the rhythm that kept the brakes from locking while cutting lap times to within a second of Fangio's qualifying effort. But problems and failures continued.

Taruffi noticed the car's handling was deteriorating badly. The rear tires bounced into the body or hopped frantically after each bump in the airport's concrete surface. Taruffi pulled in, overheated, and the car, after only 23 laps, was undrivable.

"The failure of the SS, the only factory appearance of Chevrolet in racing," Bob Cumberford explained, "came when a rear bushing failed after eight laps. Mounted incorrectly, it split. It broke because Harley Earl would not let them run the race car on the track because it would damage the paint.

"This was a styling exercise. It was not a bad car. They just should have been driving the blue car, testing *it*, developing it, proving it, correcting it. That would have made a big difference. Make a new front panel for it if it got chipped. Replace it with a fiberglass hood. As it was, it was a shameful episode."

Despite Sebring, Ed Cole saw a future in racing the SS. Duntov gave him a ride around Sebring in the mule. Cole approved construction of three more cars to race at LeMans. He let Duntov begin work on a desmodromic valve gear (without springs) for the top end of the engine. This could produce up to 400 horsepower at 9,000 rpm. A 1958 version was to be constructed. Improved SR-2 models were to be made available to private entries. Ed Cole's Chevrolet Division was going racing, publicly.

At the top of General Motors, there was another view. GM Chairman Harlow Curtice suggested to the Automobile Manufacturers Association, during its February 1957 board meeting, that AMA member companies "take no part in automobile racing or other competitive events involving tests of speed and that they refrain from suggesting speed in passenger car advertising or publicity."

All the members ratified Curtice's proposal. From the start of the American automobile industry, through all the acquisitions, mergers, and failures, car makers had avoided U.S. congressional scrutiny. GM, with the largest market share of automobile sales, had the most at stake if Washington inquisitors turned their magnifying lens on The Big Three that, together, sold more than 90 percent of the vehicles in the United States.

A tragic crash by a Mercedes-Benz entry during the 24-hour race at LeMans, France, in June 1955, brought the issue of accountability to every auto maker's boardroom. Mercedes withdrew from racing that day; unfavorable publicity tarnished the company for years. No domestic auto maker could risk the kind of public outcry and government examination such a tragedy might inspire.

"Testing and development [of the Corvette SS] would have made a big difference," Robert Cumberford concluded resignedly. "But Earl wanted the blue bullet to race. I suspect that, had the car done well, Chevrolet might not have joined that AMA ban and gone racing under the table or out the backdoor. That's how it was. It didn't stop; it just moved into the shadows."

Throughout 1957, American factory production workers' wages reached an average $82 a week. There were 7,000 drive-in movie theaters in America, and 11 percent of new vehicle registrations were station wagons. Volkswagen sold 200,000 Beetles and Ford introduced the Edsel. Government figures confirmed that more Americans died in automobile accidents than in all the wars fought in U.S. history.

The clay styling model for the 1956 production year was photographed early in February 1955 once it had passed the inspection of countless Chevrolet Division managers. The only significant change from this model to production was relocating the exhaust which here exited through the rear quarter panel.
Mike Mueller archives

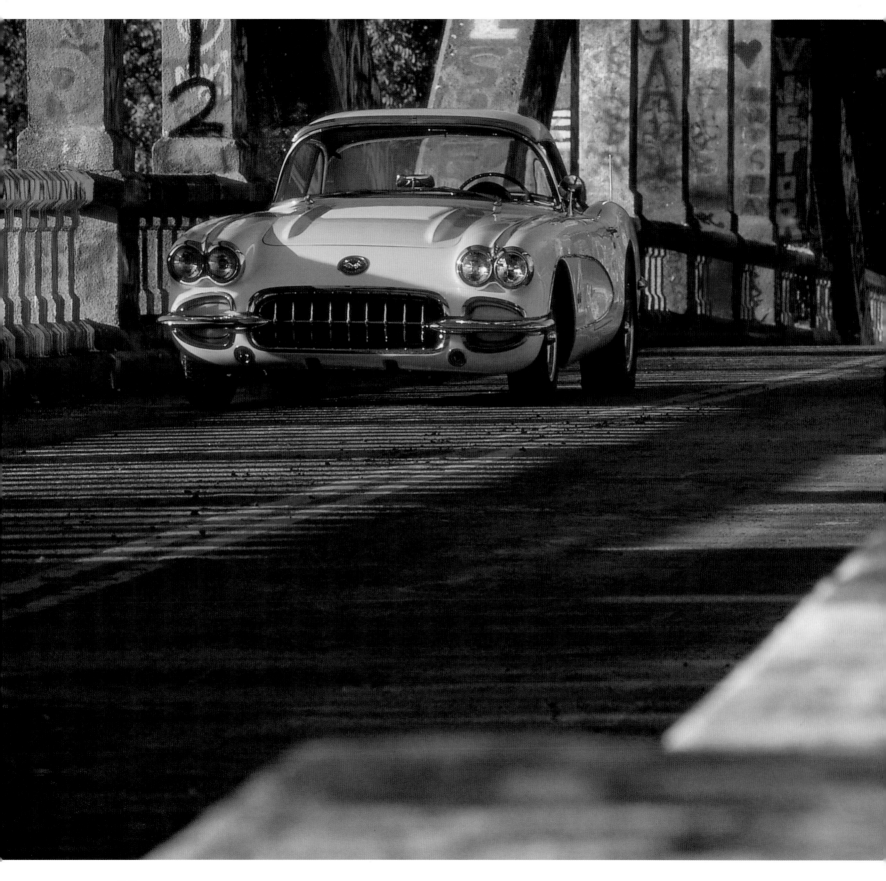

chapter 7

(XP-96) + Q = ?: 1958–1961

"The car that Tony and I wanted to do had four headlights, but none of the GM rocketship styling that I, for one, absolutely despised," Robert Cumberford continued unraveling history. He and Tony Lapine virtually lived in a small, windowless room, brainstorming possibilities for a questionable car far off in the future of these two young stylists.

"There were other designs already in the works, including an aluminum bodied-one strongly influenced by the 1956 Motorama Oldsmobile Golden Rocket. This had the Torpedo top, probably the true source of the 1963 split window. It even picked up the tubular tapered fenders with the little fins on them that Harley Earl wanted on the back end.

"We wanted to do the car on a 94 1/2-inch wheelbase, same as the VW Beetle. It looked as though it had a permanent notchback top, but it was completely retractible into the rear deck and you'd never guess the car wasn't a roadster. A car with an aluminum body and frame, aluminum V-8 in front, a full transaxle at the back. It would have given us a nice cockpit. This is what we wanted to do for the 1958 car."

The transaxle was a less radical proposal than other parts of the car. Engineering had a project in the development stages for a rear-mounted transmission and differential with the starter incorporated into the casing, all supported by a full independent suspension that would have gone into production for the 1960 model year Chevrolet sedans. This was designated project "Q." It would never have been justifiable for a sports car that sold barely 6,300 units in 1957, but it could be adopted from a passenger car line selling thousands of models.

Lapine worked out a retractable aluminum hardtop. Reynolds (Aluminum) was interested in doing the aluminum tooling in 1955. But it just takes forever for ideas to sift through.

"Tony and I were convinced that the '58 Corvette could be, and *should be* shorter, smaller, and narrower," Cumberford continued. "That Jaguar engine that predicated the design of the first Corvette was a long boat anchor of a thing. The new aluminum 4.6-liter V-8 was much smaller. Harley Earl gave us carte blanche. No specifications, but we had to deal with Zora.

"So Zora would come over and talk to us. He knew what was going on with hardware. It was fall of 1955, while Tony and I were in that studio. We wondered if there would even be a 1958 Corvette, the XP-94. The 1956 car wasn't out yet.

"So, after hours, we came up with this concept of the four-passenger Corvette. I had done this once earlier while I was working on the SR-2. Earl asked me to do the 'dachshund,' a stretched Corvette back cut off behind the seat, mated to a Corvette cut off ahead of the seat. It was clear, especially to him, that this was not something to do. It was all out of proportion, too high in the middle.

"Tony, Stan Mott, and I called ourselves Automotive Research Consultants. We wrote a letter asking what readers thought about a four-passenger sports car. We sent it to John Fitch, [*Road & Track's*] John Bond, people in the SCCA, maybe 15 people. We got 15 responses. We used Tony's address on Boston Boulevard in Detroit. It was close to GM in downtown Detroit so people might think it was GM who sent the letter.

"We got wonderful responses, a lot of well-reasoned comments. And everybody was in favor of it. People said it evoked the Bentleys, that sports cars for racing used to be required to have four seats.

Six colors were offered for 1958, including Panama Yellow, a milder color than this modified Corvette wears. Chevrolet introduced acrylic lacquer finishes, replacing the nitrocellulose lacquer from the start.

Racing, modifying, and customizing Corvettes was something done to the cars almost from the start. Zora Duntov's attention to hot-rodding and youth, the subject of a now famous memo to his bosses in December 1953, launched Chevrolet's own programs to make parts available to encourage buyers to stick with GM.

"Part of the motivation of the four-passenger car was the morality of the day. Guys didn't go out on dates by themselves with a girl. If you had a Corvette, you couldn't date. There always had to be a chaperon, or another couple, one to keep an eye on the other. Double dating was fine. A guy alone with a girl was not.

"So we got Barney Clark, who wrote the Corvette ads and who was enthusiastic about the idea, to write a description of the car as we conceived it. Big engine, so it would go as fast like European stuff. It was a chunky, high-deck, square piece of road machinery with a western theme. We had a list of names for it: Scout, Paint, Pony, Pinto, Palomino, Mustang. That was the idea, wild horses, the far West, cowboys, open spaces. America's heritage.

"We wrote a cover letter and took the car to Earl. He

was furious. Absolutely furious," Cumberford said.

"'You fellahs,' he stammered, 'you got a lot of enthusiasm. My boys are just plain garden-variety boys. But you . . . We're not going to do anything with this. But as a reward for initiative, I'm going to let you design the 1961 Buick Special. . . .'

"I think Harley Earl got mad at us not for doing a four-seater but for doing something that wasn't our job. I got the same reaction from [Harley Earl's successor] Bill Mitchell once, 'Goddammit kid, you're not paid to think; you're paid to design.'

"We thought they might cancel the car, but there was no real indication they would; it was just scuttlebutt. They had already done the '56, even though it wasn't out yet. It had the three-speed gearbox and the V-8. That caused sales

to rise and it became much more the type of car that people seemed to want. In '57, when it got a four-speed gearbox and fuel injection, it was a serious hard-charging car and sales came up again."

As a postscript, the four-door sports car didn't die, and it didn't become the Corvair. Barney Clark left Campbell-Ewald and, after another job in New York writing ads for Lincoln-Mercury, he went to work for J. Walter Thompson in New York until he retired. He became a close friend of a Ford product planner, Don Frey. Frey listened to what Clark had to say about the four-seater, and within a few years, an aggressive, ambitious Ford division general manager, Lee Iacocca, staked his career on the car Ford called *Mustang*.

The Cumberford/Lapine Corvette meant for 1958 introduction had progressed to full-size clays models, but it

was scrapped. Instead, the production studio did a quick facelift on the 1956 to have it ready for production by fall 1957. Cumberford's large dual air intakes flanking the license plate shrunk and flanked the center grille. Overall length grew from 168.0 to 177.2 inches. The car swelled 2.3 inches in width to 72.8. For sports car enthusiasts, the Corvette was going the wrong way. The car gained 200 pounds over the 1957 production car, raising curb weight to 3,000 pounds, leaving it slightly heavier than the Jaguar (2,890 pounds). Having been 5 inches shorter than Jaguar's XK-120, it was now longer and wider than 1957's new XK-150.

It was, however, a better automobile, with bumpers secured to the frame, providing true accident protection. Acrylic lacquer replaced the nitrocellulose paints. Every instrument on the dash, except the clock, was relocated in

Chevrolet's most powerful engine option for 1958 was the 290-horsepower fuel-injected 283-ci V-8. Packaged inside a substantially restyled body, about 1,000 of these were sold. The new body bowed to current styling trends, introducing quad-headlights to the Corvette.

In *Motor Trend*, March 1958, Chevrolet called their Corvette a "very special car for special people with very particular requirements." *Campbell-Ewald*

One of several proposals for the Corvair-based production Corvette were done by designer Gene Garfinkle in early 1959.

A concept for XP-96, a 1960 Corvette version was drawn November 24, 1958 by Gene Garfinkle.

A Corvair-packaged Corvette drawn in 1957 by Gene Garfinkle, offered such Harley Earl carryovers as finned exhaust towers and horizontal stabilizing fins such as those seen on the Firebird show cars.

front of the driver's eyes with a large 160-mile-per-hour speedometer surrounding the 6,000-rpm tachometer. A console housed the clock, optional heater, and "Wonderbar" AM signal-seeking radio controls.

Externally, the car collected the ideas of each successive design review. Chrome trim surrounded the headlights, trailing toward the windshield. Dummy louvers on the hood and side vents appeared in the coves. (The louvers were originally designed to be functional; Engineering discovered that engine oil blowby could mist the windshield and the top under extreme driving conditions. Styling had to fill in the slits before manufacturing began.) Prominent chrome bands curved across the trunk toward the rear bumpers.

Improvements under the hood made up for girth. Output reached 290 horsepower with the RPO 579D with Rochester fuel injection. Introduction followed Chevrolet's and General Motors' official adoption of the AMA racing ban by half a year. GM could not and would not promote racing or speed. If a customer wanted to order it, however, it only required reading the order form. A Milwaukee advertising executive, Jim Jeffords, did exactly that at Chicago's Nickey Chevrolet, ordering enough to win the SCCA B-production championship except the car's exterior color. Inspired by a popular song, Jeffords painted the car a bright purple and named it *The Purple People Eater*. Jeffords' contribution on the track and Chevrolet's own carefully created RPOs heralded the birth of the muscle car in America.

For the 1959 Corvette, Bill Mitchell removed some of the styling excesses that had marked Harley Earl's last years at GM. The 1958 chrome trim strips along the trunk lid and rows of wash-board-like simulated louvers on the engine hood, were excised from the 1959 model.

Chevrolet engineering continued to offer a 290-horsepower V-8 engine under the hood and a sophisticated four-speed transmission. While the heater was still optional, hardtops and even optional handling packages offered stiffer springs and heavily finned brake drums with road-worthy metallic brake linings (RPO 686); the Corvette base price was $3,875. A cruise-ready Corvette with a 245-horsepower 283, Powerglide, power top, radio and heater, sun shades, and other minor options cost the country club set $4,999. From 3,467 cars in 1956, production nearly doubled in 1957 to 6,339, and it moved up as much for 1958, ending the first-year, quad-headlight production at 9,168 cars off the St. Louis assembly line. The final census for 1959 reflected a further increase, albeit slight, to 9,670 cars.

If William L. Mitchell had not existed, Harley Earl would have had him designed. Drawn first in side elevation and front views, then modeled in life-size clay, he finally would have been produced as another one-off, like Earl's Y-Job and LeSabre. Only, when Earl got Mitchell, he kept him longer.

Bill Mitchell inherited the vice presidency of styling at General Motors on December 1, 1958, when Mitchell was just 46. He had worked for Earl for 22 years, starting as a

Sports Cars Illustrated and *Sports Illustrated* both ran this ad in May 1958, talking about elegance and motor sports in Nassau each December for Speed Week: "The most demanding audience any car can face is the international sports car audience." *Campbell-Ewald*

"The symptoms are easily recognizable: increased rate of respiration, a far-off look in the eyes, incessant sharp shifting motions with the right hand accompanied by unconscious 'ro-o-O-O-O-O-M-P' noises in the throat. . . . " Readers of May and June 1959 issues of the *New Yorker, Sports Illustrated,* and *Car Life* were exposed to the disease. *Campbell-Ewald*

Bob Bondurant, #51, shows the line and the body English necessary to drive his car through turn two at Pomona during the March 1959 Cal Club Regional race. He leads Andy Porterfield, #283. *Bob Tronolone*

Dick Thompson shows off the understeering problems he encountered through the 1960 season with Bill Mitchell's striking Sting Ray. Slipping through turn eight at Riverside during the October 1960 *Los Angeles Times* Grand Prix, Thompson won the SCCA C Modified national championship. *Bob Tronolone*

stylist. He learned well and the transition of power to the apprentice from Earl, the "sorcerer of styling," was seamless. Mitchell's father sold Buicks and even before Earl came in to save those, Mitchell was in love with automobiles. He worked as an illustrator for the publishing and road-racing Collier family, decorating his office with his drawings of classics. The Colliers loved and owned these kinds of cars, and they welcomed Mitchell into their close-knit circle of enthusiasts, an organization they called ARCA, the Automobile Racing Club of America. He drew quick, stylized sketches of their racing activities, and Earl saw these. In 1935, when Mitchell was just 23, Earl hired him. When Earl arrived at GM, he had to prove himself (which took a few years) to the division general managers who did not at first understand their need for him and his services, and he had to prove himself to his own staff whom he needed to be absolutely unified behind him.

Mitchell watched his mentor work. He had to fight his own battles against division chairmen who wanted to regain some control once Earl left. But Mitchell had allies, division vice presidents with "gasoline in their veins." Management oriented to finances, bean counters in gray suits, felt compelled to rein in some of Earl's flamboyance and fiscal

Dick Thompson stretched out the Sting Ray along the back straightaway at Riverside International Raceway during the October 1960, *Los Angeles Times* Grand Prix. Depending on gearing and the circuit, the Sting Ray was capable of better than 155 miles per hour. *Bob Tronolone*

excesses. Yet others, Such as Ed Cole, understood and supported Mitchell. Styling sold cars more than Ford's styling did for Ford or Chrysler's for Chrysler.

In fact, one of Mitchells' first battles was with the word "styling." To him, it represented "fashion," something here today and gone tomorrow. Design endured and from the first day he was department chief, the name changed. It was no longer styling; it was design.

Mitchell adopted Earl's technique of by giving designers no direction with their assignment. But he added a kind of volatile fickleness. Harley Earl would demand that a highlight line be raised or lowered as little as 1/32 inch. He would trumpet displeasure across a studio if it was not done. Mitchell's temper rivaled Earl's, and he used it similarly, as punctuation; but Mitchell also routinely flipped design concepts 180 degrees from one encounter to the next.

In 1956, Peter Brock, another young designer, was hired out of the Los Angeles Art Center College. After his first few assignments, Brock worked for senior designer Bob Veryzer, in Bob McLean's research studio. Mitchell had gone to the Turin, Italy, Auto Show and returned to Detroit excited by several coupes he'd seen there. He announced that he wanted to do a new Corvette to be introduced as a 1960 model, described what he wanted and created a contest within the studios to see whose design came closest. Peter Brock's concept was selected.

"I'd designed the car in coupe form according to Mitchell's direction," Brock said, "and at that point Mitchell said, 'I think we also want to do a roadster.' There was another young guy in McLean's studio, Chuck Pohlmann, and by this time, we were good friends because our design philosophies were similar. So Chuck did the roadster version while I continued with details on the coupe, and the two cars were nearly identical except for the crisp horizontal line that formed the car's distinctive shape. Chuck's version, directed by Mitchell, fell away sloped all the way to the back; mine had a slight kick-up at the rear.

"Once we had the theme there were a number of versions," Brock explained. "We had one with a fully removable roof panel, like the Porsche Targa. In another, the car didn't have A-pillars, just a single pillar in the center, windscreen/side glass wrapped completely around. But once Mitchell picked the one he liked, we went with it.

"It first went into quarter-scale clay, then into full-sized clay in coupe form. After Mitchell had made the changes on it that he wanted, we built a roadster version of Chuck's variation. My coupe also was there, in full size, so we could make comparisons on details side by side. At that point, Mitchell decided they were going to build only the roadster prototype because it was cheaper and easier to do. So they took the full-size clay model roadster and moved it out of the studio. We referred to it as the XP-96, but that car became the Sting Ray.

A study in windscreens, rollbars, and body lean as the top three finishers race through the B Production Cal Club Regional event at Pomona in June 1960. Car #222, Vince Mayell, finished second; #614, Buford Lane, remained behind him in third; and behind them, #58, cresting the rise and leaning into the apex, Tony Settember went on to pass them both and win. *Bob Tronolone*

Tony Settember, running in B Production, looks extremely determined as he drifts around the hay bales during the June 26, 1960, Cal Club Regional race at Pomona, California. Several years earlier, Settember had witnessed Corvette racing power at the hands of Dick Thompson from the driver's seat of his Mercedes Benz 300SL. It obviously had a significant impact in his future car choice. *Bob Tronolone*

"The car was built in secret," Brock continued. "With the AMA ban in force, there wasn't supposed to be anymore sports or competition stuff at all. Mitchell took it out of the research studio so it wouldn't be discovered.

"The 'hammer room,' which fronted Mitchell's secret studio, was set up behind a tool room where Design's fabrication specialists kept all the hammers and tools used to form the models. You'd go into this room and then walk around the back, through another door, and the secret studio was back there. GM's high brass walking around the building wouldn't find it because, in theory, it didn't even exist.

"The coupe was originally done with a large rear window, a single piece of glass. That split rear window was actually put on later. Mitchell imposed that hard line down the roof and rear window because he loved the Bugatti type 57SC Atlantique. He wanted the flavor of that car on the Sting Ray. That design we carried through to the first production car in 1963, although it was never seen on the roadster.

"Larry Shinoda and Chuck finished the roadster. Larry did most of the form detailing on it, the things that Mitchell wanted to put on the car like the twin windscreens, hood louvers, side vents, and such. Really, I think all three of us, Chuck, Larry, and I, provided about equal shares in developing the final appearance of that car, but the original lines were mine."

The Brock/Pohlmann/Shinoda car was built on the same 94 1/2-inch wheelbase that Bob Cumberford and Tony Lapine had developed for the proposed 1958 replacement. It carried over the technology of the Q-project transaxle as well to provide more cockpit room without a large transmission sitting between the driver and passenger. It adopted the same advanced frame and also the independent rear suspension with which Cumberford and Lapine had devised.

"There were always several engineering solutions," Brock recalled, "ideas to get room in a car when it was still in the research or design end of things. There is a kind of funny story along that line.

"Mr. Earl was always sort of bandying about engineering solutions for problems. But he was a terrible malaprop, using the wrong word for the right idea. One of his favorite engineering solutions for a lower hoodline was a 'dry slump.' Nobody dared to correct him.

"He'd be sitting there looking at a full-size elevation and he'd say, 'Jesus, fellahs, ya know, we could get that hoodline down about 2 inches, ya know; we could do that with a dry slump in it.'

"'Yes, Mr. Earl.' And we'd drop the hoodline 2 inches. He was right. These sort of engineering ideas, systems, could solve styling and interior problems. The real problem was cost. The production Sting Ray became a much larger car. But that original car was really a graceful, pretty, little automobile."

With the 283-cubic-inch V-8 equipped with a dry-*sump* lubrication system, not only did the cowl height drop, but so did the overall height. The Q-car proposal stood only 46 inches tall. Duntov advocated using aluminum not only for certain engine components such as cylinder heads but also for entire blocks, manifolds, and transmission and differential cases as well. He saw aluminum as a way to decrease the weight and to improve both the handling and fuel economy of the entire Chevrolet line. Using Duntov's directives, a Corvette would weigh less than 2,500 pounds.

However, while Duntov advocated aluminum for engine and drivetrain components, he pushed Chevrolet to build the Corvette's body out of steel.

"There was a lot of talk," Peter Brock recalled, "that the car had to reach a certain production number and then it would be feasible to do it in steel. It probably would have been cheaper, too. The way they were making the car, it was heavier than a steel-bodied version would have been. Steel would have changed the car completely, made it stiffer, lighter, and stronger.

"If you build a car in steel, then you can make aluminum panels on the same dies and then, obviously, you could build a lightweight GT version. They stuck with plastic for several reason. Certainly cost was first; the tooling was rather inexpensive compared to steel. But also, because of the possibility of working with composites in the future, and this was a way to keep their hand in on future technology. To work with the plastics companies.

"But also, they knew that they could change little details like the side scoops and hood blisters and all the little panels really quickly in glass, cheaper than in steel. And since the Corvette was going to have longer production runs . . . "

By December 1957 the Q-Corvette had passed inspection at the Engineering Policy Group show. Under

Mitchell's direction, Larry Shinoda now added working hatches and he relocated fuel caps to the left rear fender. Mitchell wanted the front fender scoops reversed, placing them at the rear of the doors. In this location, these did little more than cool the rear tires; however, he told Shinoda he felt this accentuated the "coke-bottle" taper he wanted for the car. Shinoda followed directions and finished a coupe and convertible, ready for presentation at the board of director's show, the executive show-and-tell that made or broke production plans. The full-size clay models and their accompanying engineering proposals took the Corvette far beyond what the production 1958 model would be, making it equal to the most advanced, sophisticated sports—and racing—cars built anywhere in the world.

There were critical personnel changes among the executives. Zora Duntov, as much a corporate realist as an engineering visionary, looked around and reconsidered what was really possible.

Harlow Curtice, GM chairman, retired in 1958. The GM accountant who rose to head Buick Division, who understood what Harley Earl's styling could do to car sales, had gone to the top. He drove GM through the decade that would see Chevrolet Division alone spend $90 million for advertising. Curtice may not have been born with "gasoline in his veins," Mitchell's measure of a man, but years of steady transfusions made him tolerant of Design and Engineering costs. Curtice's replacement, Frederic Donner, was immutable.

Curtice wondered about car sales; Donner worried about stock prices. Curtice knew that interesting automobiles, produced with a pleasing appearance, sold. Donner knew that reducing expenses, curbing the lavish expenditures of Design and Engineering, would increase dividends. Profits made GM attractive to Wall Street, not chrome and independent rear suspensions. Experiments like the Sting Ray were costly nonessentials.

Sitting in Mitchell's Hammer Room was the car that Duntov, with remarkable political savvy, knew was too much of a reach. He retreated from his target and wrote to Chevrolet's chief engineer, Harry Barr. He allowed that the Q-Corvette's numerous technical advances would be so costly that current management might never allow such a car to be built. He recommended sticking with the faithful separate chassis body assembly used from the start. The existing body was carried over from the 1958 and 1959 model year, and Duntov set to work with the other engine development engineers to produce aluminum cylinder heads with fuel-injected 283s. But production consistency difficulties made this a never-available option. Chassis engineers tamed the handling by deleting the optional heavy-duty springs while increasing the diameter of the front antisway bar and adding a rear one. The RPO 687 ($333.60) was really a "PRO," (Production *Racing* Option) quickening the steering and using sintered

It wasn't long before any one who wanted to race had to run a Corvette. During the SCCA/Cal Club regional race at Pomona, California, March 1960, a field of B Production Corvettes is barely interrupted by a Mercedes 300SL and a Jaguar XK120. H. Dean Geddes, #13, momentarily leads Buford Lane, #614. *Bob Tronolone*

Newton's law of gravity has been repealed by Chevrolet's V-8 engined Corvette. This physics lesson was published in *Road & Track* in June 1960 and in the next month's *Sports Car* magazine. *Campbell-Ewald*

Bob Bondurant motored easily around the vast parking lot circuit at Del Mar, north of San Diego, during the May 1959 SCCA/Cal Club Regional. His fuel-injected 1957 benefited from improved front brake cooling, demonstrating the advantages of racing fiberglass-bodied production sports cars. There was no metal to pull out to regain steering clearance. *Bob Tronolone*

metallic brake linings inside new brake drums with large cooling fins. Base price of the car was $3,872.00. The top engine option was not the aluminum head variation but the RPO 579D, the 1958–1959 290-horsepower 283 V-8 with Duntov cam, solid valve lifters, 11.0:1 compression ratio, and fuel injection.

For Briggs Cunningham, the 1960 model was a long-time coming. He entered three Corvettes (plus a prototype E-type Jaguar) in the 24 Hours of LeMans. With Duntov's quiet help, Cunningham got special cast-iron cylinder heads with the larger valves and improved porting that would appear in 1961 as the production 315-horsepower engine. But it was not an easy race. One Corvette ran off course in a thunderstorm, overturned, and burned. A second lost an hour digging out of the sand. The Jaguar's engine failed early Sunday morning, and by dawn only their last Corvette still ran, driven by John Fitch and Bob Grossman. Then it started overheating. Rules allowed adding oil or water only after 25 laps and that a car must complete four laps in the final hour before 4:00 P.M. Sunday. Team mechanic and GM employee Frank Burrell packed the top of the engine compartment full of dry ice from Cunningham's trailer behind the pits, and after each lap, Duntov coasted in, iced up, and eased away. Each pit stop took 15 minutes, and when the race ended, Cunningham's Corvette finished eighth overall, completing 280 laps, 2,363.5 miles, averaging 97.9 miles per hour, even with the ice stops. Another Corvette, Lloyd "Lucky" Casner's CAMORADI USA-entry Corvette driven by Lou Lilley and Fred Gamble, finished 21st overall, nearly 500 miles back.

In 1960, Chevrolet produced 10,261 Corvettes. After Ford had enlarged its Thunderbird, Ed Cole hoped the Corvette would absorb the two-seater enthusiasts who felt betrayed. There were very few; Corvette production inched from 9,168 in 1958 to 9,670 in 1959 before finally cracking that break-even point for the first time in its eight years.

Bill Mitchell was a racing enthusiast by

osmosis, never having competed himself. He was enthralled by the vehicles themselves. His involvement with Sam, Miles, and Barron Collier Jr. gave him a passion for motor sports. Mitchell urged along the completion of Jerry Earl's SR-2, and later he acquired, for a dollar, the 1957 SS mule chassis on which Duntov had done his development work for Sebring.

While the AMA racing ban covered corporate involvement, Mitchell saw no problem in his participating as a car owner. Mitchell asked designers Larry Shinoda and Ed Wayne to adopt the Q-Corvette theme to his own personal race car.

The result was the Sting Ray Racer, a car that had started life in the Research Studio in the summer of 1957. Mitchell and Shinoda ran it with a modified 283, similar to the SS design in 1957, developing 280 horsepower. The first Sting Ray body was 0.125-inch-thick fiberglass, nearly production thickness, reinforced with aluminum. Dick Thompson debuted the bright red racer at Marlboro Raceway in Maryland in mid-April 1959. Following a repeat of Sebring's 1957 test with unreliable brakes, too much unrestrained power, and no limited slip differential, Thompson still managed to finish fourth in his first appearance.

Bert Ruttman, #58, proves the truth of the early days racing adage: "Run What Ya Brung." While his Corvette has a rollbar and racing windscreen, competitive rubber at Santa Barbara's SCCA/Cal Club Regional in May 1959 included Firestone whitewall tires all around. Here he leads Dick Thorgrimson. *Bob Tronolone*

Dave MacDonald runs Don Steves' Chevrolet's chrome-wheeled fuel-injected 1957 through a sweeper at Marchbanks Speedway at Hanford, California, north of Bakersfield. *Bob Tronolone*

Riverside Raceway's desert run-off has bitten many drivers during its long career. Tom Franks ran out of road during the Kiwanis Grand Prix weekend in mid-July 1959 and flipped his car end-over-end, bending and breaking fiberglass and frame. *Bob Tronolone*

The fiberglass bodies for 1958 introduced the popular quad-headlight motif to Corvette. This body was among the last of General Motors production influenced by Harley Earl who would retire before these cars got to showrooms. Here painters apply lacquer in the St. Louis factory spray booths. *Mike Mueller archives*

"Aerodynamics" was still an "engineering solution" like Harley Earl's "dry slump." "The Sting Ray was terrible aerodynamically," Peter Brock remembered. "When Thompson first drove the car, the front wheels came off the ground at 140 miles per hour. The front end just packed air underneath. The lift on the hood was like an airplane wing. The front wheels were barely touching the pavement, you couldn't steer it at high speed."

Mitchell's team manager, Dean Bedford, a GM engineer who also supervised the engineering development of the road car, partially solved the problem by shimming the rear springs, creating a "hot-rod rake." This eliminated some, but not all, of the problem. The thick body panels cracked from stress. After Road America, Bedford formed a new nose and tail section of three-layer fiberglass silk, reinforced with balsa wood. This improvement saved 75 pounds over the original body. These thinner panels also gave the nose and tail such flexibility that it deformed but popped back when hit. Thompson said it literally waved at high speed. Throughout the season, one problem after another vexed Mitchell, Bedford, sometimes-mechanic

Shinoda, and driver Thompson. Mitchell's deep pockets were not bottomless; this affected how many races the car ran and how quickly it developed. Each problem was handled according to the budget that was available, and somehow the Sting Ray showed up at the next event. Designer Tony Lapine even slipped in to co-drive a 500-miler at Road America. Through the season, the car's slippery shape allowed higher speeds than production Corvettes could achieve and, coupled with its near-production car weight (2,360 without driver), it completely used up its brakes. In the winter of 1959–1960, Bedford completely overhauled the braking system, throwing out the Kelsey-Hayes system and installing a single Hydrovac booster, modified by Bendix to allow more sensitive pedal modulation. Disc brakes, the obvious solution, were ruled out once again because of costs.

During the 1960 season, the car reappeared in silver with a paper-thin fiberglass skin. With the light body and the simpler braking system, dry weight was now down to 2,000 pounds. With so many other problems to control, Bedford and Mitchell agreed to a modest tune for the

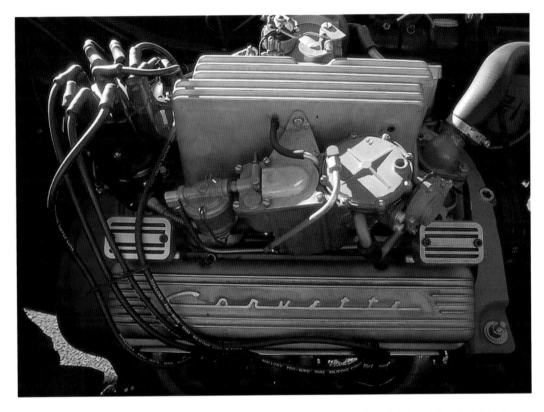

Carroll Shelby, whose initial idea was to race lightweight European sports cars using big American V-8s, wasn't discouraged by Chevrolet's reluctance to further Gary Laughlin's Corvette Italia concept. Fitted with 315-horsepower fuel-injected 283s, the cars were potent. None of the three cars was ever raced, and Shelby later took his idea from Italy and Chevy to England and Ford.

Known as the Corvette Italia, this is one of three 1959 prototype cars that Texas oil-developer Gary Laughlin had produced by the Italian styling studio Scaglietti in Modena. Laughlin, an amateur racer and friend of fellow Texans Jim Hall and Carroll Shelby, funded the project to create lightweight racers based on the Corvette running gear.

283-cubic-inch engine for reliability. They had 280 horse-power at the flywheel. With a 3.70:1 rear end, top speed was 155 miles per hour on tracks like Long Island, New York's Bridgehampton and suburban Chicago's Meadow-dale. Thompson put it to good use, thrilling spectators and chasing—but rarely beating—Augie Pabst in his Chevro-let-engined Scarab. Long before the last race of the season, Thompson won the C-modified class championship.

Mitchell retired the car after the 1960 season. It had cost him a fortune, yet it established the Sting Ray as the rac-ing Corvette. Mitchell returned it to Design for a complete renovation. It was repainted and, finally, labeled and badged as a Corvette, and it went on the GM show tour, shown first at the Chicago automobile show in mid-February 1961. After a year on show platforms, Mitchell adopted it as his fair-weather commuter car, eventually replacing the brakes with Dunlop disks and the 283 V-8 with a 427.

"Gene, go down to the basement, you're going to be working with one of the guys on the sports car." Gene Garfinkle recalled his introduction to what would become the Sting Ray production design project. He was another product of the Art Center, plucked from California before graduation. He was working in the Buick production studio when one of Mitchell's people came in and reassigned him to the basement, to the Corvette.

"Ed Wayne and I ended up doing all the drawings," he went on. "We had Chuck Pohlmann's Sting Ray roadster

Laughlin had three cars built, two with automatics and one four-speed—a car each for himself, Jim Hall and Carroll Shelby—before Chevrolet closed down the project, citing their reluctance to interrupt the assembly line to produce additional chassis without complete bodies, as Laughlin had wanted.

Gary Laughlin asked Scaglietti to produce the cars based on the bodies the Italian designer had done for Ferrari's long hooded Tour de France GT model. The new Corvette bodies, made of aluminum, were 400 pounds lighter than Chevrolet's factory fiberglass.

there to work with as a reference. We were just doing the lofting (elevation) drawings. The production car is actually on a shorter wheelbase and its body sections were a little steeper.

"We put the bumpers, windshield . . .,we even did a folding hardtop for the car. But in order to go through the complication of folding it up to fit into the trunk where all the suspension was, the cost was just way out of line for what they wanted to do. But the top that we did was very much the shape of the removable hardtop that they made for the car.

"The coupe had its split rear window. Mitchell certainly loved the Bugatti but, remember, there was also the Scaglione-designed Bertone Alfa Romeo design study BAT cars. The BAT 5, the 7, and 8 had split windows too.

"They brought in the Sting Ray, the actual Sting Ray racing car, and we had the original drawings up on the wall. Ed would lay down lines and we'd talk about ideas, how to make something look slimmer, where to place things.

"Mitchell was in there three or four times a day with Ken Pickering and Harry Ellsworth, his personal secretaries.

"'Nah, I don't want to do that,' he'd say. 'Can't you do that? Can't you move that over there? Yeah, that's it.'

"That's how they worked. And you'd be down there for five weeks and then sent somewhere else. You'd never know what happened to the car you'd worked on. Never see it again. Until one day you'd be walking somewhere else in the building and see a full-size model of it being wheeled down a hall."

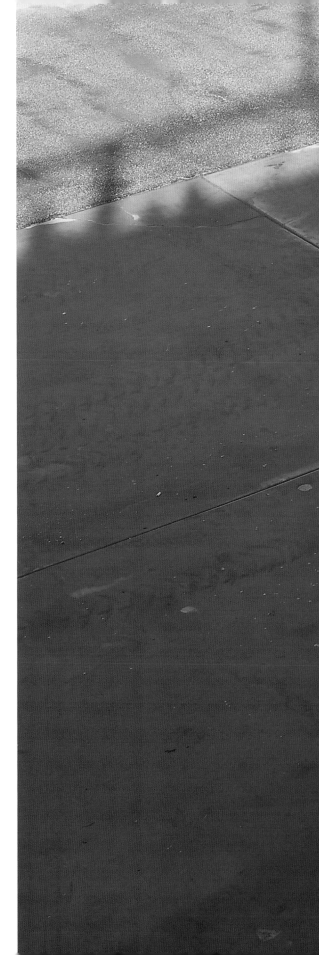

In June 1960, American sportsman Briggs Cunningham achieved a dream come true. As one of those who had chided his friend Harley Earl to produce a true U.S. sports car that he could race, Cunningham proudly entered three Corvettes in the 24-Hours of LeMans. One finished eighth overall.

Production exceeded 10,000 cars—a total of 10,261 were assembled—for the first time in Corvette history in 1960. Base price had risen to $3,872. Magazine and newspaper advertising emphasized the sporty nature of the car and its unique position in the American market once the Thunderbird got its back seat.

Sports Cars Become Mainstream: 1961–1962

"**Bill Mitchell** was very much into sharing his enthusiasm for cars. He allowed us designers to do whatever we wanted. He wanted to get us going," Peter Brock said, remembering what it was like at age 19 when he was hired.

"Mitchell would go to the shows, the Paris show, Frankfurt, Turin, or Geneva, and he'd come back with photographs. He'd pass them around. We'd all sit around and he'd say, 'I like that detail on that. We oughta try doing that on the such and such.' Or 'Here was an interesting idea, try this, do this, try that.' He was a very inspirational leader. He had excellent taste for picking other peoples' best work.

"That was the hard thing about him to reconcile. He'd pick the right line off everything—you could count on him to do that—and then as soon as he got involved with it, started doing things with it, he'd start putting chrome projections and stars and vents and stuff all over the car. It drove us nuts."

Mitchell followed Earl's precedent of producing show cars and design study vehicles, meant to introduce the public to ideas that he and his Design staff were looking at for future production. But Mitchell was restless. He loved power and speed as much as he loved distinctive style. Unlike many Earl Motorama studies, Mitchell's dreams ran.

While his Sting Ray raced, Mitchell prepared the XP-700, a road-going showpiece built in 1958. He took Cumberford's ideas such as the extended nose and grille from the SR-2 and pushed them farther. The nose of the XP-700 was three-dimensional. Its removable hardtop was a transparent plastic bubble, parted down the middle by a metal strip with air vents down the back, and a rearview mirror perched outside on top. The rear end strongly hinted at shapes for the 1961 production Corvette.

When the 1961 model hit the showrooms, enthusiasts saw a front end slightly changed from the 1960 car, but the rear end was a successful transfer from Mitchell's XP-700, becoming a new hint of what would become the Corvette in 1963.

Mechanical changes were subtle. Engineering replaced the heavy copper-core radiators with aluminum versions half as heavy while increasing capacity 10 percent. It helped weight balance and cooling. Two thirds of the buyers ordered the close-ratio four-speed transmission, while about one-fifth still wanted the three-speed manual; slightly more than 10 percent chose the two-speed Powerglide automatic.

In all, Chevrolet produced 10,939 of the 1961 models. The top performance engine was now the 315-horsepower 283-cubic-inch V-8 with Rochester fuel injection. Base price was $3,934.00, and more than half the buyers ordered the optional removable hardtop, RPO 419, at $236.75.

Private racers campaigned Corvettes around the United States, competing first, and rather successfully, with a five-car Sebring effort. Three of these were by Delmo Johnson, a Chevy dealer in Dallas, Texas, and the other two came from Don Yenko. At the end of the 12-hour event, Johnson and co-driver Dale Morgan finished 11th overall, the best finish to date for a stock Corvette.

Corvette mechanicals had evolved to the point in 1961 where its performance and reliability were never questioned. Its racing pedigree was established, and the car had earned respect. It arrived at the stage in its life where individuals wondered if a Corvette, by any other name, would smell so sweet, work so well, look so good, or race so successfully.

Fort Worth, Texas, entrepreneur Gary B. Laughlin drilled a little oil, processed some petroleum, and owned a few

Exterior appearance for 1961 got a "dental" facelift as Design removed the teeth that had been part of Corvette grilles from 1953. This was the last year that wide whitewall tires were offered. It was also the final appearance for the "coves" painted in contrasting colors, a $16.15 option.

At the back, the exhaust pipes dipped below the tail of the newly revised body, instead of passing through it as had been done previously. The back end was a hint of the new styling that had been planned for that year. With this tail, there were now four taillights. This was a design treatment, introduced for 1961, that would become an enduring trait.

Chevy dealerships. His hobby was SCCA production racing (in a Ferrari 750 Monza) where he met and hatched an idea with other Texan racing buddies, Carroll Shelby and Jim Hall. They wanted to produce a true GT version of the Corvette, lighter, perhaps lovelier. Laughlin, tired of his huge Ferrari repair bills, would finance it, Shelby would engineer it, and together they'd all race them. Their goal was enough cars to qualify it for SCCA's B-production class; they would sell cars to other competitors. Memos flew early in 1959 from Fort Worth to Warren to Modena, Italy. Sergio Scaglietti, car body fabricator for Enzo Ferrari, agreed to revise a fastback aluminum coupe to fit the Corvette chassis for Laughlin. Three 1959 mechanically complete chassis arrived.

Laughlin's oil operations took him to Europe regularly, and he always visited Modena. The car got closer to what he wanted, though Scaglietti had trouble widening his body to fit Corvette's 4-inch wider track. With a Spartan interior, the Scaglietti aluminum coupes weighed 400 pounds less than the fiberglass car.

The first car, painted silver, was completed in early 1961. Built on a chassis with a 1960 engine, the 290-horsepower 283-cubic-inch V-8 with Rochester fuel injection, the car had the close-ratio four-speed transmission and Positraction.

Scaglietti fitted the Corvette teeth into the front air intake. The interior contained two thin competition seats facing a crackle-finish instrument panel. Identification was only a hood medallion and two fender badges with the symbol of *Scaglietti & C., Modena.* The second prototype was done more luxuriously with an automatic transmission. Memories decades later recall that this car was intended for Hall, who was experimenting with racing automatic transmissions. It and the third car, another four-speed transmission version, bore Corvette crossed flags on the nose and egg-crate grilles.

Some 20 years later, Zora Duntov remembered the project only from memos he saw at the beginning and end. In the early 1980s, he recalled questions about the time the regular production line would shut down to produce these cars without bodies, interruptions too costly weighed against the increasing demand for (complete) cars. Shelby recalled Laughlin saying the project was dead. Whether it was GM's faithful adherence to the AMA ban or corporate concern over controlling the Corvette (lest someone else build something that might compete against it), neither one knew. Laughlin, after driving his car briefly, soured on the idea; it was a handful of ill-mannered handling and horsepower. He

The wildest engine option for 1961 was the fuel-injected 283, RPO 354, with 315 horsepower. Not surprisingly, even at $484.20, 1,462 buyers ordered it. Harrison's new all-aluminum radiator increased cooling capacity 10 percent, yet it weighed only half what the copper core coolers had been before 1961.

"Aficionados are made, not born" and they were readers of the *New Yorker* and *Sports Illustrated* during the middle of February 1962. "Corvette enthusiasm, like manhood, is a condition that develops slowly. . . ." *Campbell-Ewald*

The base convertible retailed for $3,934. Production reached 10,939 cars, nearly a third of them, 3,487, in Tuxedo Black. Some 7,013 buyers ordered the optional four-speed transmission, but only 698 of them paid the $59.20 for optional electric window lifts.

AFICIONADOS ARE MADE, NOT BORN Corvette enthusiasm, like manhood, is a condition that develops slowly and requires the tempering influence of experience. It begins when you're urging your faithful family sedan along some twisty bit of road and a Corvette slips by like you were just another bend in the highway. It reaches its peak with you, checkbook in hand, savoring the view from the driver's seat of that wondrous automobile, and imagining yourself expertly answering the challenge of an Alpine pass. You can shorten this process considerably; see your Chevrolet dealer and drive a '62 Corvette. It's a car worth driving. It runs like all-get-out because it has a mighty 327-cubic-inch V8 engine. It stops, it changes direction with the speed and ease of a gazelle because of its knife-edge balance and great, huge brakes. It's a car to make driving enthusiasts of us all. . . . **CORVETTE BY CHEVROLET** Chevrolet Division of General Motors, Detroit 2, Michigan.

sold his first car for about $9,200, to a business acquaintance in Chicago. Hall barely used his car and sold his by 1964. Carroll Shelby sold his soon after delivery and, undaunted, took his idea of running an American V-8 in a European car body and went shopping elsewhere.

While Laughlin worked with Scaglietti, Wisconsin industrial designer Gordon Kelly began a restyling project with Carrozzeria Vignale on his 1960 Corvette. Kelly worked with Brooks Stevens Associates styling Studebaker Hawks. He produced a one-eighth scale clay model of a Corvette body and showed it to Bill Mitchell. Mitchell offered Gordon a car if he'd find a builder who would display it at the Paris Auto Show in October 1961. Vignale agreed. Kelly's lines, stubbier, but more aggressive than Scaglietti's coupes, were striking behind an oversized oval egg-crate grille. The Kelly/Vignale–bodied car was shown at auto shows for a year before the owner finally got to drive it. The car was equipped with a fuel-injected 283, the RPO 687 brakes and suspension option, a four-speed transmission, and Positraction.

Chevrolet management changed at the top in 1961. Semon E. "Bunkie" Knudsen was promoted from Pontiac Division to head GM's biggest seller. (His father, William, had done something similar 30 years earlier.)

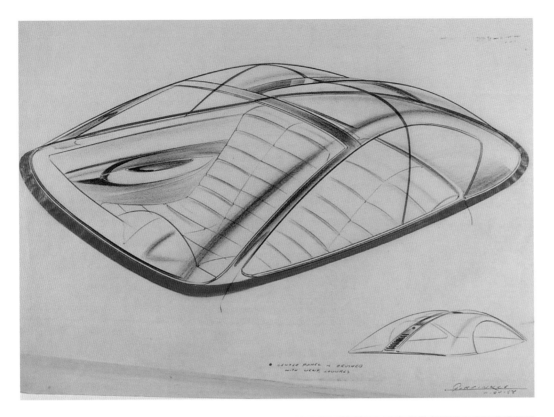

Glass bubble details drawn in late 1958 by Gene Garfinkle eventually appeared on Bill Mitchell's Mako Shark XP-755.

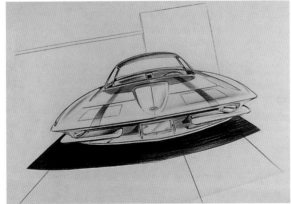

This was the first sketched attempt to develop front bumpers onto the production Sting Ray, meant for probable introduction in 1960. Gene Garfinkle worked on advance Corvette designs in late 1958 and early 1959.

Soon after Harley Earl retired in 1958, his understudy Bill Mitchell commissioned his first personal show car, the XP-700, just as his boss had done for years. It was based on a production 1958, but it absorbed ideas from designers such as Peter Brock, Bob Cumberford, Gene Garfinkle, Tony Lapine, and others. It also introduced the tail that would appear on 1961 models.
Mike Mueller archives

Bunkie Knudsen liked racing and understood what the AMA wished to deny: "speed" promoted sales. He ushered a great amount of parts, support, advice, and even money out through a backdoor at Pontiac and into the hands of stock car and drag racers. Pontiac's successes led to Ford's public repudiation of the AMA ban in 1962.

Knudsen arrived at Chevrolet just in time to enjoy the success of Ed Cole's hard work with Duntov and Mitchell and their staffs. The 1962 model year Corvette marked the introduction of another legendary powerplant in the car's history. Starting with the 283-cubic-inch V-8 and increasing the bore to 4.00 inches and the stroke to 3.25, total displacement increased to 327 cubic inches. The meekest engine produced 250 horsepower, while the solid lifter, Duntov-cam, fuel-injected engine boasted 360 horsepower. The most powerful optional engine still cost $484.20, the same fee since 1958. A car ready to prepare for racing ran $5,243.00, while a civilized back-road tourer with every civilized option actually sold for $5,014.00 in 1962.

The body retained the heavy steel and aluminum reinforcement introduced in mid-1957 around the cowl and doors, continuing to provide additional stiffness and body integrity. With all the improvements, body weight remained nearly the same as in 1953 because unnecessary fiberglass layers in some panels were deleted.

The designers and engineers labored on; each bent on answering the few lingering criticisms and improving perceptions that sports car enthusiasts carried about Corvettes. The future held great things in store. Yet, Chevrolet's only remaining competitor did not stand by idly. Jaguar understood that the V-8 was necessary for American markets; however, a dual-overhead camshaft on top of an existing inline six-cylinder engine would be perfectly adequate for its side of the Atlantic Ocean. Packaging it in a stunning body form would not hurt at all.

Jaguar introduced its new 1962 XK-E in the spring of 1961 at the New York Auto Show fully 18 months before Bunkie Knudsen could debut the new Sting Ray. Jaguar's slender cars, the coupe and roadster, threw down another challenge to Corvette, delivered in an America with a more mature attitude about sports cars. The United States had become the world's largest market for sports cars. Jaguar sold most of its cars in the United States. Its New York debut press releases boasted two bodies, a coupe and a roadster, both two-passenger cars with no jump seats. Jaguar boasted about its new body on its new chassis, with independent rear suspension and four-wheel disc brakes. It would sell for $4,915.

With what Knudsen, Mitchell, Duntov, and dozens of other engineers, designers, and managers knew about the 1963 Corvette roadster and coupe, it was very generous of Chevrolet to let Jaguar enjoy the limelight for the next year or so.

Side coves, previously done in contrasting colors, were no longer two-tone paint schemes. Even chrome trim was deleted. These coves subtly disappeared into the car sides, set off only by a single louver. This was not only the last year of the Corvette body style, but it marked the final appearance of a trunk and for other hold-overs such as the solid rear axle.

The most notable change for 1962 was one that these instruments would monitor: a new engine. Chevrolet introduced its soon-to-be-legendary 327-cubic-inch V-8. This was based on the previous 283, but Engineering increased the bore to 4.00 inches and the stroke to 3.25. In its highest state of fuel-injected tune, it produced 360 horsepower.

81

Exterior appearance was cleaned up in this last year of the second body style. Bill Mitchell's influence in Design produced folded lines and razor creases instead of Harley Earl's fleshy rounded and finned shapes. Both men tended to introduce too much but then steadily revise, tame, and improve the car's appearance over its life.

Like Corporate Tennis
CERV I: Game to Duntov

Press releases described it as "a research tool for Chevrolet's continuous investigations into automotive ride and handling phenomena under the most realistic conditions." It had no fenders or taillights, and it seated one. The "realistic conditions" certainly were not rush hour traffic on Woodward or Michigan avenues or 12 Mile Road.

It was given not a name but an acronym, CERV, the Chevrolet Experimental Racing Vehicle. In view of GM Chairman Frederic Donner's adamant support of the 1957 AMA racing ban, the CERV was inexplicable. Its appearance was a flat-out single-seat race car built to specifications close to the 1960 Indianapolis regulations. After the problems Zora Duntov had with the Corvette SS in early 1957, he began looking at new solutions, not the least of which was relocating the engine behind the driver so its heat would not roast the cockpit. But the AMA ban buried racing, and it wasn't until early 1959 when he took the risk of starting a project to test his ideas. By now, Duntov had the nucleus of a team, with Harold Krieber and Walt Zetye who had come to work for Chevrolet back in 1946. In 1958, Zetye joined Duntov and took responsibility for the chassis development up until the mid-1970s.

The three engineers created the CERV on a 96-inch wheelbase (the Indy minimum), with front and rear track at 56 inches, the actual body width was only 52 inches and overall length just 172 inches. It was nicknamed the "Hillclimber" because Duntov's first idea was to run it at Pikes Peak. Duntov developed an all-aluminum block 283-cubic-inch engine that used an alloy with a high silicon content that required no cylinder liners to power the car. The heads and most of the hang-on parts, water pump housing, flywheel, clutch pressure plate, and starter motor case were aluminum. A magnesium fuel injection intake manifold provided sufficient airflow to produce 353 horsepower. A basically stock four-speed close ratio transmission fit behind the engine, ahead of the final drive. This configuration required extra car length, but there was no money available for a final drive between the gearbox and flywheel. Duntov's design kept the weight between the axles, resulting in more neutral handling, one of the goals of his experiment.

Brakes were optional Al-Fin large-diameter drums, the rears mounted inboard alongside the differential. The rudimentary antilock rear brake system from the SS reappeared, more refined, in the CERV. He improved on the rear independent suspension for the prototype Q-Corvettes for the CERV, while its front suspension was basically carried over from the SS racer.

All this was mounted on a chrome-molybdenum alloy steel tube frame, surrounded in a two-layer fiberglass paper-thin body designed by Tony Lapine and Larry Shinoda in the Hammer Room. Without liquids, the completed CERV weighed only 1,450 pounds.

Other projects interrupted Duntov, Zetye, and Krieger through spring and summer 1960 (including Briggs Cunningham for his LeMans Corvette effort). Duntov couldn't run his first trials up Pikes Peak until September. He felt fast, but bystanders with no accurate records of others' test times exaggerated the recollections, telling the Chevrolet engineers they were off the pace.

Disheartened, the CERV returned to Warren, Firestone withdrew its support, and everyone returned to work. Of course, after the event, when winning times were published, Duntov learned his CERV set records.

The real value of the CERV then appeared. Its formidable power-to-weight ratio, less than 5.25 pounds per horsepower, provided both Firestone and Goodyear with an excellent platform on which to test and develop wider tires they wanted to introduce. Walter MacKenzie, former Racing manager for Chevrolet who was now director of product information, renamed the CERV Chevrolet Engineering Research Vehicle. This kept the management calm while Duntov continued to work.

In 1960, NASCAR founder Bill France challenged racers to lap Daytona speedway at 180 miles per hour, offering a $10,000 award. Duntov had already topped 170 miles per hour at GM's Proving Grounds, again at Riverside and once more in testing at Sebring. He thought 180 miles per hour was achievable.

Back in Warren, he and his crew tried supercharging and then twin turbochargers. Working when time permitted through 1962, they developed the engine's reliability. Dynamometer

tests measured 500 horsepower with an 8.5:1 compression ratio. Then work began with the 377-cubic-inch engines destined for other competition projects, filling most of 1963. But Duntov used one of the 377s, with Hilborn fuel injection, an extremely efficient cross-ram induction intake, and a slightly cleaner front body nose cone, and he reached his magic 180 miles per hour. And he kept going. The run wasn't at Daytona, but where the clocks recorded his fastest laps, he'd averaged 206 miles per hour around GM's Milford Proving Ground 4.5-mile oval.

While it was nicknamed *The Hillclimber,* it was one of Zora Duntov's most cherished road racing projects. Officially it was known as Chevrolet's "Engineering Research Vehicle," used beginning in early 1960 to develop engines, chassis, and suspensions for the Corvette and other production cars. Duntov first showed its potential in demonstrations here at Riverside Raceway near Los Angeles in November 1960. In 1964 it lapped GM's Milford, Michigan, 5-mile test track at 206 miles per hour. *Mike Mueller archives*

chapter 9

Race Cars Are Built in Loopholes: 1962–1966

Appendix J, *Chapter IV, Group 3, Article 264: Definition*

Paragraph 1: Grand Touring Cars are vehicles built in small series for customers who are looking for a better performance and/or a maximum comfort and are not particularly concerned about economy.

Article 265: Minimum production—Recognition

Paragraph 1: in order to enjoy recognition in the "Grand Touring" category, cars will have to be produced at a minimum rate of one hundred identical units as far as mechanical parts and coachwork are concerned in 12 consecutive months.

Duntov had a tremendous ally in General Manager Bunkie Knudsen, who liked seeing his cars in the spotlight. In March 1962 Ford announced it would return to racing, blaming GM for side-stepping the AMA ban for years. Frederic Donner, embarrassed, repeated General Motors' intentions to honor GM's 1957 commitment. Knudsen could guess what Ford's "Total Performance" program was. So even though a Corvette Z06 had beaten Carroll Shelby's single Cobra at Riverside in October 1962, Duntov's description of Shelby's car made clear its threat. Knudsen encouraged Duntov to be discrete but to think ambitiously, as Ford and Shelby were doing. Duntov's idea for a four-wheel-drive, CERV II midengine coupe to take to LeMans in 1964 was too blatant a project after Donner's latest declaration.

Zora Duntov knew LeMans; he knew what it would take to win overall, because he had won his class there once before in a small Porsche. He understood the Federation Internationale de l'Automobile (FIA), and knowing the organization, he recognized that the rule change that made Grand Touring cars eligible in the contest for the World Championship for Manufacturers was really a veiled invitation to U.S. manufacturers to bring their cars out to play.

Falling back on alternatives, Duntov then considered his own "lightweight," an 1,800-pound Corvette. He still needed 600 horsepower to propel the car, with its aerodynamic disadvantages, through the French countryside at competitive speeds.

Duntov and his chassis engineer Walt Zetye fabricated an aluminum frame using two large-diameter parallel tubes joined at the back end by three transverse tubes and at the front by a massive 6-inch diameter cross-member. Aluminum saved 94 pounds over steel, and Zetye and Duntov transferred onto the car the independent rear suspension (IRS) devised for the CERV that would appear later on the production Sting Ray. They cast an aluminum differential case, and fitted a Dana limited-slip differential to replace the GM Positraction. The body was shortened slightly, from 175.3 inches to 172.8. It also was lightened considerably by using paper-thin fiberglass carefully laid over an aluminum substructure. Overall height grew 2 inches because the seats rested on top of, not inside of, the two major longitudinal frame members. Ground clearance, however, dropped from 7.4 to 4.3 inches. Because the race car weighed nearly 1,000 pounds less than the production car, Duntov decided to try four Girling disc brakes.

There were many pages to the FIA racing regulations and thousands of words. Nowhere in the rules for 1963 did it limit engine displacement, this being another invitation to the Americans. Still, Chevrolet Engineering's 427 Mark II "mystery motor" could produce the power Duntov wanted, but it weighed too much. Boring out an all-aluminum 327

The Monterey Historics offer living history lessons. In the foreground, Roger Penske's Nassau ride, #50, reminds enthusiasts of Grand Sport power. The bulbous hood accommodated the four twin-choke Weber carburetors and fender flares were needed to contain the 11-inch-wide rear Hallibrand. Behind it is Mecom's #3 car in Sebring trim.
Maggie Moore

block to within a couple of thousandths of its life might meet the same ends through different means. A 4.00-inch stroke and 4.00-inch bore would give him a lightweight 402-cubic-inch engine. Zora and Yura Duntov, his brother, had devised the Ardun head, a hemispherical combustion chamber, for Flathead Ford V-8s in the 1940s. For the aluminum 402, they created twin-plug hemi-heads. The engine was assembled and tested and was soon discarded as too far stressed. Back at the drawing board, they reconsidered the stroke at 3.75 inches, which required less intrusive modifications to accommodate the spinning crankshaft. This engine measured 377 cubic inches. Duntov even produced three prototype dual-overhead cam versions, which produced an estimated 550 brake horsepower. This was less than his target of 600 horsepower, but it was more than any other option they had tried.

Duntov took this first car, known by now as the Grand Sport (GS), to Sebring in mid-December 1962. Equipped with a race-prepared 327-cubic-inch engine, he used it for shakedown runs and tire testing with Firestone and Mickey Thompson. The GS outshined Thompson's purely production-based car; however, the Girling disc brakes proved inadequate. Actually, the Grand Sport shined a little too brightly:

The Grand Sport invaded Nassau during the December 1963 Speed Weeks. Roger Penske (#50), in Grand Sport #004, driving for team owner John Mecom, leads Mecom's team Lola GT coupe, a courageous Volvo P1800 (driven by Art Riley), and Penske teammates Jim Hall (#65), in Grand Sport #003, and Dick Thompson (#80), Grand Sport #005, during the first lap of the five-lap preliminary heat for the Tourist Trophy. *Dave Friedman photo collection*

Roger Penske proved Zora Duntov right in the engineer's assessment of what it would take to make a competitive Corvette. Penske finished third overall in the Nassau Governor's Trophy race. *Dave Friedman photo collection*

As they replaced the Girling rotors with new 1-inch thick factory-produced ventilated discs, word came down from the corporation—Chevrolet was too visible behind Donner's back. There would not be 100 lightweights. The five prototypes that were underway would be "scrapped, sold, or used as testing and evaluation vehicles." But they would not race.

Chevrolet had already filed specification papers with the FIA in Paris when Donner's edict hit Duntov's operation two weeks later. The specifications promised completed assembly of 100 identical cars before June 1, 1963 (with LeMans running June 15 and 16). Duntov had wanted his prototypes to be followed by 125 "production" cars for sale to customers to meet the FIA "homologation" (legalization) requirement and then later 1,000 street-legal production cars for public sale would follow. Engineering had spoken with outside vendors about manufacturing the customer racing cars and the street cars as well. However, Knudsen had authorized only 25 cars total and just 40 of those special 377-cubic-inch hemi engines.

It was over in a heartbeat.

Dick Doane, the Dundee, Illinois, car dealer and racer, and Grady O. Davis, president of Gulf Oil and an enthusiastic car owner, were the beneficiaries of Donner's

John Cannon, driving Grand Sport #65 enjoyed the moment passing John Everly in the Nassau Trophy Race's solo Cobra entry. *Dave Friedman photo collection*

Dr. Dick Thompson joined the Grand Sport forces during the Nassau Tourist Trophy race as part of Nassau Speed Week in December 1963. *Dave Friedman photo collection*

Just before the start of the Nassau Tourist Trophy, Roger Penske talked quickly with driver Dick Thompson. Team owner/official entrant John Mecom (in the tennis sweater) held the door. Jim Hall sat in #65 in the background. *Dave Friedman photo collection*

edict. Duntov sent out one of the completed cars to each of them, with instructions to keep their activities "low key" and not cause Chevrolet any embarrassment. Each car was white and equipped with a production stock 360-horsepower 327-cubic-inch fuel-injected engine. Because there were only five built, these cars did not qualify for production racing classes but instead had to go up against modified sports racers like Jim Hall's Chaparrals and Lance Reventlow's Scarabs. This class elevation, however, allowed Doane and Davis to build real racing engines. The privately held Grand Sports went through teething troubles but eventually came to hold its own.

Grady Davis put Dr. Dick Thompson in his car. After a shaky start, Thompson and Davis had the car sorted to the extent that, by early June, it consistently finished in the top five overall. Through July and August, Davis' crew reworked and improved the "modified" Corvette, and when it re-emerged in late August at the Watkins Glen, New York, Nationals, it was closer to Duntov's original vision. Somehow, when the points were totaled, Thompson finished fourth for the year in the C-modified category.

This frustrated Chevrolet engineers and its general manager, who recognized how close they had come with the car. Carroll Shelby and his drivers steadily teased them. Discretely, through Chevrolet's back corridors, a word was whispered: escalate. Texas oil heir John Mecom Jr. ran a Cooper-engined sports racer, the Xerex Special, throughout 1963. He acquired the car, its builder, Roy Gane, and its driver, Roger Penske, and during the year, he added Augie Pabst and A. J. Foyt to his stable. The team was highly regarded, thoroughly professional, and extremely successful. Because Mecom was a newcomer, he owed allegiance to no one, making him the perfect team owner for Chevrolet's whispered plans.

Duntov arranged to ship Mecom several engines to install in a variety of sports racers. He called back Doane's and Davis' Grand Sports and pulled a third car from the storage garages and set to work, preparing cars for Nassau Speed Week, scheduled for early December 1963, with Knudsen's unwritten but enthusiastic blessing.

New body modifications accommodated 11-inch-wide Halibrand wheels, necessary to fit the Mickey Thompson–inspired new wide Goodyear low-profile racing tires. Ventilation, to engine and driver, was improved by liberally perforating the nose, hood, sides, and rear of each car. Duntov dropped in the 377-cubic-inch all-aluminum block aluminum head engines originally developed for the car. These engines used four twin-throat Weber side-draft carburetors for induction. Duntov's dynamometers saw 485 horsepower.

The three Corvettes, chassis 003, 004, and 005, were painted in Mecom Racing's Cadillac Blue and shipped to Nassau, timed to arrive on November 30, the day before their first race. Several Chevrolet engineers arrived as well, all vacationing at the same time. Along with the Grand Sports, Mecom sent his three midengined Chevrolet-powered sports racers, his Lola GT, Cooper-Monaco, and Scarab.

Fresh off the Bahama Star, the three Grand Sport Corvettes underwent scrutinizing by a most interested group of observers. One young man at the left even has a tuning idea to try on the Weber 58-mm side-draft carbureted engine. It was reported to produce 485 horsepower at 6,000 rpm. *Dave Friedman photo collection*

Team owner/entrant John Mecom brought new meaning to rush hour commuting vehicles as he thundered through the traffic rotary outside the Port of Nassau. This car and his two others (driven into town by Roger Penske and Augie Pabst) would soon bear numbers, stripes, and Goodyear and Mecom racing stickers. *Dave Friedman photo collection*

Except for covered headlights, it could be Sebring, 1964. John Mecom's #3 car, wearing race number 2, was driven by A. J. Foyt in an incredible performance. He started 62nd and in the first lap, used the Corvette power and handling to full extent, passing 50 cars! Foyt shared the 12 hours with John Cannon. At its best, it ran 8th, but a broken wheel in the 11th hour dropped it to 23rd overall at the finish. *Maggie Moore*

With this stable, piloted by some of racing's best drivers, Duntov believed that if the Corvette lightweights themselves did not win, at least a Chevrolet engine was likely to come home in first.

The Corvettes won the five-lap qualifying race, but Mecom's Lola took the 99-mile Tourist Trophy on December 1. The Grand Sports' final drives, not broken in before the races, couldn't handle the torque of the 485-horsepower engines or the pounding of the old airport course. Carefully seasoned rear axles were flown down in the baggage of another Chevrolet engineer who was suddenly overcome with the need for a Caribbean vacation.

The second weekend's 112-mile Governors Cup was a better show. A. J. Foyt won in Mecom's Chevy-engined Scarab, and the Grand Sports finished third (Roger Penske), fourth (Augie Pabst), and sixth (Dick Thompson), beating Shelby's best-placed Cobra by two places. The next day's finale, the 252 Mile Nassau Trophy, ended with Dick Thompson in fourth, a Cobra in seventh, and new Mecom inductee John Cannon in eighth. But this race pointed out once again the fearsome aerodynamics of the cars. Air pressure built up under the hoods and continually blew the fasteners. Each driver endured several pit stops to cut in new vent holes and apply racer tape to the panels.

Somehow, Nassau escaped Frederic Donner's sharp eyes. The Grand Sport operation returned to Warren for some improvements and modifications before the 1964 season openers at Daytona and Sebring. Each race presented specific problems. Engineers fitted a new Rochester fuel-injection system to even out the engine power curve and they installed a pneumatic air-jacking system to speed pit stop tire changes, changes that would benefit the Mecom team at both venues.

Grand Sport roadster #002 was campaigned by driven George Wintersteen, running a cast-iron 427-ci engine. At a Grand Sport reunion at Watkins Glen in August 1988, it led the Foyt/Cannon car (rear left) and the Penske Nassau car immediately behind it. *Maggie Moore*

Daytona was a track where maximum speed was beneficial, as it would be at LeMans and a few other circuits in the world. Duntov knew the Corvette was a brick punching a big hole through the air. A sports-racer body like Mecom's other cars, or like his originally planned CERV II, would have been ideal but would introduce all new development problems. Instead, he decided to cut down the big brick, knowing that he'd pick up speed.

Duntov removed the roofs from two coupes, chassis 001 and 002. Engineers replaced the tall windshields with low windscreens and incorporated roll bars into lower fiberglass fairings. But the spies were loose in the back halls at GM Engineering, and shortly before the Daytona Continental 2,000-kilometer race in mid-February, Bunkie Knudsen was called before his bosses. A press release stated that Chevrolet was not associated with John Mecom Racing, ever. Donner applied effective leverage over Knudsen, and he recognized the threat. This left one more permanent blotch on his record. More clearly than ever, he saw his future ending at General Motors.

Quickly Chevrolet sold the three coupes, two to Mecom and the third, chassis 005, to Jim Hall. The two roadsters were wrapped under covers and buried in storage in Warren. The three coupes began an odyssey of owners and races and

The fiberglass 36.5-gallon gas tank was different from production Sting Rays and it was fitted much farther forward in the frame to improve weight distribution. A complete 327-ci 360-horsepower Rochester Ramjet fuel-injection engine sat where Duntov had hoped his wilder 377-ci V-8s might fit. This is chassis number one. *Mike Mueller archives*

Grand Sport Roadster #001 wore race #10 at Sebring in 1966. Entrant Roger Penske, known for meticulous race preparation, matched wheel paint to exhaust pipes to Sunoco's logo color and his dealership name. Engine power by this time was a single Holley four-barrel carburetor atop a 427 ci. Dick Thompson left the track trying to avoid a slower car and the roadster did not finish. *Maggie Moore*

modifications that has filled other books, most notably Lowell Paddock's and Dave Friedman's informative and entertaining 1989 history, *Corvette Grand Sport*. The cars campaigned privately, valiantly, and with some success for another three seasons, beating in major international events the best that Ford of Dearborn, Venice, and England could throw at them. In the late winter of 1966, Roger Penske, retired from driving but active as a team owner, acquired the two remaining roadsters from Chevrolet, selling one quickly to friend George Wintersteen. Prior to Sebring in 1966, Penske fitted a 427-cubic-inch Mark IV engine into 002, and during practice his crew bolted on aluminum heads, a first for the Mark IV and an indication that creative thinking was not dead, only in hiding within Chevrolet.

Both roadsters and the coupes soldiered gamely on through the 1966 season, thrilling fans and inspiring loyalists. But insightful racing observers saw something that Zora Duntov never predicted, though he'd already envisioned it. In his CERV I, Duntov had experimented with the future: Midengined race cars offered enormous handling advantages over the nose-heavy front-engined Grand Sports.

In late 1962, as Chevy gave birth to the Grand Sports, Peter Brock moved back to the West Coast,

joining Shelby's organization. where he watched Chevrolet and GM's board futzing and fidgeting from the long view in Venice. Decades later, he wrote about it in his excellent, insightful history of racing in the era in Shelby's most intriguing car, the Cobra Daytona coupe, which Brock designed.

"This dilemma [to race or not to race] split the board of directors," Brock wrote. "In the GM board room the battle lines were redrawn: bean counters versus engineers and marketing experts," he observed. "Neither group seemed capable of convincing their adversaries of the wisdom of their self-held philosophies, and it was obvious that any solution to the dilemma was going to be expensive. There was, however, one fact both sides could agree on. The Texan's Cobras were just too strong. A new Chevrolet racer was needed to meet the Ford Challenge, and this, of course, was going to cost even more money. Could they afford to meet the challenge? Obviously yes, but was it worth it . . .? Chevrolet realized a serious retaliatory racing program would take time and money."

Soon after its homologation application was filed, Chevrolet heard that FIA vehicle inspections were being more effectively enforced. One hundred cars in the rules called for 100 cars in the parking lot.

Gulf entered the car in Sebring with Duncan Black and M. R. J. Wylie as drivers. It qualified second fastest, but at the start it was the last car to leave. Wylie explained, "I flooded the damned thing. Couldn't get it started." Twelve hours later he and Black finished first in class, 18th overall.

Historically, the Italian car builder had made continuous, minor modifications to all its models. The FIA accepted these changes on the 250 GT SWBs as "a normal evolution of type." Through the fall and winter of 1962–1963, Ferrari developed a new body for the 250 SWB, but it was not complete when it had to file its 1963 application. So Ferrari instead included photos of the existing 1962 SWB and, on subsequent pages, it listed the options available including an entire body. With no photos, the FIA questioned Ferrari's engineers who shrugged it off as a "normal evolution of type"; this was, they said, the complete, final evolution. The FIA didn't buy it. So Ferrari contacted racing promoters and track owners and threatened to cancel his 1963 racing efforts because approval was being withheld for reasons he could not understand. The FIA had passed all his previous evolutions of type without hesitation. Racing organizers, threatened with loss of revenue, pressured the FIA and Ferrari won. The 1963 Ferrari 250 GT was accepted, homologated, *omologato* in Italian, hence the 250 GTO designation.

Ferrari manufactured only 36 GTO models. Under the current rules interpretation, the FIA had to accept it though everyone knew it was a new automobile. The precedent for production variants had been established.

"Came time to homologate the Cobra," Brock said, "only eight [roadsters] were completed when the FIA inspected our paperwork and approved the car. But Carroll had signed an affidavit to the FIA that 100 *would* be built. More than that eventually were built. When the Daytona Coupe came along as 'normal evolution of type,' the FIA had to let it through on the same loophole. Ferrari, now threatened with serious competition, protested. That raised the hackles on the back of all the FIA delegates' necks.

"The FIA was caught between the realities of commerce and sincere attempts to keep racing equitable for all involved." So in an attempt to tidy up its mess, the FIA pendulum swung back completely in the opposite direction. They would enforce the letter of their law.

"Chevrolet's plans to produce the lightweight Corvette Grand Sport were dealt a severe blow when Chevrolet was formally informed by the FIA that it would have to complete 100 cars before it could race its radical new car in the production GT [group] III category.

"Not having a guarantee from the FIA to accept the car as 'production' prior to the actual completion of 100 units had much to do with Chevrolet's plans to cancel the program. Chevrolet engineers realized there was no way to build that many cars prior to the first event of the '64 season, and they knew they would have to participate in these events to qualify for championship points or be out of the running," Brock wrote. The entire series of events caused a ripple effect.

"Then Ford came in with the GT40," Brock continued. "The FIA asked to see all 100 copies. Well, there weren't and so, in spite of its 'GT' name, it was forced to run

Following the Daytona 24 hours and Sebring 12 hours, Gulf sold the second 1962 car and resurrected one of its 1961s so that it could compete in both A and B production SCCA events. The strategy worked and Don Yenko, most often driving the 1961, won the National B Production title while Dick Thompson, in this car, won the national A production championship. Don Yenko raced the car again at Sebring in 1963.

"In the early '60s," Brock explained recently, "the FIA would accept the manufacturer's word that all 100 would be produced. A few completed cars would be shown. All manufacturers submitted chassis numbers of scheduled—but unbuilt—cars to the FIA. Preapproved FIA homologation meant buyers could place an order for a limited-production car early in the year, and they'd be certain it would be accepted in international competition even before the required number of cars had been completed." The FIA knew that by trusting the manufacturers, it encouraged other competitors to purchase new FIA-legal vehicles and compete in FIA events.

"The word 'identical' was subject to interpretation," Brock noted. "Slight variations to the production model were accepted as 'normal evolution of type.'" This rule meant that wider fenders to accommodate fatter tires, or new air intakes for engine or cockpit ventilation, the kinds of running changes that occur on any racing team, were allowed without building another 100 identical cars."

Enzo Ferrari had a more creative interpretation in mind. From 1960 to 1962, he built about 200 of the 250 GT short-wheelbase Berlinetta (SWB) coupes. By early 1961 it was clear that the car's flat nose and crude aerodynamics produced front-end lift similar to Bill Mitchell's SS. Ferrari recognized that a new body was essential to stay in front.

only as a prototype. Enzo Ferrari appeared at Sebring in 1964 with his 250LM, basically a P2 with a roof, a prototype sent in to defeat the Daytona Coupes. He had attempted to homologate this car as his new 'production' GT car and he submitted his papers to the FIA stating his intent to build 100 identical examples. But only this car had been completed and everyone on the FIA board knew he had no plans of building 100 of these. Since the FIA officials had made their formal statement to Chevrolet turning down the Grand Sport. There was no way they could accept the 250LM. The rule that [Ferrari] called on Ford, that was enforced on Chevrolet, blew up in his face."

It created a racing conundrum for all makers. Private competitors would not buy a car that was not yet homologated. Duntov could not get the Grand Sports homologated unless there were 100 cars completed, and Chevrolet would not build 100 of them unless there were firm orders for at least 90 cars. Further clouding the issue was the matter of public visibility in Europe versus America. Ford, for example, had a vested interest in competing in Europe. The blue oval logo appeared on cars built in Germany and the United Kingdom. Chevrolet had no such presence in Europe; in fact, at times GM had de-emphasized its ownership of Vauxhall in the United Kingdom and Opel in Germany. For Chevrolet to have won in Europe might even have necessitated an expensive advertising campaign just to explain to Europeans what it meant and who should care. The Corvette was neither sold there nor was it well regarded compared to other European sports cars.

Donner would not consider risking public embarrassment by circumventing the AMA ban by racing in Europe. The fabulously expensive prospect of producing so few cars, which it might not even be able to sell (at a reported $9,200 each), made the accountant's blood boil. It had only been during his rule that Corvette had begun to pay for itself. He understood that little projects like the Grand Sport served to keep his engineers excited and loyal, so long as they didn't cast the wrong light onto an observant public. Yet the car simply couldn't be. The corporation he believed, should not spend the money, the division would not have the Grand Sport.

In a master stroke of public relations good fortune, Donner turned a purely economic decision into a safety conscious issue. He was still smarting from the secret, seamy Ralph Nader investigations and from congressional subcommittee questions on Corvair safety. He had blurted out that GM had expended less than 1 percent of its net profit on safety-related research. It was an awful moment. The Grand Sport was the perfect project to shut down. In the newspapers, it would read as purity of motive: Donner was upholding the June 6, 1957, AMA speed and racing ban. In the eyes of the wary public, he had begun to redeem himself and General Motors. In the eyes of Wall Street stockbrokers, individuals who were far more important to Donner, he had exercised fiscal responsibility.

Like Corporate Tennis II CERV II: Set and Match to Donner

Zora Duntov's champion, Bunkie Knudsen, had approved the CERV II in early 1962 as a follow-up project. This was to be an alloy-tube frame, 92-inch wheelbase, 1,800-pound sports racer powered by a new 244-cubic-inch engine (to meet 1962 FIA regulations for 1963 prototype race cars' 4.0-liter maximum engine displacement). There was the possibility of using Mark II 427-cubic-inch engines in this car and, with 550 horsepower on hand, other opportunities arose. All-wheel-drive was one. Knudsen and Duntov believed in using racing and competition as a means to improve and promote regular production vehicles. They understood that racing forced fast engineering solutions to problems, short-cutting normal development times from months to days between one race and the next.

Duntov worked on the all-wheel-drive CERV with Frank Winchell, Chevrolet's head of research and development. As Bill Mitchell had his locked design studios, so Winchell had secret engineering labs. He was responsible for the engineering of the Corvair rear engine. He didn't care much for racing, but he loved engineering problems. The solution he and Duntov created for an all-wheel-drive CERV II was dual torque converters, one front and one rear. The sheet-steel, unit construction chassis used the engine as a stressed member, surrounded by a tubular substructure to carry the other loads.

Word of the CERV II slipped out and got downtown. Donner knew Knudsen was the leader of a pack of division managers aiming to go racing again. The corporation slapped Knudsen's wrists, but it closed down CERV II, which was already past wind tunnel testing as both a coupe and roadster. Chevrolet racing in internationally sanctioned events against the likes of Ferrari would not happen. At least not in the prototype category, not in anything so radically, noticeably different as a tiny, midengine, sports racer.

This immediately set Duntov and Knudsen to wondering about a Plan B—something not quite so obvious, something that looked much more like a regular production product.

chapter 10

All New, Everywhere Improved: 1963–1967

If anyone doubted Bill Mitchell's influence and power, all questions were answered when the 1963 Sting Ray arrived. Its rear-end design was startling and derivative. The coupe—itself a Corvette first—incorporated a boat-tail taper adopted from the classic sporting roadsters of the 1930s. Breaking its rear window was that controversial center spine, adapted from the Bugatti Atlantique and the Bertone BAT design studies.

Zora Duntov and others protested the intrusion of the spine on rearward vision. Mitchell retorted: "If you take that off, you might as well forget the whole thing." That was a hollow threat; because Corvettes had always belonged to Design, he had the highest authority. The solid threat hit Duntov where he lived: If there was no spine, there might be no independent rear suspension, no disc brakes. Mitchell made it clear that Engineering's contributions were accepted when they did not interfere.

Yet, startling as the Sting Ray was visually, it was equally impressive mechanically. The car derived material benefits from the Q-Corvette project, from Mitchell's Sting Ray race car and also from Zora's pet project, the CERV I.

For the production Sting Ray, called the XP-720 internally, the designers shortened the wheelbase 4 inches from the old XK-120 dimensions of 102 inches. Built on a 98-inch wheelbase, the new car improved maneuverability and quickened handling response. Engineers lowered the center of gravity roughly 2.3 inches, accomplished through a new ladder-type frame with five cross-members, replacing the original car's X-frame. This allowed them to place passengers inside the frame rails for the 1963 car rather than on top of them as before. Engineering ran its designs through computer analysis to predetermine the necessary steel wall thicknesses and

structural placement. Test frames were built too stiff, intentionally too rigid, to determine what was proper not only for the average customer but for more sophisticated buyers or potential racers. The convertible frame was 10 percent and the coupe fully 90 percent stiffer than the 1962 car.

Zora Duntov understood he had only so many dollars to spend to improve the car. A new frame took some, but he and his colleagues wanted the car to have a new rear axle with fully independent rear suspension (IRS). One could be devised from the Q-sedans and Q-Corvette prototypes. Engineering and development work had been accomplished years before and written off against other budgets, but the production passenger car was killed and there was no other big-volume item to pay for it. Whenever Duntov stated his need for an IRS, he was challenged about its cost. By this time he had learned the car business was a numbers game. He prevailed, by constantly telling the naysayers that the new car, with IRS, would sell 30,000 units, despite larger logic that questioned how many drivers would even recognize the difference.

The system that Duntov, Harold Krieger, Walter Zetye, and the Corvette Engineering staff devised also adopted technology from CERV I. It incorporated twin half-shafts coming out of a frame-mounted differential, connected (and suspended) by a transversely mounted nine-leaf spring bolted to the back of the differential housing. This system used the drive shafts as part of the suspension system, and this economy of design saved a great deal of money over more complicated European systems and a great amount of weight over the 1962 solid tube rear axle.

The front suspension was carried over with subtle changes devised using mostly passenger car production parts that had

The Sting Ray represented some of the best work by some of America's finest automotive designers who began to conceive the car as early as 1958. Design possibilities were as wildly radical as was Engineering's proposal of adapting a passenger car-based rear transaxle.

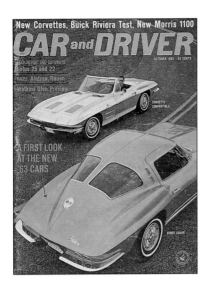

Car and Driver tantalized its readers in the October 1962 issue with a cover photo that announced detailed cover stories and technical analyses inside about the new 1963 Sting Ray.

On April 4, 1960, Design rolled out the XP-720 clay model for comparison with a production 1960 convertible. The contrast was striking, not withstanding the new tail end coming with the 1961 models. Even at this stage, the development of Peter Brock's sketches done in late 1957 is apparent. *Mike Mueller archives*

Bill Mitchell's elegant split window coupe graced the cover of the 1963 dealership sales brochures. Black was chosen to accentuate the elegance of the new sports car. *Chevrolet*

appeared in new configurations on CERV I. A faster steering ratio, 2.9 turns lock to lock instead of 3.4, capped the intricate efforts resulting in greatly improved road feel, steering response, and ride comfort. What's more, the Corvette offered hydraulically assisted (power) steering for the first time, available on all but the two most powerful engine options.

Duntov's few development dollars were nearly all spent. So the 11-inch diameter cast-iron drum brakes all around were carried over. Buyers could order optional sintered metallic linings and finned aluminum brake drums. These provided greater fade resistance and better cooling. Power-assisted brakes were introduced as well.

Once all this was gathered together, Duntov had development mules built. These he and other engineers drove daily, living with their work and constantly tweaking their systems. Bill Mitchell wanted his own mule but knew that was not possible without giving away the design. So he devised another show car that he could drive.

Mitchell again called on Larry Shinoda. He had done all the production drawings of the Corvette and probably knew the car's lines better than anyone. Mitchell gave him a new project number, XP-755, and turned him lose. Mitchell devised a design study theme for it on a fishing trip to the Caribbean. Where his first car had been fashioned after a sting ray, this new one would honor the ocean's great predator, the shark, with a paint scheme to match. Shinoda's car picked up the best features of the Sting Ray racer and the upcoming production car, exaggerating some of them to a great extent. The double-bubble glass top from Mitchell's first show car, the XP-700, was adopted as well.

Design from the earliest days had its own mechanical assembly area where Harley Earl's and later Bill Mitchell's ideas were given motion. Leonard McLay had labored long and hard to keep Earl's supercharged Buick running in Earl's

LeSabre, and over time he had tamed a great number of temperamental engines. He and his crew supercharged a 327 for Mitchell's commuter car. (Over its 10-year life, the Shark's engine compartment swallowed power steering pumps, power brake boosters, and eventually a 427-cubic-inch Mark IV engine. It was first shown at the New York Auto Show in April 1962, and journalists covering the show theorized aloud and in print that if this proved to be like Motorama 1953, then what they saw was what they would soon see in production.

While Mitchell's car sported a supercharged engine, under the hood of the production cars, the 327-cubic-inch small block was carried over just as it had been offered in 1962. Four levels of performance ranged from 250 horsepower from carburetors to 360 horsepower from fuel injection. Three- and four-speed manual transmissions and the Powerglide automatic were still offered. Interestingly, Corvette engineers placed the engine into the frame 1 inch

By September 6, 1960, Larry Shinoda, one of the Corvette's principal production designers at the time, was tweaking and revising various details. Mitchell saw the first drawings for the coupe and he soon wanted a convertible as well. In this photo, possibly taken before the board of directors' review of the car before production approval, Shinoda had relocated side air vents at Mitchell's direction. The car was still known as the XP-720.
Mike Mueller archives

Regular production 1963 Sting Ray coupes were assembled at St. Louis. Unlike Zora Duntov's racing Grand Sports, production cars lacked the trunk lid for spare tire and suitcase access.
Mike Mueller archives

to the right. This increased footroom for the driver while, naturally, decreasing passenger foot space.

Designers created a new instrument panel and gauge cluster, giving the tachometer and speedometer equal importance. The center console still carried the clock, radio, heater controls, and between the seats, the gearshift lever, its marked pattern, and ashtray. The steering column offered 3 inches of length adjustment (albeit a job only accomplished in the engine compartment with a wrench). Behind the seats in the coupe, designers and engineers created a large luggage area, although both Duntov and Mitchell ran out of production dollars before a working trunk lid could be funded. The only access to the luggage was from inside, lifted over the seats.

It was, of course, the Sting Ray body that seized viewers' attention. Design staff had first seen a full-size clay model in late October 1959 of something that looked like Mitchell's Sting Ray racer with a boat-tail teardrop molded on. Through the winter, Design nipped and tucked at it, giving it the taper at the doors that visually lightened the car. Management approved the full-size clay coupe body in April (and the interior, done in a studio separate from those

doing the body, in November) 1960. Sold on the coupe, Design created a convertible in the fall only after being told to do so. Once management decided to build the new car in fiberglass, Engineering and Design combined efforts to make the new body stronger, tighter, and quieter. They used twice as much reinforcing steel within the fiberglass panels as they had on the 1962 car. Yet they thinned the panels enough to get the body weight for coupe or convertible down below that of the previous model.

With engines ranging from 300 horsepower out of the 327 ci up to 425 horsepower from the 427-ci V-8, Campbell-Ewald's writers offered Corvette buyers a choice, via word play, of "whether you spend your time on the observation deck or the flight line." This ran in April and May 1966. *Campbell-Ewald*

First rear and then front suspension assemblies for 1965 model year cars were bolted into place along this subassembly line. At the end of this line the white claws grabbed each four-wheel disc brake chassis, flipped it over, and deposited it onto the next assembly line for engine, transmission, and drive shaft installation. *Mike Mueller archives*

Design solved the dilemma of aerodynamic resistance from quad headlights. (It subjected both coupe and convertible bodies to three-eighth-scale clay model wind tunnel tests out at CalTech before final approval.) They devised a rotating housing to hide the lights in a retractable body panel. Further aft, limousine-style doors not only launched a new design trend but also provided welcome headroom for entry and exit. With so much of the form of the car following function, it's worth noting that the vents on the hood and behind the doors originally had functions. When all the design and development sums were totaled, however, there was nothing left to make that plumbing work.

Ever since the impact of the AMA racing and high-performance promotion ban became apparent throughout GM, Zora Duntov skirted the issue, explaining logically and accurately that Corvettes would be raced by private customers whether GM approved or not. It was therefore in the best interest of the company to continue parts development to benefit racers.

Zora and his cohorts created RPO Z06. This Special Performance Equipment package included a vacuum brake booster, a dual master cylinder, sintered metallic brake linings within power-assisted Al-Fin drums, cooled by front air scoops and vented backing plates, a 20 percent larger diameter front antiroll bar, larger diameter shocks, and springs nearly twice as stiff as standard. Initially, a 36.5-gallon gas tank replaced the new 20-gallon container. This package, which also included the 360-horsepower 327-cubic-inch engine, M-21 close-ratio four-speed transmission, Positraction and cast-aluminum knock-off wheels cost the buyer an extra $1,818.45 over the base coupe price of $4,257.00. Initially, the package was offered only for coupes (because the oversize tank could not fit in the convertible). It was a pricey, race-ready package; deleting the heater and defroster saved $100, but the total tipped in at $5,975.45. Later in the model year, Chevrolet discovered problems with air leaking through the porous aluminum wheel castings. The knock-off wheels and the extra-large gas tank were deleted from the Z06 package (although the tank was available on any coupe separately), and its price was revised down to $1,293.95. At that point, Chevrolet offered it for the convertible, as well. A total of 199 Z06s were built.

In *Car and Driver* and *Road & Track*'s June 1965 issues the text announced, "It's not rumor. You may have heard talk of a new 'mystery V-8' from Chevrolet." *Campbell-Ewald*

Cubic inches, that is. We're ready if you are.

It's no rumor.

You may have heard talk of a new "mystery" V8 from Chevrolet. You probably discounted some of what you heard as exaggeration. It wasn't just talk, and chances are it wasn't even exaggerated.

This is the genuine article. Officially, the Turbo-Jet 396 V8. Unofficially, it's a production engine raised to the nth power, an outright masterpiece, almost the kind you could expect to get only with cams and gadgets and exotic labels hung all over the outside. The 396 gets everything it needs on the inside.

425 bhp at 6400 rpm. 415 lb-ft of torque at 4000 rpm. (Nice, round figures that give a specific output of 1.073 horsepower per cubic inch.) 396 cubic inches. 4.094-inch bore, 3.76-inch stroke. Solid lifters, one 4-bbl. carburetor, dual exhausts. That's just the bare bones of the story.

The rocker arms are separately mounted, which allows individual placement of valves, inlet ports, and exhaust ports. That in turn allows precise control of combustion chamber shape, unshrouding of the valves, better heat dissipation, remarkably good "breathing" characteristics. The rest of the engine is similarly advanced, but the big story is the breathing.

Remember the 265-cubic-inch V8 in 1955? It became the 283, and the 327 was based on it. It was so good because it breathed so well. This one's better. A *lot* better. You can get it in a Corvette.

Chevrolet Division of General Motors, Detroit, Michigan

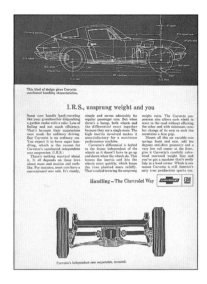

Enthusiasts got another physics lesson in June 1966 issues of *Car and Driver, Road & Track,* and *Sports Car Graphic.* "There's nothing mystical about it. It all depends on those laws about mass and motion and such like." Well, perhaps not a physics lesson. *Campbell-Ewald*

By 1966, Design had cleared up much of the extraneous clutter from the hoods as these cars show, coming out of final inspection. The nearest convertible was equipped with the optional removable hardtop and a small block engine. The next two rag tops, however, had big blocks. *Mike Mueller archives*

Production began at St. Louis just as Bill Mitchell introduced his Shark in New York. About 25 pilot 1963 models were manufactured in the plant, outside the regular production line, since the new model involved entirely new body pieces. These cars were completed by late June and were quickly parceled out, a number of them going to enthusiast magazines so they could publish their stories at the same time dealers unveiled the new car.

The car was a success with the enthusiast magazines. *Road & Track*, the least gee-whiz of the publications, spent most of its October 1962 three-page road test discussing and examining the handling. It hadn't tested a Corvette since 1960, finding too little different since then to merit the effort. The previous car, its reviewer reminded readers, had "a tendency for the rear wheels to spin freely on acceleration and for the rear end to come sliding around rather quickly during hard cornering. . . . That production-component live rear-axle," the magazine concluded, "could hop and dance like an Apache with a hot foot.

"Now, with the advent of full independent rear suspension . . .," the magazine continued, "the new Sting Ray sticks! Whether you slam the car through an S-bend at 85 or

pop the clutch at 5,000 rpm at the drag strip, the result is the same—great gripping gobs of traction."

Where the 1953 through 1962 cars had balanced 52 percent of the weight on the front, magazine publisher John Bond, in his technical analysis of the new car, pointed out the new balance, by their scales, at 48 percent front, 52 percent rear. In examining the rear suspension, Bond pointed out that the transverse rear spring, the only use for such a system in the United States (and something he said recalled the 1937 Cord front suspension), was necessary because there was no room in a smaller car for rear coil springs, and these would have increased overall and unsprung weight. With the 360-horsepower 327-cubic-inch engine and four-speed, Bond's testers recorded 0-to-60-mile-per-hour times of 5.9 seconds, and they accomplished the standing-start quarter-mile times of 14.9 seconds at 95 miles per hour.

"The 1963 Corvette," Bond concluded, "has come a long way in 10 years—from a stylist's plaything to a full-blown, out-and-out dual-purpose sports car."

Jim Wright, *Motor Trend's* technical editor, led off his May 1963 reexamination with a three-quarter rear view of the car sliding through dirt and a headline in letters 1 inch

Bob Bondurant was one of Corvette's finest racers in the late 1950s and early 1960s. He ran with Number 614 on his entries. When the first four Sting Ray Z06-cars appeared at Riverside, Bondurant drove this coupe, competing along with Dave MacDonald, Jerry Grant, and Doug Hooper in the other three cars. Number 614, shown here at the Monterey Historic Automobile Races, was driven in this event by Vic Edelbrock.

Mitchell argued with Zora Duntov several times about the split window. The chief stylist's concept was a much narrower spine, but manufacturing limitations widened it into something capable of hiding a pursuing motorcycle policeofficer.

tall: "For the first time in its 10-year history, the Corvette String Ray is . . ." and then the text jumped to the next page, where it continued: "in such demand that the factory has had to put on a second shift."

As John Bond reminded readers of past prognostications, so did Wright, recalling a comment of the previous year's review (they did test a 1962 model): "The factory has never made any big profits on the Corvette but . . . Chevy brass was more than satisfied as long as it carried its performance image and prestige over to the bread-and-butter lines. We also ventured an opinion that as long as the factory kept building the car on this basis, it would be a great automobile, but if they ever put in on a straight dollar-profit basis, the Corvette would probably be ruined."

Wright reflected, after driving the test car and others, that Chevrolet had let a few quality-control glitches slip by that concerned him in a $4,500 to $6,000 car, including fiberglass body quality and the interior fit and finish. He had no fault with the chassis, suspension, and handling, or the engine and transmission, however. He recorded 0 to 60 times of 5.8 seconds and the quarter-mile in 14.5 at 102 miles per hour.

In *Car & Driver's* April 1963 report, technical editor Jan Norbye wrote that "the key to the personality of the

[1963] Corvette lies neither in the power available nor in the revised design, but in the chassis. Up to now the Corvette has been struggling to rise above a large number of stock components, notably in the suspension, where their presence created all kinds of problems that required extensive modifications for any competition use beyond normal road rallies. The new all-independent suspension has completely transformed the Corvette. . . ."

Norbye selected not the wildest, hairiest optional engine for his review but the much more commonly purchased 300-horsepower 327 and found it up to anything any average motorist could put to it. It didn't outrun its handling or brake options (all three reviewers expressed strong preference for the sintered metallic brakes over the standard fade-prone units).

"Vastly more practical than any previous Corvette," he concluded, "the Sting Ray Sport Coupe appeals to a new segment of buyers who would not be interested in a convertible. . . . As an American car it is unique and it stands out from its European counterparts as having in no way copied them but arrived at the same goal along a different route. Zora Arkus-Duntov summed it up this way, 'For the first time I now have a Corvette I can be proud to drive in Europe.'"

The Sting Ray brought the introduction of cast-aluminum wheels with knock-off center hubs. Total production for 1963 topped 21,000, of which 10,594 were the split-window sport coupes.

There are those who will argue that this is the most beautiful Corvette body ever produced, that Bill Mitchell was a design genius and that the split rear-window made a clear statement at the height of a designer's career. Others hate it.

Chevrolet issued a press release late in the fall announcing double shifts at St. Louis. The production goal for 1963 model years was 16,000 units. When the counting was done, the company had sold 10,594 coupes and 10,919 convertibles, a total of 21,513 cars. It hadn't quite achieved the numbers Duntov predicted would flock to the independent rear suspension, but it far exceeded Chevrolet's own estimations; and it beat 1962 by nearly 50 percent.

In racing, Duntov's Z06 coupes proved formidable in their first outing, the Times Three-Hour Invitational Race at Riverside, California, in October 1962. Three cars, a silver, a white, and a blue coupe were driven out from the St. Louis factory by racers Bob Bondurant, Dave MacDonald, and Jerry Grant (another car had been trucked out earlier) to break them in, and then prepared for the A-production race. At the start, the race quickly settled down to a Sting Ray driven by Dave MacDonald and one of Carroll Shelby's new Cobras driven by Bill Krause. Both of them broke after the first hour, and two more

Corvettes retired by the end of the second; but the fourth car, entered by Mickey Thompson and driven by Doug Hooper, won the race. Thompson was pleased, but Duntov was concerned. He knew Shelby, and what broke on the Cobra was something that Shelby would find and fix. Next time it could win and soon it would dominate.

By June, the championship was secured and it didn't go to Corvette. Duntov was philosophical; he could afford to be because, while Cobra won on the race tracks, it didn't compete in the race that management cared about most, the one for the pocketbooks of regular folks who never raced cars.

For 1964 production, Bill Mitchell sacrificed his split-rear window. In preparing the body for production, the spine had become much wider than Mitchell intended. It was as much a victim of journalist and customer criticism as for the desire merely to perform a facelift on an otherwise successful design. The new year dropped the fake hood grilles but left behind the indentations. Design made the left roof vent functional (but not the right). Engineering

replaced the front coil springs with a progressive rate version to improve handling without sacrificing ride quality. Revised valving addressed the shock absorber problems on the 1963 models. Engines got stronger, as a Holley 4150 carburetor was added, and peak power of the solid-lifter engine rose from 340 horsepower to 365 horsepower. The fuel-injection version increased to 375 horsepower by virtue of better breathing accomplished through a new intake manifold design. Engineering also replaced the Borg-Warner gearboxes with four-speeds produced at GM's Muncie, Indiana, transmission plant, a change implemented during 1963. In the coupe, a small fan circulated air in the rear, answering the complaint of sweltering heat under the large back window, and in all the bodies more insulation and revised body and transmission mounts quieted the complaints about too much interior mechanical and road noise. Duntov fought to create a true European sports car, but the real nature of the American grand touring customer kept crying for attention.

Another group within GM found a new direction to take performance automobiles. Muscle cars, born in the 1950s at Chrysler as big cars with bigger, powerful hemi-head engines, spawned a new generation of imitators that were quick studies. Pontiac Division General Manager Elliott M. "Pete" Estes, its former chief engineer, fired the opening salvo of the marketing and product-planning muscle car wars. He launched the Tempest LeMans and GTO

After years of offering convertibles only, Chevrolet introduced its first coupe body style for the Corvette in 1963. In fact, the car was conceived first as a coupe in a series of drawings done by Peter Brock under Design chief Bill Mitchell's direction. Sometime after seeing the coupe, Mitchell considered it necessary to offer an open car as well.

The walnut grain plastic Sting Ray steering wheel was standard equipment. New to the Corvette was the ability to adjust it forward or backward a total of three inches to accommodate arms—and driving styles—of any proportion. The seats also were new and they provided better support and greater comfort. The Am-Fm radio was delivered in nearly every 1964 car.

options in 1963 and 1964. These packages stuffed 389-cubic-inch three, two-barrel carb-equipped "Tri-power" engines into what were conceived as fuel-efficient commuter cars. These small vehicles generally were not engineered quite well enough to take on all the extra power. They were cheap, costing thousands less than a fully optioned Corvette. Yet they went just as quickly at the stoplight grand prix that took place on any Saturday night on Main Street. What was worse, they offered the politically correct benefit of room for four, allowing two couples to double date. All of this interest in big engines led in a direction that went diametrically against Zora Duntov's goals for the car. And yet Chevrolet's product planners and, more significantly, its general manager, Bunkie Knudsen, fresh from Pontiac himself, knew the sports car could not be left out of this new definition of sporting cars.

For 1964, total production reached another record, 22,229 cars, broken down into 8,304 coupes, and nearly twice as many convertibles, 13,925. The models retained their 1963 introduction prices, the coupe at $4,252.00, while the convertible still sold for $4,037.00. The racers' package, now assembled from a variety of RPOs, not one alone, would set the buyer back a total of $6,526.40, including the 375-horsepower "Fuelie" engine, four-speed, aluminum wheels, sintered brakes, Positraction, the F40 special front and rear suspension, and a few other necessities. By comparison, a 389-cubic-inch dual-quad, fully performance-optioned GTO coupe sold for less than $3,800.00. The boulevard grand tourer got off scarcely any easier than the racing coupe, at $6,514.00 for a 300-horsepower convertible with air

While only one engine was offered, the 327-ci V-8 was available in four levels of tune. Standard equipment was 250 horsepower; about 4,000 of those sold. More popular was a 300 horsepower option at $53.80 (10,471 were produced.) Rarest was the 375 horsepower version using Rochester fuel injection. Costing $538.00, only 1,325 buyers ordered the engine.

Of the more than 22,000 cars sold in 1964, only 804 were delivered with the finned, cast-aluminum knock-off wheels, a $322.80 option. Output of the L84 fuel-injected 327-ci V-8, an option at $538.00, was increased to 375 horsepower. Only 8,304 buyers selected the $4,252.00 coupe, while 13,925 preferred the $4,037.00 convertible.

The optional L79 engine produced 350 horsepower out of the carbureted 327-ci engine. A $107.60 option, some 4,716 buyers chose it. Chevrolet introduced its first big block, the L78 396-ci V-8 with 425 horsepower. However, 1965 was the last year that the L84 fuel-injected 327 was offered.

Silver first appeared as a Corvette color with the 1957 model year called Inca Silver. It disappeared in 1958 but returned in 1959. In 1960, 1961, and 1962 it was renamed Sateen Silver. It was called Sebring Silver with the 1963 Sting Ray, Satin Silver in 1964, and by 1965, it was relabeled Silver Pearl.

conditioning, automatic transmission, optional hardtop for winter, whitewall tires with racey aluminum knock-off wheels, an AM-FM radio, and another few bits and pieces.

Design did more with an eraser for 1965 than with pencils. They cleaned off the hood, wiped out the roof vents, and slit open the former "speedlines" behind the front tires to make real working vents.

After years of battles, Engineering prevailed. The 1965 model year introduced disc brakes at the four corners as standard equipment at no extra cost (although for reasons few people understand, some 316 individuals ordered cars with drum brakes for which they received a $64.50 credit). In fairness, Engineering had, by this time, elevated the sintered metallic Al-Fin drum brake to a level approaching fine art and near perfection. Still Duntov and his colleagues listened to critics and journalists who wailed that the Corvette simply was not yet a sports car without discs.

Outside suppliers took on the task of developing a disc brake system, but success eluded them. Management would not approve the expense of developing a power boost solely for the Corvette, and this was a requirement of the systems brought in from outside. So Chevy engineers working with Delco-Moraine devised a completely new approach. Their system let the pads barely touch the disc at all times. This provided instant pedal response and satisfactorily addressed an early criticism of discs, that when they got wet, they failed to work adequately. With the pads against the rotor, this kept the disc swept clean of moisture and road grit.

Convertibles outsold Sting Ray coupes in 1965 nearly two-to-one, with 15,376 open cars produced versus 8,186 closed cars. The Sting Ray did away with a rear trunk on open and closed cars, making luggage storage a bit more challenging.

Of the total 23,562 Corvettes produced in 1965, 231,107 of them left St. Louis with four-speed transmissions and 22,113 left with the AM/FM radio. The base coupe retailed for $4,321.00 and the big block added another $292.70 to the window sticker.

The discs selected for production were ventilated and 1.25 inches thick, a full quarter-inch thicker than those used on the Grand Sport racers. The brake system dual master cylinder, similar to what had first appeared in the Z06 racing package in 1963, was fitted as standard equipment on all cars with disc brakes, ahead of expected federal safety standards. It was the introduction of the mid-1965 engine, however, that made these new brakes more important.

Chevrolet had first revealed its "big block" V-8—its 427-cubic-inch V-8 "mystery motor"—at the Daytona 500 stock car race in January 1963. Nicknamed the "porcupine head" because of the odd angles that the overhead valve stems stuck out when the valve covers were removed, the engine was internally known as the Mark II. Events in the racing world had come full circle by 1963, and the AMA racing ban fell by the wayside.

GM's pursuit of performance resumed publicly within months of Ford Motor Company's announcement in mid-June 1962 that it would no longer adhere to the AMA agreement. Once the first manufacturer broke ranks officially, no car maker wanted to be last. Zora Duntov and the other

engineers had continued developing new products, just as, it turned out, every other major car maker had done. Once these engines appeared, everyone understood that the gloves were off. A good fight was brewing.

For 1965, Chevrolet introduced its powerhouse 396-cubic-inch engine, the L78, with 425 horsepower on tap. The rating was conservative, as a number of enthusiasts discovered when they simply had their engines blueprinted. Available as an option for only $292.70, some 2,157 buyers exercised the option. The price included a visual cue, a new hood that swelled in the center in a subtle "power bulge" to accommodate the engine's bulk. Option N14 was much more visible. This new $134.50 package put exhaust pipes along the side of the car, as they had been on countless Bill Mitchell show cars. Only 759 buyers had the flamboyance to announce so clearly to local police what they intended.

Carroll Shelby found a home for his car-building ideas in a hybrid using car bodies and heavily reworked frames from the English builder, A. C. Into this package he installed Ford running gear, briefly the 260-cubic-inch V-8 but then the 289. With this lightweight package, he proved a potent

Off-road exhaust system and L72 427-ci V-8 with its special engine hood: with those elements, who needs more words? This simple message ran in March 1966 in *Car and Driver, Road & Track,* and *Sports Car. Campbell-Ewald*

Brute-strength performance was what the big-block engines were all about. Various magazine tests achieved 0-to-60 mile-per-hour times at around 5.7 seconds. The standing-start quarter-mile took 14.1 seconds at 103 miles per hour through the speed traps, and top speed was above 135. Fuel economy was unimportant in those days of 29-cents-per-gallon gasoline.

A serious performance machine, this L78-equipped big block put out 425 horsepower from Chevrolet's 396-cubic-inch iron V-8. This was Corvette's first big block. With the side-mounted, off-road exhaust, the cast-aluminum knock-off wheels and its standard four-wheel disc brakes, the Corvette was becoming both a muscular sports car and America's sportiest muscle car.

rival to Corvette racers. Shelby took on Europe, setting his sights on an old racing rival, Enzo Ferrari. But Shelby's cars, with their pushrod V-8s and cluttered aerodynamics, were no match for the Italian maker's sleek shapes and high-revving V-12 overhead-cam engines. In the best of the homespun engineering tradition, he got a bigger hammer. Ford had its own 427-cubic-inch V-8, and Shelby squeezed it into a bulging body on a new, computer-designed frame. The results were stunning.

Against Shelby's 427 Cobra, Duntov and company were forced to compete with a 427 of their own, the L72. The engineers enlarged the 396-cubic-inch engine's bore to 4.25 inches. With 11:1 compression, the engine produced an advertised 425 horsepower. The engine was introduced for 1966 production, and quickly the magazines reported astonishing performance. *Sports Car Graphic* magazine tested acceleration on a 1966 coupe with the 4.11:1 rear end. Runs from 0 to 60 miles per hour took a scant 4.8 seconds, and the run hit 100 miles per hour only 11.2 seconds after leaving the line. *Car & Driver* ordered a longer-legged hardtop with 3.36:1 gears and their 60 mile-per-hour time took 5.6 seconds. The standing-start quarter-mile came after only 12.8 seconds, at 112 miles per hour, however. Plus, they saw a top speed of 152 miles per hour.

Model year 1966 was Corvette's biggest sale year up to that time. A total of 27,720 cars sold. Of them, just 2,967 were delivered in Silver Pearl. A total of 17,762 were convertibles. Base price was $4,084.

Beginning in 1966, option codes became mantras for performance junkies. Young men, many just eligible for the draft, preferred to know the codes—L72 (427 cubic inches, 425 horsepower), M-22 (heavy-duty, close-ratio four-speed) C48 (heater/defroster delete), G81 (Positraction), N14 (side exhaust) or N11 (off-road exhaust system), F41 (special front/rear suspension), J56 (special heavy-duty brakes)—than to think about draft status. Earlier in that year, Lyndon Johnson had asked Congress for another $3 billion for defense. The United States already had 400,000 soldiers in Vietnam. It was a pleasure to know that fully equipped

Corvette coupes cost $5,434.75. The baby-boomer generation, born after World War II into the greatest period of prosperity in the United States since the mid-1920s, had trouble accepting that their times were becoming the worst of times. It was far more enjoyable to discover at year end that Chevrolet's Corvette had another banner year, selling 9,958 coupes and 17,762 convertibles, a total of 27,720 cars.

For Corvette, 1967 was the best Sting Ray yet. While its replacement was supposed to be introduced, delays in engineering once again held up introduction for another year, and so mild design updates had to do. "Rally" wheels

arrived. But while exterior and interior changes were subtle, under the hood, the changes yielded big results.

New code numbers entered the Corvette lexicography. Enthusiasts learned the meaning of L71, the 427-cubic-inch V-8 with a trio of progressively linked two-barrel carburetors, producing 435 horsepower. Some 3,754 buyers paid $437.10 to go this route. There was an option available for the optional engine: By checking RPO L89, the buyer got aluminum cylinder heads for the L71, although only 16 of these were delivered at an additional $368.65 over the engine cost. The other new engine became legendary: the L88. With 427 cubic inches and 12.5:1 compression, Chevrolet hinted at but never officially quoted 430 horsepower, and it vigorously discouraged buyers by sticking it with a $947.90 price. Topped with a single Holley sucking 850 cubic feet of air per

This was the age of muscle cars and Corvette was prepared to join the street fights. With the 1966 cars, Chevrolet introduced the Mark IV 427-ci V-8s, with ratings up to as much as 450 horsepower. A tamer option was the 350 horsepower RPO L79, 327-ci V-8. Engineer Zora Duntov fought hard to keep the 327 in the line-up, preferring the car's handling with the small block 327s to what it did with the 427s in front.

121

Beneath the special big block air-induction hood, getting the power to the ground was as important as the power itself. In 1966 and 1967, Chevrolet offered three four-speed Muncie gearboxes including the base equipment transmission. The second was the M21 close ratio (11,105 delivered) and the last was the M22 (just 20 delivered), nicknamed the "rock crusher" for its strength and noisiness.

The Sting Ray body design was carried over one year longer than intended for 1967 and it offered Chevrolet another successful year with 14,436 convertibles and 8,504 coupes sold. This Tuxedo black coupe was one of an astonishing 3,754 cars sold with the new Mark IV big block L71 427-ci V-8.

minute (cfm), and capable of running on 103 octane fuel, the true output of this engine was closer to 560 horsepower. By suggesting a horsepower rating below the L71, Chevrolet sought to keep power-mad, speed-hungry youngsters from buying something they'd find beyond their abilities. Buyers could get the car only with the transistorized ignition, Positraction, F41 suspension, and J50 power brakes. Ordering the engine automatically deleted the heater and radio "to cut down on weight and discourage the car's use on the street," according to a release at introduction. Only 20 individuals paid for it, whether or not they saw it for what it was—a flat-out racing engine with a Regular Production Option code.

The end of the Sting Ray marked a similar turning point in American history. It was a bittersweet time. The car had become the best that it could be. Years of anticipated replacements delayed for one reason or another provided the time to correct the few remaining faults. This happened with the first generation cars before it, those in production through 1962, and it certainly was the case with the 1966 and 1967 versions. Ultimately, unmatched performance was available with the aluminum-headed L71, for $6,625.25, for a no-nonsense boulevard (or nearly-track-ready) racer with an AM-FM radio. No car available with American reliability matched that performance for that price, except Carroll Shelby's outrageous 427 Cobra, a car in which one could only hear the radio with the engine off. By the end of model year 1967, Chevrolet had sold 22,940 Sting Rays, a total of 117,964 over all five years.

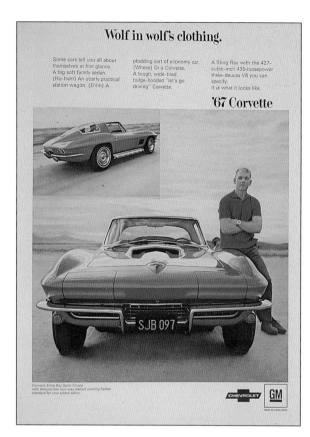

"Some cars tell you all about themselves at first glance," the text said. The big-block-equipped 1967 Sting Ray coupe "is what it looks like." This ran in February and March issues of the *New Yorker, Sports Illustrated,* and *Sports Car Graphic. Campbell-Ewald*

By 1967, all the appearance bells and whistles, trim and shimmer was removed from the car, making it the purest form that the Sting Ray body ever achieved. Coupled with the possibility of astounding performance from a $437.10 optional 425-horsepower engine, with standard four-wheel disc brakes and new, wider 6-inch wheels, it was the best of the best.

Students and practitioners of automotive design will argue for hours on end over the relative merits of the Chuck Pohlman\Peter Brock\Larry Shinoda-designed 1963 through 1967 Sting Ray. The cars that would follow were striking but none were so beautiful.

125

The five angular slot vents along the fenders are functional as they had become with the 1966 model year (when there were three). Aftermarket wheels and 60-series radial tires do a much better job of keeping the car's power and handling on the ground.

While there was nothing wrong with Chevrolet's optional L71 with the three Holley two-barrel carburetors and aluminum heads, there is always more to do. In this case, however, the owner replaced the factory 427ci with a 454 with aluminum heads and a Crower roller cam. Horsepower is estimated at closer to 500.

Big Blocks

In 1958, Chevrolet introduced its W engine, the 348-cubic-inch V-8. It didn't take long before the engine development engineers found ways to increase its capacity to 409. But the W block was heavy and large. It had many of the characteristics that Zora Duntov and others felt were exactly wrong for the Corvette.

When Jim Premo (the engineer who had visited Bob Morrison's operation in Ashtabula, Ohio, on a snowy day in 1953) was promoted to replace Harry Barr as Chevrolet's chief engineer, he found vigorous support in Bunkie Knudsen and Zora Duntov. Everyone knew that Corvettes would have larger engines; however, Duntov's high-performance engine group had been working on its own solution to that inevitability, with Knudsen's blessings.

Richard Keinath developed heads for a completely new big block, with an odd configuration of intake and exhaust valves that allowed much better breathing. The seemingly random angles of the valve stems earned Keinath's work a nickname, the "porcupine" heads. This engine, completed and running well before the end of 1962, was known as the Mark II, and it was developed for stock car racing. It first appeared at the Daytona 500 in 1963 and established the reputation for Chevrolet's "mystery motor."

California racer Mickey Thompson got one late in 1962 and stuffed it into a Corvette that Bill Krause drove to third place overall in the Daytona three-hour sports car races prior to the 24-hour international enduro. But GM Chairman Frederic Donner had decreed his own racing and speed ban and, while outside racing fell under a blind eye, any regular factory production of these engines was ruled out.

That is, they were ruled out until end-of-year sales figures spoke to Donner. When the numbers became clear, authorization came from on high to begin manufacture of a street version of the Mark II. In deference to increasing federal government attention and scrutiny from the automobile insurance industry brought on by troubles with Corvair handling and Donner's handling of that embarrassment, GM management did attempt to keep a rein on the tendencies of the product planners and engineers to produce larger and more powerful engines. The intermediate-size cars, Chevelle, Pontiac Tempest, and the like, those most suited to muscle car performance, were limited to engine displacements below 400 cubic inches. With that in mind, the engine developers produced the Mark IV with a 4.09-inch bore and 3.76-inch stroke for total capacity of 396 cubic inches. Peak horsepower offered from the 327 with carburetors was 365; the new 396 was rated at

The city of Warren, Michigan, has hundreds of complaints on file against Chevrolet because of the noise from "Dyno Row." When Chevrolet had L88s to test, as here with Zora Duntov and a fellow engineer, it didn't want to plug up the engines with the dyno exhaust systems' back pressure. *Mike Mueller archives*

425 horsepower. Compression ratio was 11.0:1 with modified wedge-shaped cylinder heads. This extra power came at a penalty of an extra 150 pounds for the fully dressed engine.

For 1966, the muscle power wars turned serious. By the end of 1965, Chevrolet Division had a new chief executive, Elliott M. "Pete" Estes, fresh from Pontiac Division where he and fellow collaborator John Z. DeLorean had intensified—if not invented—muscle cars. Estes followed a similar route as Ed Cole. Both had been division chief engineers prior to their promotions. Both liked products.

The Mark IV had been stretched closer to its full potential. Bore was increased to 4.25 inches, pumping displacement to 427 inches. It was available in two versions, an L36 with 390 horsepower using a single four-barrel carburetor, high-performance camshaft, hydraulic lifters, and 10.25:1 compression ratio to help accomplish the output. The higher output L72 for 1966 production was quoted at 425 horsepower, assisted by valve lifters. Soon everyone knew that the 425 horsepower was an extremely conservative rating. Magazines tested the Mark IV–equipped Corvettes and found 0-to-60 times around 5.4 to 5.6 seconds, and yet it ran up to better than 135 miles per hour.

chapter 11

The Shark Bites: 1968–1972

Even before the St. Louis production plant started its preassembly runs of the 1963 Sting Rays, Bill Mitchell told his designers to think about the next Corvette. The Sting Ray would remain in production only through 1965, possibly carried over into 1966, and so it was not too early to begin.

He set Larry Shinoda on a flight of fancy, a wild excursion with an open-wheeled single-seater not unlike Duntov's CERV I. It drew technical inspiration from the Frank Winchell, Chevrolet Engineering Center's R&D chief. Winchell had developed the production Corvairs and the Monza GT and SS prototypes in 1962 and 1963. Mitchell called his new car the X-15, a project named after the Air Force's black rocket plane. Shinoda worked with John Schinella and a small group of designers and modelers in another one of those invisible, locked studios. While few people ever saw the car, it became the reality check at the far end of the spectrum from down-to-earth production products all the way to pie-in-the-sky daydreams. From it, Mitchell refined and defined what he wanted in his next personal car and in the next Corvette.

In his book *Corvette: America's Star Spangled Sports Car*, Karl Ludvigsen recalls Mitchell's description of the car: "He wanted a narrow, slim, 'selfish' center section and coupe body; a prominently tapered tail; an all-of-a-piece blending of the upper and lower portions of the body through the center, avoiding the look of a roof added to a body; and a sense of prominent wheels which, with their protective fenders, were distinctly separate from the main central body section, yet were grafted organically to it. This was the launching pad for the missile known as Mako Shark II."

Shinoda's design, known internally as the XP-830, actually filled in at the last minute as a future Corvette when earlier plans failed. Duntov's work on CERV II had led to suggestions that the next generation Corvette, perhaps now delayed until the 1967 model year, could be a midengined two-seater, reflecting the racing technology that Duntov believed Corvette customers wanted and deserved. Winchell's group had promoted the idea of a true lightweight (2,650-pound) rear-engined car, using the 327-cubic-inch V-8. The handling was frightening with weight bias of 70 percent on the rear. Duntov's idea was a midengine with the Mark IV 427, but with more neutral handling. But because the Corvette had always been built out of parts produced for other Chevrolet models and no pieces existed to build such a car as Winchell, Duntov, and Mitchell imagined, it was impossible. The costs to develop such pieces, even to a wealthy corporation such as General Motors, were prohibitive balanced against the volume of Corvette sales and the likelihood of those expenses ever being repaid. Design exercises produced cars with shapes as striking as Lamborghini's midengine Miura. But while Europe and exotic car buyers might accept a price tag above $20,000, GM management was sure Corvette buyers never would. It was purely economic considerations, plus Donner's displeasure at the public exploits of the Grand Sports and CERV I, that doomed the ambitious midengine next-generation Corvette.

The effort to make a Corvair chassis handle Corvette engines took time. When that possibility was eliminated, Engineering and Design found themselves fighting an unforgiving timetable. In something like a forced march pace, the two sides worked to bring a new car into existence.

Bill Mitchell's designers blended Mitchell's Mako Shark design with Zora Duntov's engineering accomplishments to produce a street car worthy of desire. In its highest, rarest incarnation, the L88-engined convertible, the car became a legend even while in production.

The L88 was unchanged for 1969. Only 80 of the L88-engined cars were sold in 1968, while 116 were sold in 1969. It was an expensive option—$947.90 in 1968, $1032.15 in 1969—and its power was underrated in promotional literature. That's because its power was highly rated on the race track or drag strip.

Shinoda's car became known as the Mako Shark II. Mitchell's earlier 1961 Shark show car, the XP-755, was renamed Mako Shark I to give consistency and longevity to styling exercises that would lead to the 1968 car. The Mako Shark II premiered at the New York International Auto Show in April 1965. By October, a running, functional model, powered by a Mark IV 427-cubic-inch V-8, was shipped to the Paris Salon. Throughout the rest of 1965, the two prototypes, created for something like $3 million, toured North America and Europe. They created a huge firestorm of publicity and speculation. Magazines pronounced themselves certain that viewers were seeing the next Corvette when they looked at Mitchell's Mako II.

Meanwhile, in Washington, D.C., lawmakers proposed rules and wrote regulations that would greatly affect the products of Detroit and its suburbs for nearly 20 years. As early as 1965, Congress began discussing legislation to set

Bill Mitchell's most exaggerated Sting Ray was the Mako Shark II, a car he commissioned first as a show car and then as his personal transport. The first version for the New York Auto Show in April 1965 was not driveable but it showed off sleek outside exhausts. By fall, engineers installed a Mark IV 396-ci engine. After several years of shows and use, this car was redesigned as the 1970 Manta Ray, fitted with an aluminum-block 427 ZL1 engine. *Mike Mueller archives*

One easy way to differentiate 1968 Stingrays from those built in 1969 was the addition of the Stingray logo—as one word with these cars—on the front fenders. Overall production for 1969 soared from 28,566 in 1968 up to 38,672. Of these, 16,663 were convertibles. The L88s, in either coupe or convertible form, remained among the rarest, with just 116 manufactured and sold as a $1,032.15 option.

acceptable levels of auto exhaust gas emissions. Some of these would go into effect with the 1968 model year. In 1966, the Traffic Safety Act began setting front, rear, and side impact and visibility standards for cars sold in the United States. It also established procedures requiring manufacturers to recall vehicles on which mechanical and safety flaws were found. California introduced its own auto emissions standards, stricter than the rest of the country, to become mandatory with 1969 models sold in that state.

At the same time, the Chevrolet studios worked to revise the Mako Shark II into something that could be produced. They built it on the Sting Ray chassis, carrying over virtually everything mechanical from the production cars.

By November 1965, Chevrolet's production Studio under Hank Haga had produced full-size clay models that were very close to what the finished car would look like. Haga's designers replaced Mitchell's boat-tail rear window of his Mako II with a scooplike treatment evolved from one of Duntov's midengine prototypes and similar to two of Haga's favorites, Ferrari's angular 1964 250 GTO and Porsche's Type 904 GTS. But as soon as Engineering tested these prototypes in its wind tunnel, Corvette's perpetual aerodynamics problems reappeared. The new shark nose proved even more airworthy than the previous Sting Ray had been. A ducktail lip at the rear helped hold that end down but, of course, that brought the nose up farther. Duntov fitted a

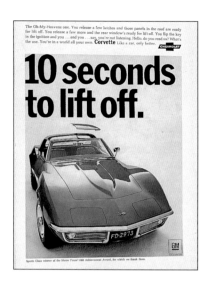

That quickly the readers' hair can blow in the wind. In March, this ad ran in the 1968 New York *Auto Show* program and *Sports Illustrated*. It appeared next in June issues of *Road & Track* and *Sports Car Graphic*. Campbell-Ewald

The cowl-induction hood was a tell-tale signal of power under hood. It served aerodynamic functions as well, reducing acceleration times and increasing top speeds while drawing in cool outside air from the high-pressure area at the base of the windscreen.

133

Mismatched tires were not unintentional but went toward improving weight transfer during acceleration. Perhaps only 12 of these were produced for 1969. Motion's performance put the car across a quarter mile in 12.35 seconds at 117 miles per hour.

The complete Motion Phase III option package cost the buyer $7,672 including the car. Motion improved the L72 iron block 427 to closer to 500 horsepower using a single Holley 950cfm carburetor.

small chin spoiler across the front, well below the small grille and slender fenders. It helped some.

Design had carried over into the prototype the tall front fender bulges from the Mako Shark II. Once again Duntov found himself fighting against Mitchell. The design chief's dearly held design preferences ran counter to engineering practicality and driver visibility. Duntov marshaled support from Chevrolet's new general manager, Pete Estes, who came to the division from Pontiac in 1965, replacing Knudsen. Estes, like Cole, had been a division chief engineer (at Pontiac) before his subsequent promotions. He also was displeased by the sight lines. The car went back to the drawing boards. Work piled up in the Engineering and Design departments, already overburdened with the brand new Camaro, Chevrolet's response to Ford's Mustang and Pontiac's GTO. It was Chevy's entry into the nationwide muscle car wars. Chevrolet had to introduce this car in 1967.

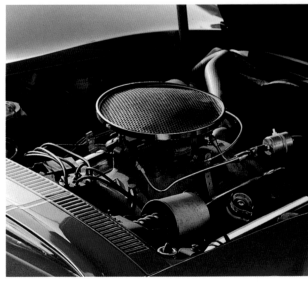

Product planners could count sales lost to Pontiac and Ford. So everyone involved with the Corvette agreed to hold over the Sting Ray replacement until 1968.

Under supervision from Chevrolet's chief designer, David Holls, Larry Shinoda collaborated with Production Studio chief Hank Haga and his staff to reduce the excesses of Shinoda's Mako Shark II that had continued onto the prototype.

One Design idea that had appeared in the small experimental studios since the late 1950s was resurrected: the removable roof panel. By the time the Corvette final clay models were approved, Porsche had introduced its 911 Targa, a model with a completely removable roof center section and rear window. Chevrolet Design wanted to do the same, but it learned a similar lesson to Porsche Targa designer, Butzi Porsche. The 911 was not stiff enough to support a completely open car, so its roll bar added the necessary stiffness to the steel-bodied Porsche. For Corvette, its fiberglass body and steel frame were not even stiff enough to accommodate an open roof. By incorporating a center beam that tied the windshield to the rear section, Design adapted an innovation from outside industrial designer, Gordon Buehrig, and introduced the T-roof.

Shinoda's hidden headlights and windshield wipers from the Mako II were carried over to the production

This was the golden age for performance automobiles in the United States. Vince Piggins in Product Promotion, worked Chevrolet's Central Office Purchase Order (COPO) system to a great advantage. Piggins "invented" cars, preselling them to a handful of American dealers, keeping Chevy "bow tie" loyalty high.

This was a factory-approved hot rod. In the late 1960s Chevrolet encouraged high-volume dealers to purchase specially equipped high-performance models. Baldwin Chevrolet on Long Island, New York, was one such dealer. A speed shop up the street, Joel Rosen's Motion Performance, took what Chevy built and went from there.

135

prototype, causing problems and delays. The headlights, when closed, hung down into the air stream available for engine cooling. Yet the retractable headlights had become part of the iconography of Corvette. They would stay. Developing the vacuum plumbing to operate lights and wiper covers, powerful enough to punch through snow or ice, took time. Through the winter of 1966 and early 1967, there were still problems to solve.

One of those problems was engine cooling. Duntov took time off in the spring of 1967 to recover from a serious illness, and somehow engine cooling tests performed during the winter were forgotten. He returned to work three weeks before the press introduction for all the 1968 models, which he was to supervise. Public relations had specified the press preview Corvette to be a heat-absorbing dark blue, powered by the Mark IV 427 big block. Duntov nearly panicked when he learned that engine cooling had been forgotten. In a typical racer's response to a problem, he lengthened the front chin spoiler and then sliced two large scoops into the bottom bodywork just ahead of the spoiler to channel more air in for engine cooling. The combination worked well and the journalists never noticed. It was immediately approved as a last-minute design change. Still, through the 1968 model year, cooling was barely sufficient for big block engines with air conditioning. What's more, air conditioning was a popular accessory. Buyers learned that inside the pinched cockpit, the newly introduced flow-through Astro-Ventilation system was not adequate.

This was the litany of challenges that Design and Engineering had faced to get the Corvette (it would no longer be called the Sting Ray) completed for 1967. When the launch was delayed a year, it benefited the other engineers faced with meeting U.S. emissions and safety standards.

Soon after the press introduction, Chevrolet reorganized its division management, disbanding Corvette Engineering. Duntov was shuffled into special assignments as a roving Jack of all trades. Others were not so lucky, relocated to more plebeian Chevrolet passenger car responsibilities.

Then the magazine reviews of regular production Corvettes began to appear. Most notable was *Car & Driver*, known for its quick wit and tart voice. Editor Steve Smith pulled no punches, writing in the December 1967 issue about his plans to road test the 1968 Corvette he had just driven out to Watkins Glen. "But we won't," he wrote. "The car was unfit for a road test. No amount of envious gawking by the spectators could make up for the disappointment we felt at the car's shocking lack of quality control. With less than 2,000 miles on it, the Corvette was falling apart." With fewer strokes of the typewriter keys, Smith succeeded in restoring Corvette Engineering. Duntov and his group were reassembled, and Duntov was named chief engineer–Corvette. The group worked tirelessly. By year end, in the sweetest of ironies, *Car & Driver* readers voted the 1968

Corvette the "Best All-Around Car In The World," beating out the hyperexotic, midengined $21,900 Lamborghini P400 Miura with its transversely mounted V-12 as the car they wanted most.

Under the hood, Chevrolet carried over all the engine combinations offered in 1967 models. The 327-cubic-inch 300-horsepower model formed the base engine. At the top of the option list, Chevrolet still offered the L71 aluminum head L89 427-cubic-inch engine with its three two-barrel carburetors, underrated at 435 horsepower. The Powerglide automatic transmission was dropped, in favor of the three-speed, the Turbo Hydra-Matic, which boasted of a third gear, improving economy, performance, and efficiency along the way. No one could argue with the car's straight line performance, as blisteringly quick as the previous year's had been. The L-88-engined models wore new cowl induction hoods sculpted by Design based on Duntov's ideas, and the car scorched the pavement with its acceleration. Timed runs from 0 to 60 miles per hour took 4.2 seconds, and barely 8.0 seconds to 100 miles per hour.

By the end of the model year, the initial problems were mostly resolved. Sales reflected enthusiasts' appreciation for its dramatic appearance, phenomenal performance, and fairly reasonable price. When the numbers were counted, Chevrolet had sold 9,936 coupes with their removable roof panels and rear windows, and 18,360 convertibles (more than 8,700 of which went with auxiliary hardtops), for a total production run of 28,556 cars. Division chief Pete Estes even added a third assembly shift at the St. Louis plant to keep up with demand. Prices rose only slightly from 1967: The coupes rose only $274.25 to $4,663.00 base price, and convertibles climbed $79.25 to $4,320.00. A fully equipped boulevard cruiser convertible with the 350-horsepower 327-cubic-inch engine and an AM/FM stereo radio set the buyer back $6,216.95 (about $5.00 less than 1967) while a no-compromise/no-heater/no-radio street racing rocket coupe with the $947.90 L88 engine option meant parting with $6,594.45 (roughly $275.00 more than in 1967).

Bill Mitchell, ever in search of a more provocative commuter car, began to get antsy once his Mako Shark II–based production car appeared in showrooms. Advanced Design studio artists reinvented Mitchell's car, creating something that looked as though modeling clay had been pulled, stretched, extruded like taffy into a new sea creature that Mitchell called the Manta Ray. By 1969, the elongated Mako Shark/Manta Ray was out on the show circuit, stopping viewers in their tracks, hinting at things to come in the future from Bill Mitchell's multimillion dollar playground.

For 1969, the name Stingray returned to the regular production Corvette, now as a single word. Duntov's group further improved the new car, reducing the steering wheel diameter an inch to 15 inches to improve seating comfort and ingress/egress. Federal standards led to more padding,

Car Life and *Hot Rod*, in January 1969, and *Car Craft* a month later, kept it plain and simple. A blurred center line said enough. *Campbell-Ewald*

This car was purchased by Jack Cheskaty, a Denver amateur drag racer who liked the specifications when he read them and could afford the nearly $10,000 sticker price. Once he dialed it in, he won often. Historian Anthony Young reports that Chevy built 154 ZL1 engines of which 59 went into Camaros. A third complete car was built for Zora Duntov as a development mule.

Engineering used a different alloy for the ZL1 block and heads from the aluminum-headed L89 big blocks introduced in 1967. Advertised power was 430, to make it seem less appealing to uniformed buyers. In reality 500 to 525 was common. It was a regular production option for Corvette buyers although only two were ever sold, at $4,718.35 plus the cost of the car.

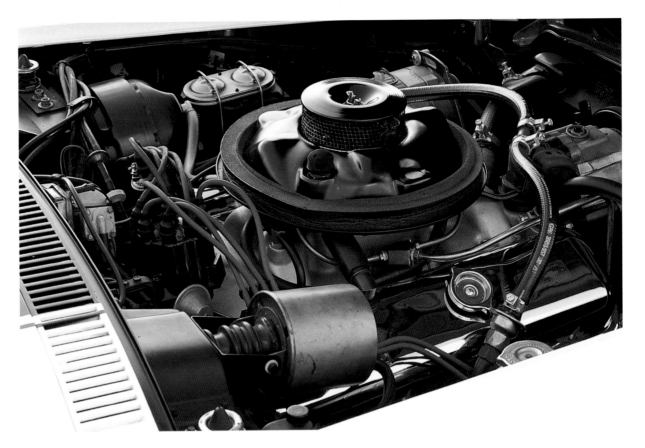

redesigned door handles, and introduction of antitheft steering column ignition switches.

Up front, Engineering stretched the 327's stroke to 3.48 inches, increasing overall capacity to 350 cubic inches. In addition to the base 300 horsepower 350-cubic-inch engine, there were seven optional powerplants, including the limited edition L88 and ZL1 427s. This was a new production application of Duntov's experimental all-aluminum engines for the Grand Sport. Both engines, conceived as purely racing powerplants, were underrated at 430 horsepower to confuse amateurs and to keep the engines off the streets and out of the hands of those unaware of their temperamental natures and true potential. With exhaust systems unplugged, in road or drag racing applications, power output was something closer to 560 horsepower from the L88 and perhaps as much as 585 horsepower from the aluminum engine, which weighed nearly 100 pounds less than the iron block version. In addition, the option pricing, $1,032 for the L88 and a staggering $3,000 for the ZL1, dissuaded the unfamiliar and uninformed. In the third year offering the L88, scarcely 116 sold and only two ZL1 aluminum block 427s were reported sold, although more may have been produced during its single year of availability.

Beneath all this, in attempts to improve ride and handling, engineers stiffened the chassis and changed wheel widths to 8 inches. It met with mixed success, as magazine reviews and owners alike complained of continued shakes, rattles, and body roll. This didn't deter an increasingly wealthy population from buying even more Corvettes, though. Dealers sold a total of 38,762 cars—22,129 coupes and 16,633 convertibles—the first time that closed cars outsold the open models. Prices rose only slightly, $117.95 for the coupe to $4,780.95 and $217.95 for the convertible to $4,437.95.

A two-month autoworkers' strike created a backlog of orders for the 1969 model. John DeLorean, the new division general manager and another Pontiac graduate, was promoted in February 1969. He set back the new model introduction to February 1970 (which partially explained the very high sales number for the 16-month 1969 model year). The corresponding eight-month 1970 season, however, recorded only 17,316 total sales, split 10,668 for coupes versus 6,648 for the convertibles.

Chevrolet announced late in the 1969 model year an engine option that did not appear until 1970. This small block 350-cubic-inch engine came much closer to Zora Duntov's own hopes for the car. He had never pushed the big block Mark IV engines. Even the aluminum ZL1 was too heavy for his liking, unbalancing a car he had worked so hard to get into shape. With this solid lifter-equipped 370 horsepower LT1, it symbolized in its own way the high-performance motivation of the muscle car era. With Frederic

Donner long out of the front office, replaced by former Chevrolet chief Ed Cole, performance no longer was a dirty word. It had become such a battle cry that even the LT1, with its lighter weight but inferior output to the outrageous 427s, could find a slot on an option list. Product planners, marketing personnel, and advertising executives, however, were aware of public sentiment and a rise in insurance premiums. The LT1 probably produced more than 370 horsepower, but like the L88s of the previous years, its output was down rated to keep the safety-conscious less mindful of Chevrolet's products. Of course, at the other end of this spectrum, engine builders stretched out the Mark IV further, increasing stroke from 3.76 to 4.00 inches, pumping up displacement to 454 cubic inches. And new designations appeared: the LS5 was a 454 with hydraulic valve lifters that, at a loaf, rated 390 horsepower. An all-aluminum LS7 was listed, but never offered, its price hinted at about $3,000 while rating a conservative 460 horsepower. Prices of the Corvette topped $5,000 for the first time, at $5,192 for the base coupe but still $4,849 for the convertible. The Corvette now provided tinted glass, choice of four-speed manual or three-speed automatic and Positraction at no extra cost. A custom interior trim option included not only the leather seats but also woodgrain appliqué on door panels and the console and special carpeting. To address the embarrassing quality-control problems, DeLorean sent every single

Once Jack Cheskaty got this car home to Denver, he replaced the stock exhaust with headers and the stock carburetor with a Holley 1100 cubic-feet-per-minute monster. A 5.13:1 rearend and wrinkle-wall slicks helped to routinely get him down a quarter-mile in 10.5 seconds at 132 miles per hour.

Production of these cars was so limited that they have an exclusivity approaching the rarest of all 1969 ZL1 with its all-aluminum block 427ci engine. Records indicate that only eight of these solid-lifter LT1 "ZR1" cars were produced in 1971, at a price premium of $1,010 for the package.

Corvette through a water bath with an inspector riding inside, looking for something like six dozen possible leaks. After that, the car was run over a 2-mile "Belgian Road," exaggerated cobblestone and potholed surfaces followed by a short stint on a vibration table that flexed and torqued the car repeatedly. DeLorean allowed no failures to leave the plant.

Once Ed Cole arrived in the chairman's suite, his perspective changed slightly. He was still undeniably a friend of performance, but his concerns assumed broader views and encompassed a greater variety of legitimate voices. On the one hand, the financial climate outside his doors was fairly healthy, if inflationary. America was in a wartime economy. The gross national product was up 7 percent, inflation up

5.7 percent, and unemployment at a decade-low 3.5 percent. The average U.S. salary was slightly more than $7,500, enough, by popular rules of thumb, to purchase or finance any product sold in any GM line. In December 1970, Congress passed the Clean Air Bill in the National Environmental Policy Act. This established regulations specifying fuel economy and emissions standards. It set targets the big blocks could never meet, giving auto makers less than six years to develop engines that would reduce toxic emissions by 90 percent.

Cole, who had loved and perhaps already saved the Corvette, set out to ensure its continued existence. He began eliminating all the options that didn't sell well. He ordered

The ZR1 package included not only the modified 330-horsepower 350-ci V-8 but also the Muncie M22 "rock crusher" transmission, heavy-duty power brakes, aluminum radiator, and special springs, shocks, and front anti-rollbar. It was a factory-prepared race car with a regular production option number and full warranty.

engineers to rework all GM engines to run on low-lead 91-octane fuel. He told Engineering, Marketing, Advertising, and Public Relations to use Society of Automotive Engineers (SAE) net measurement standards for engine horsepower output, numbers substantially lower than the gross-horse-power ratings previously published.

The result was a slight improvement in auto insurers' regard for GM. The LT1 dropped to 370 horsepower gross/275 net rating, but the LS5 454 dropped to 365 gross/285 net. The LS7 never appeared, but an aluminum head 454, called the LS6, rated 425 horsepower gross/325 net, and provided 0-to-60-mile-per-hour times of 5.3 seconds. The LT1 followed quickly behind at 6.0 seconds, and it offered far better ride and handling. Throughout Duntov's career as Corvette's chief engineer, the compromise between ride and handling had vexed him. He was in charge of building a production car with a top speed of more than 140 miles per hour in a country where that was illegal everywhere but in one single state. Yet to Duntov's mind, if any Corvette owner should need to drive at 140 miles per hour, for whatever reason, the car should do so safely. The dichotomy of Corvette buyers—some who wanted the car simply for its looks in front of the country club or nightclub, and the others who wanted its 140-mile-per-hour capability—would

frustrate him to his final days with Chevrolet.

Recognizing that racers were Chevy customers, the company introduced the ZR1 and ZR2 packages similar to the earlier Z06 options. No radio, power steering, power windows, or air conditioning were available with either of these options. The ZR2 used the LS6 454-cubic-inch 425-horsepower engine, and only 12 hardy racers bought in. The ZR1 was an even rarer breed, based on the LT1; just eight buyers shared Duntov's vision of what the Stingray could be. Total sales crept back up for 1971, totaling 14,680 coupes and 7,121 convertibles—21,801 in all.

The real impact of the new U.S. clean air standards was apparent in the 1972 model year. Cole's cleanup had its effect as well: The LS6 454, which had sold only 188 copies in 1971, disappeared. The legendary Muncie M22 close-ratio four-speed gearbox, known as the Rock Crusher, because of its durability and gear whine, remained available through 1972, but only as part of the ZR1 package. The only 454-cubic-inch engine left—of which 3,913 sold—was rerated down to 270 SAE net horsepower. The solid-lifter LT1, listed at 255 horsepower, sold 1,741 copies, while the ZR1 package saw its last year on the options lists with only 20 copies delivered. In all, 28,004 Stingrays sold in 1972, with 20,496 coupes delivered against 6,508 convertibles. It

The ZR code was also applied to another "factory racing option," one that was called the ZR2, used the LS6 454-ci V-8. Only 12 of those were built and production continued only through 1971. The era of muscle cars was ending. Clean Air legislation required a switch to unleaded gasoline for 1975 and this required lower compression engines that developed less horsepower.

was a nice position for a new general manager to inherit, and that's what Jim McDonald found on October 1, 1972. Another Pontiac graduate, he knew the value of building a car in great demand. He increased production slightly, knowing too well the drawbacks of excessive supply. Those who thought that the Clean Air Bill threatened either their livelihood or their enjoyment of private automobiles were in for a worse shock. In mid-January 1971, members of an 11-year-old group called the Organization of Petroleum Exporting Countries (OPEC) failed to negotiate price increases with 17 western oil companies. In frustration, OPEC members agreed to set prices by themselves, ending the previous courtesy of consulting customers beforehand.

Through 1971, the price of a barrel of Mideastern crude oil nearly doubled. Western companies dug in their heels, and so did OPEC, which reduced production and export volume by nearly 75 percent before the end of 1973. Gas prices in the United States climbed steadily.

Auto insurance premium rates for an unmarried 20-year-old male driving his own high-performance car to work or school reached $1,000 a year in 1968 and nearly $2,000 in 1970. Massachusetts introduced the country's first no-fault automobile insurance. On Earth Day, April 22, 1970, a nationally televised teach-in painted a grim picture of the world's environmental pollution, indicting the automobile as the chief perpetrator.

Frank Winchell and Zora Duntov Built GT40 Killers

Ford in Dearborn and in England produced the GT40, the FIA racer for the World Manufacturers' Championship. After Henry Ford II failed to purchase Ferrari in Italy, he set out to beat the Italian on his own turf. Once Ford Advance Vehicles tamed their 427-cubic-inch engine, the GT40 Mark IV (as they too called their big engine race car), won LeMans and did humble Ferrari. Ford then planned to take the car to the street to humble the Corvette with a road-going GT40, the Mark III. There was talk of introducing it in the fall of 1967.

Frank Winchell heard of the plan and he saw a Mark III. He set one of his engineers, Larry Nies, to work designing a midengine Chevrolet two-seater that could beat Ford's Mark III on the public roads. To be sure, his research and development staff had it right, he bought a Mark III GT40. The Design staff helped with a body, labeled the XP-880, much like a forward cab, midengine version of Mitchell's Mako Shark II. It was built around Nies' steel backbone frame whose central member and large side rails made deep, natural seat wells. It proved exceptionally stiff, and Nies improved its weight balance by placing the cooling radiators in the rear, which allowed Design to move the driver's position farther forward since no room was needed to vent air through the radiator. Overall length was 181 inches, front and rear track was 60 inches, and overall width was a beamy 74 inches. Suspension pieces came from other divisions, and the hybrid was powered by the Mark IV in 390 horsepower tune. Weight distribution settled at 40 percent front, 60 percent rear, with total weight of 3,400 pounds. The weak link here was a Pontiac Tempest transaxle to fit between the rear drive wheels for his prototype. By 1967, this was an obsolete, out-of-production part never intended to handle 390 horsepower.

Duntov had his own solutions in mind. Zetye and the rest of his crew developed another midengined prototype known as XP-882, spinning off technology from Duntov's all-wheel-drive CERV II.

Zetye adopted drivetrain bits from the 1966 Oldsmobile Toronado, a front-drive transaxle designed to handle massive amounts of power and torque. But this system was meant for a taller vehicle than they had in mind. So they rotated the engine, mounting it transversely and, using bevel gears, ran a long drive shaft rearward. Through masterful engineering, they fit in an existing three-speed manual gearbox where automatics had gone before. Duntov's entire vehicle fit on a 95.5-inch wheelbase and measured 174.5 inches overall. But it was wide: wide in track at 61.5 inches and wide in body at 75 inches. Fears over anticipated legislation against convertibles dictated a coupe-only body style, and Design's XP-882, done by Hank Haga and assistant Alan Young, stood just 2.5 inches taller than Ford's GT40. The front end of the car looked like nothing else out of GM Design, but the rear was pure Mitchell/Mako/Manta Ray with a louvered back window.

John DeLorean, Chevrolet Division's new general manager, a stylish personality with a whiz-kid reputation from his successes at Pontiac, looked at both Winchell's midengine project and Duntov's XP-882. Despite wide support of midengine ideas, DeLorean saw only tank traps into which he did not want to fall. Despite Duntov's three-speed prototype gearbox, Engineering really could provide only an automatic transmission for any midengine version. This would be the situation for several years, until budgets relaxed enough to cover the big cost. It didn't matter that four or more out of every five Corvettes sold then were automatics. DeLorean saw only high development costs on an unproven product that would have his name on it if it failed. DeLorean shelved both concepts during the summer of 1969.

Ford also shelved plans to produce its Mark III GT40, going instead after the stylish if imperfect DeTomaso Pantera that would debut at the New York Auto Show in April 1970. American Motors also had a midengine show car to introduce at the New York show.

Bill Mitchell had come to think of auto shows as GM Design shows. Duntov, disappointed over DeLorean's dismissal of the XP-882, did an end run around him and showed the prototype to Mitchell and Chevrolet's chief engineer, Alex Mair. When the New York Auto Show doors opened on Thursday April 2, 1970, Mitchell and Duntov trumped the competition. Rumor told the automotive world that Chevrolet's midengine Corvette was dead, and yet there it was, labeled a Corvette prototype.

DeLorean put the XP-882 back in business, approving funding to design a transmission for the big block Mark IV 454. A stretched-out 400-cubic-inch small block and Turbo Hydra-Matic was fitted for testing purposes. DeLorean asked Mitchell to design a new body and XP-895, a running prototype, was born in late 1971. DeLorean contacted Reynolds Aluminum to produce an aluminum body. Starting in mid-March 1972, Reynolds delivered a completed body in mid-June that weighed roughly 700 pounds, some 450 less than the steel prototype Design had done. When all the mechanical pieces from Design and Engineering's prototype steel XP-895 were transferred into Reynolds' car, the finished, running midengine, aluminum-bodied Corvette weighed barely 3,000 pounds. DeLorean was impressed enough that he began to explore ways to produce the car. Factory production cost analyses within GM facilities made the car too expensive, too costly to the customer. He took the idea offshore, looking at lower-cost assemblers in Europe. The numbers just would not work for GM. DeLorean pulled the plug after learning a great deal about midengine, alloy-body auto making.

chapter 12

More of the Same but Less: 1973–1982

The Corvette was born from a flamboyant designer's idea of what an American sports car could be, given the limits of time and money available. Just before the end of its second decade, it had been finessed into what a flamboyant engineer thought the car could be, given the same limits. Ironically, as the car began its 21st season, a pendulum had begun to swing back perhaps toward the Corvette's roots. Some of this change fell on Duntov, Winchell, Mitchell, McDonald, and Estes from federal regulations, rules that required Corvette to forsake its recent high-performance identity if it was to survive.

Soon after the 1963 Sting Ray's introduction, the new body began to make its name on race tracks. Carroll Shelby's Cobras, running with Ford's 427-cubic-inch V-8 starting in 1965, were less of a threat by 1968 because they'd gone out of production. The 427 Cobras never could be made smog and safety legal, and so he simply discontinued them. Private racers soldiered on, but Shelby's "factory" support disappeared when Shelby was drafted to lead Ford's endurance racing program with the GT40s in Europe and to supervise production of the higher volume Mustang GTs that bore his name. It all dried up when Ford itself withdrew from racing around Thanksgiving 1970.

Mark IV L88s had SCCA events to themselves. Actor James Garner bought three to run at Daytona, and longtime racers Don Yenko, Tony DeLorenzo, Jerry Hansen, and John Greenwood made racing history year after year starting in 1968 and continuing to the end of the Stingray design in 1982.

Off the track, however, the car took on a different identity. A flurry of emissions standards and skittish insurance companies strangled performance. Even the car's appearance was affected. The 5-mile-per-hour impact-resistant bumpers were the law of the land. While most manufacturers simply thrust large shelf-like projections out in front, David Holls' more talented designers produced something nicer, more innovative, cloaking the energy-absorbing bumpers in urethane plastic skin painted in body color.

To satisfy their own standards, for 1973, Design revised front fender side vents and eliminated the cowl door that too often left owners without working windshield wipers. The removable back window, carried over since its introduction in 1968, was discontinued. Engineering fitted radial-ply tires. Cast-aluminum lightweight wheels, planned for delivery were never available except across parts counters due to quality problems. Under the hood, the 454-cubic-inch engine was carried over, but revised to provide an additional 5 horsepower, now rated at 275 and renamed the LS4. The small block, hydraulic-lifter L82 offered 250 horsepower from the 350-cubic-inch cast-iron engine. Duntov's chassis engineer, Walt Zetye, and body engineer, Bob Vogelei, changed body and engine mounts and applied more sound insulation throughout the body, however, stiffening the car while decreasing road and mechanical noise.

Model year 1974 was the absolute end of high performance. It had been under serious attack for some time. After 1974, there would be no 454, and the small blocks would lose true dual exhausts. Exhaust, instead, was collected into a single catalytic converter from which it would emerge and split again into twin mufflers and tailpipes. Petroleum refiners introduced unleaded fuel, and General Motors cars were re-engineered to run on the lower-octane, low lead gasoline. It began nearly a decade of temperamental engines producing lower power, poorer fuel economy, hesitations, stumbling

Safety and comfort were paramount issues to Design and Engineering for the 1973 models. Radial tires appeared and new rubber-wrapped steel-sleeve chassis mounts were developed to stabilize the body on the chassis yet isolate road vibration for passenger comfort.

145

The LT1 solid-lifter 350-ci V-8 was deleted from the engine line-up, replaced by a hydraulic-lifter 350, the L82. This was done as much to quiet underhood noise as for any exhaust emissions requirements. Substantial sound-deadening material was added throughout the car as Corvettes left performance behind and headed for luxury.

idle quality, and uneven performance. So many standards were introduced and enforced between 1975 and 1984 that engineering staffs swelled at domestic and foreign car makers.

In mid-March 1974, OPEC, now 13 members strong, settled with its western customers and crude oil that had sold for $2.11 per barrel in early January 1971 went to $14.08 38 months later. A gallon of gasoline in America would never again sell for 19 or 26 or 33 cents. Lines formed at gas stations and some states proposed rationing supplies and even closing stations on Sundays. Fuel economy all at once made a difference. To make sure it did, the White House ordered a nationwide 55-mile-per-hour "energy conservation" speed limit.

Despite this gloom and doom, Corvettes sold better than ever in 1973, topping 30,000 units. The units were split into 25,521 coupes and 4,943 convertibles, with many more buyers preferring the T-topped cars to pure open air motoring. The grand total was 30,460 all together. Nine-out-of-ten buyers went for power steering, eight went for power brakes, and seven went for air conditioning. Barely a third purchased an optional engine yet nearly two-thirds ordered the automatic. The nature of Corvette buyers was changing and the car kept pace.

For 1974, the trend away from convertibles continued. Some 32,028 coupes sold while only 5,474 convertibles were delivered. Again, it set new production and sales records with 37,502 cars sold. Base price of the coupe crept up to $6,001.50, including the 350-cubic-inch 195-horsepower engine. The most popular option was the $117.00 power steering (35,944 delivered), followed by power brakes ($49.00, 33,306 sold), and then the $82.00 telescopic steering column (27,700 ordered). Only 3,494 buyers ordered the 270-horsepower 454 with close-ratio four-speed, while 25,146 accepted the no-extra-charge standard equipment M40 Turbo Hydra-Matic automatic gearbox.

The rear bumper adopted the front's energy-absorbing technology hidden with body color painted with urethane plastic, done subtly and successfully in Hank Haga's Production Studio. Inside the passenger compartment, standard equipment three-point lap and shoulder belts were made standard on convertibles as well as coupes.

Model year 1975 marked the end of several Corvette mainstays. James McDonald moved out as general manager, replaced in December 1974 by Robert Lund who came from Cadillac but who had been sales manager at Chevrolet. Convertible sales dwindled to only 4,629 cars, accounting for less than one-eighth of another record annual production total of 38,469 cars. Management killed the open cars. This was not only a production decision based on poor showroom performance, but it was also the result of outside pressures. An increasingly intrusive federal government made loud noises about convertible rollover safety as early as 1970. Congressional hearings and investigations led Detroit

car makers to expect a governmental mandate. That it was no longer an economically viable product made the decision easier, even though the legislation never appeared.

The only engine option for the Corvette was now the 350-cubic-inch L82 with 205 horsepower. Base prices took a huge jump, the result of meeting federal clean air and vehicle safety regulations. The 1974 base coupe that listed for $6,001.50 increased to $6,810.10 for 1975, while the convertible rose from $5,765.00 to $6,550.10. The standard engine was strangled down to 165 horsepower. Astro ventilation, a barely efficient flow-through fresh air system, breathed its last gasp in 1975. But the greater loss to the car was a human one.

On New Year's Day 1975, Zora Arkus-Duntov, Corvette's chief engineer for nearly 22 years, retired and was replaced by his heir-apparent, Dave McLellan, a GM engineer since 1959 and one who, like Zora Arkus-Duntov, brought to the job a full head of already graying hair.

Through 1976 and 1977, Corvette forged ahead, producing two more record sales years and increasing prices. Engineers improved standard engine performance as they got a grip on air pumps and exhaust gas recirculation systems. Base power output returned to 180 horsepower. But this was enough for nearly 85 percent of the Corvette buyers both in

Steel beams spanned the doors to provide enhanced side-impact safety for drivers and passengers. Despite these changes adding weight and diminishing performance, production and sales crept up from the roughly 21,000 cars in both 1971 and 1972. Some 25,521 coupes and 4,943 convertibles rolled out of St. Louis, for a total of 30,464.

1976 and 1977. Those who wanted more bought the L82 with 210 horsepower for an additional $481.00. All but 173 buyers of 1977 models ordered power steering, while every car received the $59.00 optional power brakes. Both of these and the leather interior were made mandatory options in late 1976 and continued thereafter. Suggested retail price for 1976 was $7,604.85 and $8,647.65 for 1977. The interior was redesigned for model year 1977. This was done mainly to make use of the full line of GM Delco radios that could not fit into the previous console.

By mid-March 1977, Corvette had reached a landmark when the 500,000th car drove off the assembly line in St. Louis. But this was only a precursor to the facelift that appeared in 1978 to commemorate the 25th anniversary of the Corvette and the 62nd annual running of the Indianapolis 500.

Both cars represented GM's getting the most out of the least. Behind locked doors in Engineering R&D and in Mitchell's Design studios, dreamers created midengine prototypes using small blocks, big blocks, and even multiple rotary engines, clothed in fiberglass, thin sheet steel, and aluminum that were meant to commemorate 25 years of the car. But cold budgetary realities—and even differing opinions of what was a true Corvette—doomed each of these creations to auto show stands.

Instead, quick and easy changes sufficed. The sugar scoop rear window treatment was replaced with a large, intricately shaped back window. Plans called for this to open, giving access to this space, but a tight economy cut this function. Inside the cockpit, the glovebox got a working cover and the theft alarm system expanded to include T-roof panels. Under the hood, federal Corporate Average Fleet Economy (CAFE) restrictions for entire product lines limited the 350-cubic-inch L48 base engine to 185 horsepower (except in California where its own emissions standards pulled another 10 horsepower from the engine). The optional L82 offered 220 horsepower. Total production reached 46,776 cars, including 15,283 delivered in the B2Z optional 25th Anniversary paint and trim, a $399.00 option that included two-tone silver—light on top, darker on bottom. Another 6,502 cars were painted and sold as replica Indy 500 pace cars, one for each Chevrolet dealer. While the standard base coupe sold for $9,351.89, the Pace Car Replica, RPO Z78, soared way over the next price hurdle of $10,000.00, reaching $13,653.21, for a specially equipped car. The L48 engine was standard (with the L82 optional), and front and rear spoilers added to its appearance and stability; black-over-silver paint reproduced the color scheme of the actual Pace Cars. The decal came inside the car, to be applied by the dealer at the customer's discretion. Special seats, intended for introduction with the 1979 models, were fitted, and badges and trim filled out the package.

The 1979 models gained in horsepower due to an across-the-board adoption of the L82s twin-snorkel air

Model year 1973 saw the first of many environmental considerations that affected performance in all cars. The 5 mile per hour impact front bumpers were introduced, adding 35 pounds to the weight of the Corvette. The hardtop's rear window was no longer removable, an effort to limit exhaust fumes entering the cockpit.

With the L82, the cars would reach 60 miles per hour in 7.4 seconds. Production for the year set a new performance record with 38,465 cars sold. However, convertible sales had been shrinking and the U.S. government had previously made noises about safety and rollover standards for open cars. Convertibles disappeared from the line-up at the end of the 1975 model year.

Under the hood, the optional 205-horsepower L82 engine was the highest performance package available in the emissions-controll period of the mid-1970s. The car was ordered with the Z07 Off-Road Suspension and Brake Package, air conditioning, AM/FM stereo radio, close-ratio four-speed transmission, and the vinyl covered auxiliary hardtop.

Bill Davis, a sports car dealer in Kentucky, ordered the convertible from a local Chevrolet dealer on speculation. He chose every option possible and in cases of similar possibilities, selected the more expensive. Davis had heard a new body style was coming along and convertibles were going away. The window sticker read $9,077.10.

cleaner, ingesting cooler outside air. This, plus adoption of the L82's lower back-pressure mufflers, gave the base L48 a 10-horsepower boost, to 195 in all 50 states. The L82 also gained 5, to 225 horsepower. Thinner, lighter seats from the Pace Car were standard for all Corvettes in 1979. The Indy Pace Car spoilers became a $265.00 option (D80) for all Corvettes. Base price settled in at $10,220.23, and a new record of 53,807 cars were produced. This level of output made GM corporate management question the need to change something that was doing just fine. Corvette had been enormously profitable for several years.

Few people remained in the division who would buck the status quo. Duntov, the leading advocate of midengine technology, had long since retired, as had Ed Cole and Bill Mitchell who retired in 1978 Chevrolet's newly named director of engineering, Lloyd Reuss, had no preference. David McLellan, Duntov's successor, resonated contentment, pronouncing his preference for front-engined Corvettes.

In 1980, California buyers suffered from the state's own emissions standards that were even tighter than the federal

CAFE requirements. Californians got cars with a recently introduced 305-cubic-inch small block, rating of only 180 horsepower. Throughout the rest of the United States, the standard engine remained the L48 350 with 190 horsepower, and buyers from the other 49 states had the option of the L82, which now had increased to 230 horsepower.

All of this was packaged within a newly revised, lower drag nose with a standard front chin spoiler. Between this more aerodynamically friendly front end and a weight reduction of nearly 250 pounds, 1980 models weighed 3,179 pounds—a welcome improvement. One change inside the car was highly unwelcome, if not downright silly. Federal standards that lowered national speed limits to 55 miles per hour required that all speedometers provide calibration no higher than 85 miles per hour, no matter what the actual top speed of the car might be. Suggested retail price of the base Corvette rose by nearly $3,000.00 to $13,140.24, a result of countless federal safety and emissions requirements. Sales and production totals dropped nearly 20 percent for 1980 as buyers recognized that as weak as the car was that they bought in 1978 or 1979, it was more car than what they could purchase now for 30 percent more money. Still, 40,614 buyers were undeterred by these facts and forked over the down payment or the first lease payment— a form of car financing that had steadily gained in popularity since the mid-1970s.

Improvements continued in fairly undramatic fashion in 1981 and 1982. The 49-state 350 was certified in California, but optional engines disappeared; 190 horsepower was all any buyer could get. Nationwide, under the hood, a new Computer Command Control (CCC) module managed fuel and air mixture in the carburetor and ignition timing to produce optimum exhaust emission performance and fuel economy, though the latter was a distant second in importance. This system first appeared in 1980 on California-only 305s. The four-speed manual transmission was discontinued at the end of the 1981 model year. Engineering devised a fiberglass-reinforced leaf spring for the rear suspension, saving another 36 pounds.

Complaints from magazine reviews and buyers alike continued about the car's fit and finish. Quality control still seemed to be an elusive quantity for Chevrolet's most expensive, most visible product. To finally control that problem,

The black-over-silver Indy Pace Car replica was the first Corvette to cross the $10,000 price hurdle; it cleared it by a good margin: $13,653. (The base sport coupe, of which 40,274 were produced, retailed for $9,351.) Chevrolet intended to build only 2,500 of these cars, but each of the dealers demanded one. In the end, 6,502 were built.

Some 15,283 of the 1978 buyers ordered the Silver Anniversary paint and trim, a $399 option providing them with a light silver-over-dark silver car. Just six months before the 1978 introduction, St. Louis completed the 500,000th Corvette. It was an event that few in General Motors would have believed possible on the fifth anniversary.

production began at a new high-tech assembly plant in Bowling Green, Kentucky, on June 1, 1981. Before General Motors acquired this structure it had been Chrysler's AirTemp Division air conditioning manufacturing plant. Corvette assembly overlapped at the old St. Louis facility until model year production ended on August 1. Bowling Green's new equipment offered not only tighter assembly standards but also new paint: Enamel based colors finished with clear topcoats came from Kentucky, while the remaining St. Louis cars finished up with the old, standard lacquer.

Prices jumped another $3,100.00, as the standard car reached $16,258.52, about $1,660.00 more than Cadillac's El Dorado. The basic Corvette, it must be said, was highly civilized and the only remaining options really just gilded the lily. In all, 40,606 sold.

By 1982, most enthusiasts knew about the arrival of a new Corvette in 1983. The existing body had first appeared in 1968, assembled on a chassis that first showed up underneath the 1963 Sting Rays. Chevrolet certainly had paid off development and improvement costs. Still, even in a lame duck production year, Chevrolet chose to make important introductions. Fuel injection reappeared, in the form of throttle-body injection called "Cross Fire Injection," which pumped engine output up to 200 horsepower for all 50 states. The CCC module was given more power and responsibility, including shutting off fuel supply with the ignition to prevent dieseling. It also opened a cold-air intake direct into the air cleaner under maximum acceleration. A four-speed overdrive automatic replaced the previous three-speed Turbo Hydra-Matic.

This final "shark" was available not only as a well-equipped base model at $18,290.07, but also as a special order Collector Edition. Product planners watched sales of the 25th Anniversary and Indy Pace Car replica and produced a special exterior paint and interior trim option to honor the end of the longest production run and celebrate 30 years of production of Corvettes. The silver-beige metallic paint was capped with bronze-tinted glass T-roof panels

The 1981 models retailed for $16,258, having climbed steadily once they broke the $10,000 price barrier with the 1978 Indy Pace car replicas. A total of 40,606 cars were produced not only from the St. Louis plant but also from Corvette's new assembly facility at Bowling Green, Kentucky. Production began on June 1. The last St. Louis car was finished on August 1.

Weight loss was the name of the game for the waning years of the Corvette body style known to many as the fourth generation. Engineering developed a single reinforced plastic, transverselymounted rear spring that saved 34 pounds over the previous steel versions (which remained in production on FE7 Gymkhana suspension cars and those with manual transmissions).

Chevrolet Engineering introduced its 200-horsepower "Cross-Fire Injection" engine for all 50 states. The Computer Command Control system introduced in 1980 managed two injectors per cylinder with this new system and provided smoother acceleration and idle, and better fuel economy even with the 10 horsepower improvement over 1981 cars.

The "Collector Edition" was Chevrolet's first Corvette to break the $20,000 price barrier. Just as the 1978 Indy Pace Car did at $10,000, this new one passed the point and kept going to $22,537. These were wrapped in a striking silver-beige paint set off with graduated beige-to-brown panels on the sides and hood. Several badges attested to each car's provenance.

No manual gearbox was available for 1982 and the now-three-speed-plus-overdrive automatic transmission confirmed Corvette's steady drive away from pure, traditional uncivilized sports cars toward highlycivilized personal luxury automobiles. Some 25,407 cars sold including 6,759 known as the "Collector Edition," commemorating the end of three decades of production.

It was no longer a secret. The "Shark" was dead; long live the shark. The next Corvette that anyone would see would be new. The body style known for some time as the fifth-generation Corvette would not arrive in 1983 as a 30th anniversary but would appear mid-1983 as the very first of the 1984s.

and fitted hinges to the large back window, making the fastback a hatchback at last. The Collector Edition sold for $22,537.59. Dealers sold 6,759 of them and another 18,648 standard coupes, as well.

Enthusiast magazines had published spy photos and descriptions for nearly two years that revealed to their readers the looks and performance of the new Corvette. While total production for 1982 was 25,407 cars, it was anticlimactic as an end to production. Throughout its 15-year lifetime, Chevrolet had sold more than half a million Sharks—542,861 in all. The car had poured tens of millions of dollars into General Motors.

Despite that, in 1981, General Motors announced its first loss since 1921, coming up $763 million short for the year. Throughout the corporation, all new projects were

either delayed a year or canceled outright. While inflation dipped to only 10.2 percent, down from a high of 14 percent in 1974 and 1975, President Ronald Reagan, authoring the concept of "trickle-down" supply-side economics, signed a 25 percent tax cut spread over three years. Into this shaky economy, former Chevrolet General Manager John Z. DeLorean introduced his stainless-steel-bodied, four-cylinder midengined Irish-built sports car, priced at $25,000.

By the end of 1982, when the Stingray went out of production, inflation had dropped to 6 percent, while unemployment had jumped to 9.7 percent of the population. Federal courts reported 20,365 bankruptcies, the most since the early 1930s. And John DeLorean had been arrested for possession of too much cocaine for an occasional user.

Rotary: Not a Monthly Luncheon Meeting

In many ways, this was the last hurrah of an old breed within General Motors. Bill Mitchell, having been present for Corvette's birth, and Zora Duntov there at least for its first birthday, these two collaborators had learned the techniques to avoid management scrutiny. General Motors was, by the late 1970s, one of the largest corporations on the planet. It was presided over by men—there were very few women on any board of directors in American industry at the time—who increasingly were more excited by the performance of the New York Stock Exchange than of an uncorked Mark IV. More discussions involved return on corporate investment than value per customer dollar. The business of General Motors had become making money more than making automobiles. The corporation that once led America in innovative design and engineering under Alfred P. Sloan, Harley Earl, and inventor Charles Kettering, was almost afraid of its own ideas. Risks had become too costly. The Corvette, which was GM's test bed for new technologies, the vehicle through which GM's customers were introduced to the future as GM saw it, had become gun shy.

In the early 1970s, the gun was still blazing away. Back in November 1970, General Motors signed an agreement to manufacture, under license, Felix Wankel's rotary combustion engine. The Engineering staff produced one prototype engine using two rotors and another using four rotors, to be installed in two prototype Corvettes. Ed Cole, promoted from Chevrolet general manager to GM president, told his chief engineers that the Wankel Rotary would eventually power every GM product. Duntov recognized that, with Cole's support, this might yield a midengine Corvette, using the Wankel behind the driver.

In early 1971 Mitchell assigned Clare MacKichan (chief stylist for the 1953 Corvette and now chief of advance design) to supervise the appearance of new rotary coupes to be designed by Dick Finegan of the Experimental Studio. The two-rotor car was given the number XP-987GT (a production sedan using the same engine was the XP-987). By June Mitchell and others saw Finegan's work and approved a full, running prototype. Pininfarina in Italy was to fabricate the body while Duntov and Walt Zetye were to make it run.

As Karl Ludvigsen reported in *Corvette: America's Star Spangled Sports Car*, Duntov shortcut a great deal of development time by starting his work with an existing midengined chassis, using a Porsche 914. Zetye shortened it to a 90-inch wheelbase, but he retained Porsche's front and rear running gear. In mid-January 1972, the chassis was shipped to Turin to Pininfarina, which shipped the completed car back in mid-April. The engine was installed, the GM powerplant RC2-266, rotary combustion 2 (rotors) 266 cubic inch. It produced 180 horsepower fed by a single Rochester four-barrel carburetor. The finished car weighed just 2,600 pounds, which with its power, gave it performance similar to the 1972 base production coupe.

Duntov, ever hungry for more power and higher performance, asked fellow engineer Gib Hufstader to build for him a four-rotor engine. He accomplished this by siamesing two 195-cubic-inch twin-rotor engines on either side of a shaft running between the two. This configuration would never fit in the smaller XP-987GT, but a chassis from the XP-882 which had once accommodated a Mark IV 454, would handle 390 cubic inches of twin two-rotor Wankels. Power output was estimated at 350 horsepower. Within two months of agreeing to build Duntov a hot rotary, Hufstader had it completed, almost in time for the GM board review in June 1972. Cole drove Duntov's much faster version a month later. The car went through many hands, each pair liking what they felt and touched. In January, Chuck Jordan delivered an assignment from Bill Mitchell to Hank Haga, chief designer of Chevrolet Studio 3, to create a totally new body for Duntov's four-rotor. Haga described Mitchell's assignment to Peter Licastro writing for *Corvette Quarterly*. It was to be "the breakthrough to get away from all the cut-off Kamm rear ends that were fashionable at that time. He wanted to take a page out of the German racing book from the thirties and have a teardrop shape." Haga gave the new car a more Corvette-like nose but overall lines similar to his earlier XP-882, and he added folding gull-wing doors. The car was hurriedly completed in Warren to make its flight to the Paris Auto Show in October 1973.

Rotary engine development continued until the engines' fuel economy, dirty exhaust, and reliability problems related to their oil seals became apparent. By late 1974, GM suspended Wankel rotary production indefinitely. Hufstader and his crew refitted the lovely rotary body with a traditional V-8 reciprocating piston engine. GM abandoned the rotary enterprise.

In a final repudiation of the four-rotor project, the now V-8 engine chassis was redone as another show car, the AeroVette. The four-rotor project represented the best of the Mitchell/Duntov flights of fancy. It cost millions. Its ultimate purpose, once management saw it and drove it, was to continue promoting Chevrolet Design and Engineering throughout Europe.

chapter 13

Missing Time, Quick Recovery: (1983)–1989

In 1983, President Ronald Reagan began to get hold of the inflation wracking the economy early in his term. In his third year, he cut inflation in half, knocked unemployment down slightly, doubled the nation's gross national product from 3.7 percent in 1982 to 7.6 percent in 1983. However, he ended the year with a $189 billion deficit. What was turbulent for America was turbulent for General Motors. Nevertheless, this was not the reason that Chevrolet Division produced no model year 1983 Corvette. That goes back to 1977 when C4, the fourth-generation Corvette, as this model is now called, was first imagined.

In 1977, Bill Mitchell retired as General Motor's vice president of Design and was replaced by Irvin W. Rybicki, a conservative, modest man who had directed the Buick-Oldsmobile-Cadillac studios. Unlike Mitchell and Earl who were leaders, Rybicki was more direct.

Mitchell had nurtured a relationship with Jerry Palmer, who had designed Corvette show cars for him in 1969 and had begun affecting the production models with the 1973 version. In 1974, Mitchell named Palmer chief designer of Chevrolet Studio 3, the home of the Corvette and Camaro. These kinds of appointments generally came with career-long tenure.

Across the Warren campus in Engineering, Duntov's protégé, Dave McLellan, a veteran of similar training, was in equal position to affect what any new Corvette would become. Both Palmer and McLellan learned of corporate plans to replace the profitable (more than $100 million annually) current product with a completely new car for 1983, in time for the car's 30th anniversary. This would be the first car produced without a direct, tactile link to Harley Earl's 1953 model. Its chief engineer and chief designer were not even employed by Chevrolet before the 1963 Sting Ray.

Options floated to the surface once engineers and designers got input from management. Rotary Wankel engines had not worked out, but the AeroVette's transversely mounted 400-cubic-inch reciprocating V-8 still held promise for midengine configuration. The newly introduced X-body cars, Chevrolet's Citation X-11 and Pontiac's Phoenix, used transversely mounted V-6 engines to drive front axles. This technology was available to Corvette. Yet Citation/Phoenix drivetrains engineered for 90 to 110 horsepower would fail instantly if subjected to the Corvette's 205. Engineers walked a tightrope over this question, because federal regulators proposed an added sales tax punishing fuel inefficiency, a "gas-guzzler" tax. Fleet average for 1983 had to be 19 miles per gallon. Corvettes, no matter what performance parameters were agreed upon, would not ever be subject to that tax. While John DeLorean was Chevrolet general manager, he proposed downsizing the Corvette to fit the F-body platform, belonging to the Firebird and Camaro. It would share development expenses and chassis pieces. But Design and Engineering both vigorously fought an idea that seemed too clearly profit motivated rather than improvement oriented.

The Corvette's heritage was in everyone's mind as they started doodling and sketching ideas and concepts for the 1983 replacement. The question of midengine versus front engine arose. Midengines had become buzz words when cast-iron big blocks skewed weight distribution to 65 percent on the front axle. Duntov and others wanted the hallowed 50/50 split, but that had been met in recent front engine production.

This was the first new Corvette in 15 years. Zora Duntov retired January 1, 1975. He was replaced by Dave McLellan who inherited a program in 1978, but this soon was canceled. This and other delays led to the delay in introducing the new body style to the public until midyear 1983.

Introduced as a 1984 model, the new Corvette was forced to meet increasingly stringent safety, emissions, and fuel economy standards. Its new shape, clearly derived from the previous generation, improved aerodynamics by nearly 25 percent and reduced weight by 250 pounds. Wheelbase shrunk 2 inches and overall length decreased 8.8 inches.

The Cross-Fire V-8 produced 205 horsepower and the base price reached $21,800. The lift-up fastback window, offered on the Collector Edition in 1982 was standard now. So was a remarkable "clamshell" hood that seemed to open the entire front end for engine access. Chevrolet sold 51,474 cars in the extra long 1984 model year.

More important, midengine cars provided marginally superior handling at the expense of load carrying. High-performance midengine cars were often second or third cars in wealthy households. Corvettes often were only cars. They had to go to the grocery store, to the golf course, on vacation with luggage, and back to work. Despite Zora Duntov's long-held dream of producing a sports car he could proudly drive in Europe, the Corvette was and always will be an automobile built for American habits. McLellan remained resolute in his support of Corvette's traditional configuration.

Then, ironically, Porsche, a European exotic car maker with a history of producing cars with weight bias to the extreme rear, produced its own Corvette, the 928. One of Chevrolet's own designers, Tony Lapine, who had labored in Studio X for Bill Mitchell creating Corvette SS racing cars and numerous production Corvettes, left GM's Opel operation in Russelsheim, Germany, to work for Porsche in 1969. One of Lapine's finest, most notable designs for the German sports car builder was its first front-engined sports car, the V-8 Type 928. Begun in 1974, the car was introduced in Germany in the fall of 1977. There were complex decisions that had led Porsche to produce a Corvette. It feared that the U.S. government, so safety conscious and regulation happy, would regulate handling in a way that would eliminate rear engine cars from U.S. markets. These rules, like those earlier hints about convertibles, never came to pass; but Porsche's product catalyzed Corvette's creators.

No product is developed in a vacuum.
Ideas or products of collaborators or competitors directly impact most accomplishments, whether it's heavy industry or fine art. Factors of seemingly little importance can bear enormous consequence. Such was the case with Ferrari's rule bending at the time of Duntov's Grand Sports. Such was the case now with Goodyear and tires.

From the time of Duntov's Grand Sports, Corvette supported the introduction of the highest performance tires within GM. When Dave McLellan assembled performance targets for the 1983 Corvette, everyone agreed the new Corvette should be the best-handling sports car in the world. To McLellan that meant wide, low-profile tires on 10-inch-wide wheels. Duntov's rule of thumb that Corvette's suspension remain compliant at full speed over uneven roads remained clear in his successor's mind. Such compliance meant vast suspension travel, but it ensured that no driver at top speed would be thrown out of control because the suspension bottomed out.

Design chief Jerry Palmer wanted 16-inch wheels for styling purposes. When the first specifications went down on paper, McLellan set minimum ground clearance at 5.25 inches, up 0.25 from the 1968 to 1982 car. And he placed four fat tires at the corners. From there, the design began.

Goodyear developed a special tire based on its work on Formula One rain tire development. McLellan's crew wanted tires that would hold up to the new car's top speed, in the 140- to 145-mile-per-hour range. Yet they must handle crisply, ride quietly, shed water efficiently, look interesting, and last longer than 10,000 miles, even under enthusiastic use. Goodyear returned with the VR50 "Gatorback" tires, which met all Corvette's parameters with room to spare.

Actually, "room to spare" was the only parameter the Gatorbacks didn't meet: Front tires with enough room to clear the engine and suspension pieces required the car be widened by 2 inches over the 1982 model to allow full-lock turning. As it was, Corvette wheel width shrunk greatly from McLellan's target 10-inch width to only 8.5 inches front and rear, because the tires stuck out beyond the body otherwise. Yet this and a major design strategy provided an increase in interior space.

Owners had complained that the Coke-bottle shape of the existing car created a claustrophobic cockpit with too little shoulder room. The 2-inch increase helped remedy that. McLellan and Palmer, conscious of the weight and size increases that Corvettes had endured over 25 years, found that their performance goals and safety requirements were in conflict with corporate mandates to downsize each vehicle. Good enough: Straightening out the pinched waist added 6.5 inches to interior shoulder room.

Then, because human shoulders are wider than waists, the added interior width provided extra room in the center tunnel below the cockpit for the drive shaft, exhaust, catalytic converter, plumbing, and wiring. No longer feeding these below the seats permitted lowering the seating floor an additional 2 inches to the bottom of the chassis. Despite a tiny increase in ground clearance, the lower seat position added headroom while it lowered the entire vehicle an inch. This reduced frontal area, decreasing aerodynamic drag and improving fuel economy. Efficient packaging made the overall length of the car 8.4 inches shorter than the 1982 model.

By early spring 1979, McLellan's engineering staff had a few development mules already out testing. Palmer's Studio 3 design staff began creating the new car's look. Randy Wittine, called "Mr. Corvette" because of nearly 15 years of involvement with the car, worked alongside a new kid on the block, John Cafaro. Cafaro produced a rendering of the new car with its back hatch up and an XK-E Jaguar-type hood opening revealing not only the engine but front tires, suspension, and chassis, as well. The hood opened like a clamshell, split along a seam that ran around the entire car, a styling element adopted from Ferrari's midengined 308 GTB. In one drawing, the studio's youngest designer created two of the most significant design features. With this mammoth hood, Palmer recognized that the engine and mechanical parts should appear integrated. McLellan agreed and engine castings, forged suspension pieces, and even spark plug wires were designed for appearance as well as function, and they were color coordinated to add visual impact. Cafaro's seam simplified molding and joining the fiberglass body panels and began to make possible tighter quality control in both fit and finish.

As the body continued its design evolution, Palmer's chief assistant, Roger Hughet, spent more time with Charles Toner and his design staff aerodynamics engineers testing the shape in several wind tunnels at speeds of up to 140 miles per hour to ensure valid results from a variety of conditions. Tests confirmed the viability of continuing a grilleless front end with a chin spoiler to shovel air from the ground up to the radiator. The high-speed experiments in the wind tunnels reintroduced fender-side "gills," the air extractor slots. The same air pressure buildup that popped hoods on Duntov's Grand Sports at speed induced lift under the vast wide front end. The "gills" gave that air pressure somewhere to go. Aerodynamic testing examined the retracting headlights (should one need to turn lights on at 140 miles per hour) and turbulence caused by the turbine-bladed wheels.

This was the age of space exploration and NASA's preoccupation with getting more of its astronauts back to the Moon. Americans had first walked there as part of Apollo 11 in July 1969, and in September 1976, the agency unveiled the space shuttle. Light-emitting diodes and liquid crystal display technology were high-tech and trendy. As early as 1978, Corvette's interior designers worked hard to match the instrument panel and interior seating to the sleek, new design coming from Palmer's exterior body studio. However, the interior staff had other considerations to worry about. One

One of the most distinctive design features of these Corvettes was its clamshell hood. Designer John Cafaro sketched it as a study idea and Jerry Palmer encouraged him to develop it further.

The convertible returned midyear to Corvette's line-up after a ten-year absence. The 1986 convertible was designated as Indy's 500 pace car; all the convertibles were called pace car replicas.

In shades of high-performance eras gone by, Chevrolet announced aluminum cylinder heads for the L98 V-8 for 1986. These saved some 125 pounds of weight up front.

was a cluster of troublesome federal regulations—Motor Vehicle Safety Standard (MVSS) 208, for driver and passenger safety in the event of front-end collision. The driver had the collapsible steering column in the event of a head-on crash; the passenger got a padded structure nicknamed the "breadloaf" because of its looks. MVSS 208 was introduced in 1977 to be in effect for model year 1982. It became a political issue, postponed eventually to 1985 introduction. In October 1981, President Reagan revoked it altogether. By this time, the breadloaf was part of the car and buyers found it where a glovebox would have been.

The V-8 engine that now looked marvelous under Cafaro's huge hood remained Chevrolet's rock-solid, death-and-taxes reliable pushrod small block. The throttle-body cross-ram induction introduced with the 1982 model year Shark carried over with improvements to engine management, a serpentine belt accessory drive and the inclusion of an electric cooling fan in front of the radiator.

Behind the engine, however, was a new, innovative four + three-speed manual transmission, a clever variation on the standard Warner gearbox, re-engineered by Doug Nash. Coupled to the Delco Electronics onboard computer—the "electronic control module" (ECM)—the Nash transmis-

sion provided what were essentially short shifts in second, third, and fourth gears. It was something like an automatic manual transmission, configured specifically to beat the best figures out of the EPA test. (When introduced, the car's window sticker stated 16 miles per gallon city mileage, 28 highway. The EPA balances these figures 55/45 percent to arrive at Corvette's 19.8 miles per gallon, exceeding the 1984 CAFE number by 0.3 miles per gallon.) There was still an automatic transmission, the four-speed Turbo-Hydra-Matic, which provided good launch times for standing starts but also was efficient and strong enough to propel the car to its 142-mile-per-hour top speed. To haul the car down from those speeds, McLellan and his engineers replaced the earlier, heavy, iron Delco-Moraine disc brakes with Australian Repco (formerly Girlock, from Girling and Lockheed) aluminum-and-iron versions. This saved more than 70 pounds between the four brakes.

McLellan's people improved the suspension as well. They set out to accomplish an ambitious handling target of 1.0G of lateral acceleration cornering power. Their achievement was due equally to their innovations with the chassis, the work they did on suspension configurations, and Goodyear's Gatorback tires.

The chassis was made of thin sheets of high-strength, low-alloy (HSLA) steel, spot welded into boxes and other shapes to support front and rear suspension, engine, differential, roof, doors, and windshield. Previously, Corvette frames involved two separate elements, one chassis/frame and the other a bird cage of much smaller members fitted above the chassis/frame that supported the body. With the new car, and unlike most other unit frame cars where the body is a structural element of the car, all the fiberglass surface panels are simply "decoration," camouflage to hide the frame and running gear. In addition, where past ladder frames required cross-members to tie outer frame rails together and add structural rigidity to the car, the 1983 car was fitted with only one bolted-in cross-member as a front engine support. The entire frame weighed just 351 pounds, yet was rigid enough to accommodate the engineering challenges of a completely removable roof center section that no longer required the T-roof support.

Onto this chassis, suspension engineers hung all-aluminum forged suspension pieces. The independent rear suspension (IRS) used a five-link system instead of the previous 1982 model three-link system. The new IRS more positively located the rear axle, eliminating its tendency to steer the car from the back in certain suspension load-unload transitions. Springs were fiberglass leaf-type springs and were mounted transversely on both front and rear suspensions. Fiberglass was not only lighter, but it was more resilient and it won't sag even after millions of jounce and rebound cycles. Engineers devised another use for the transverse springs as antisway bars. Any transverse spring holds tires on the ground and tries quickly to return them there after crossing, for example, railroad tracks. Yet in cornering, transverse springs, if attached to the chassis well inboard from the wheels, adopted a kind of S-bend that the leaf fights. The arch of the spring, induced in the molding process, served the same function as a normal add-on antisway bar, by seeking to equalize the position of the unloaded wheel with that of the heavily loaded wheel. It worked so well that engineers were able to greatly decrease the diameter of the supplemental antisway bar.

The car was scheduled for a 1983 model year introduction. Yet there were intricate, delicate systems to perfect. McLellan's engineers raced against time and the perfectionist's desire to get everything right. They couldn't get everything finished. The effects of this delay were compounded when, owing to a smaller than expected demand for the 1982 model, assembly line engineers began dismantling the production line in anticipation of the model changeover at Bowling Green. It developed into a three-way race of bad public relations: The new car is delayed one year; an unfavorable image because there would be no new model for 1983 to commemorate 30 years of the Corvette, and the worst disaster possible—releasing a car that was not ready.

Thus the 1984 model year was 17 months long. When it was over and inventory was complete, 51,547 buyers became enthralled with the new car and drove one home. The first 70 cars or so were kept within GM as continuing engineering development vehicles. The base price was now up to $22,361, which included the one-piece lift-off roof section, an opening rear hatch window, and the Goodyear P255/50VR16 tires and wheels. A most popular option was the remarkable Delco/Bose sound system. A fully optioned Z51 coupe (equipped with the performance handling package) delivered to a buyer in California with that state's mandatory emissions package, retailed at $26,936 plus shipping, tax, and license charges.

The first 1984s trickled into California showrooms around the end of March, as magazines published mostly favorable reviews of the car. The engine, with 205 horsepower, was sufficient to shoot the new car to 60 miles per hour in 7.1 seconds and to see a top speed of 137 miles per hour or so. Most reviewers had hoped the car would weigh less, and most of them disliked the video gameboard instrument cluster. Others complained about the ride harshness that came as a by-product of the Z51 handling package's 0.868G skid pad handling.

A $1,295 Z51 performance handling package (for manual gearbox coupes only) offered new Goodyear 275/40ZR17 Eagle tires on 17x9.5-inch "Cuisinart" wheels. This big size greatly improved handling over the standard 15-inch rubber. Brake rotors were replaced with thicker units and the front brakes received two piston calipers for improved stopping power and better pedal sensitivity.

The year 1988 was another milestone in Corvette history, representing 35 years of production. A commemorative package, Z01, was offered at a $4,795 premium (2,050 buyers went for it). While the body was unchanged, numerous improvements went into place under the skin. Coupes with the optional 3.07:1 rear axle ratio gained 5 horsepower, to 245, by using less restrictive mufflers (which were too loud for convertibles).

Two other factors influenced the decision to push back model introduction to early spring 1983. Chevrolet liked the opportunity to be the first 1984 model available rather than the last 1983 model launched. Then it also would be the first car introduced that met 1984 emissions and barrier impact standards. Once it became apparent that the Corvette would not be available for introduction in September 1982, the engineers slowed down a bit and set out to completely conquer the 1984 regulations. Production fired up on January 3, 1983, and each of the cars bore a vehicle identification number (VIN) indicating it was a 1984 car.

Two years after its introduction, Chevrolet's chief engineer, Don Runkle, talked to *Road & Track's* John Lamm about the 1984–1985:" We more or less moved the Corvette away from the classic Corvette customer. It was

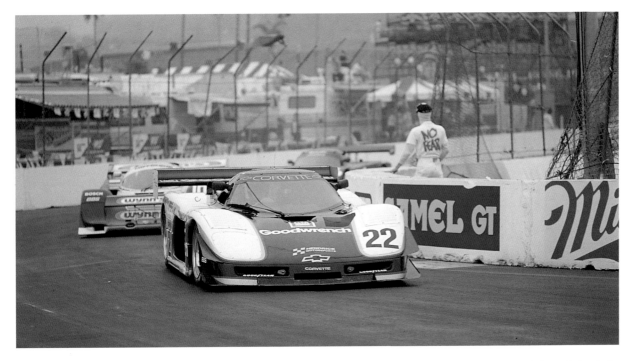

Originally based on Lola T-600 Group C prototype cars, a total of five chassis were built during the mid-to-late 1970s by Lola to accommodate aluminum block 6-liter 366-ci Corvette racing engines. The body was modified to look less like designer Eric Broadley's Lola. Hendrick Motorsports ran several of the cars from 1985 to 1989 as the GM Goodwrench Parts entry.

deliberate on our part; we didn't exactly fall into it. We decided to move the Corvette primarily because we wanted to make a technical statement with it, but we couldn't figure out how to keep it where it was price-wise and also make that statement.

"We didn't have to make the car cost as much as it does. But if we hadn't put all those features (aluminum front suspension arms, plastic springs, tuned port injection, etc.) into it, the car wouldn't be as good as it is right now. . . . I don't hear many people making fun of the Corvette anymore. But they used to. They would say 'That's not really a sports car. [It's a] Dumb Detroit . . . two-passenger sedan.'"

For 1985, Dave McLellan's engineers addressed ride harshness complaints by adjusting shock valving on both the base shocks and the Z51 Bilstein gas shocks, and by altering spring rates in the fiberglass transverse leaves. The rear wheels grew to 9.5 inches wide during the 1984 production run; the fronts were upsized as well for 1985.

Under the hood, Chevrolet continued chasing EPA numbers while incorporating remarkable performance improvement. True fuel injection, dubbed Tuned Port Injection, replaced the CrossFire Throttle Body injection. The result was engine output up to 230 horsepower, a much faster 0-to-60-mile-per-hour time of 6.6 seconds and top speed nearer the magic 150 miles per hour while still meeting GM's CAFE requirements.

Production for the 1985 model year slipped compared to the long 1984 numbers, but the second year of C4 was a 12-month year, and the total reflected more accurately the continuing interest in the car. In all, 39,729 cars sold, with base retail price set at $24,878. Fully optioned, the car took it to just shy of $30,000, another breakthrough level for America's sports car/luxury two-seater.

Model year 1986 brought patient enthusiasts a convertible Corvette near the middle of the year. Steve Kimball, writing in the February 1986 issue of *Road & Track* a month after production began at Bowling Green, waxed nostalgic: "What the Corvette convertible is—always has been—is a fantasy car of large proportions, head-turning shape, stunning acceleration and vivid romanticism. It is a car of dreams and it announced to the world like nothing else just what your dreams are.

"Has anyone ever forgotten his first ride in a Corvette convertible? Not very likely."

While the chassis had easily accommodated the Targa-type removable roof, the open car required substantial reinforcement. The bolt-in cross-member ahead of the engine was enlarged, as were the braces connecting that piece to the frame rails. In addition, Engineering fitted a large X-brace below the passenger compartment and added two more cross pieces behind the seats. Convertible buyers could not get the still-stiff Z51 suspension, but the 9.5-inch wheels were part of the convertible's own dedicated Z52 suspension. Chevrolet introduced the convertible in bright yellow Indianapolis Pace Car replica trim, at a $5,000 price premium over the coupes. Base convertible price was $32,507 while the base coupes retailed at $28,502. Clearly at such prices "base" cars were nearly fully equipped and the prices reflected the addition of a number of mandatory options. One new standard item was an intelligent ignition key, the PASS key, with an identification sensor. This was part of the Vehicle Anti-Theft System (VATS). Any other key fit into

Very few copies—reportedly only about 40—of the 1989 ZR1 slipped out of Chevrolet, each of these destined for the hands of journalists and reviewers.

The six-speed transmission, developed primarily for the ZR1, was introduced in regular production 1989 models. Another joint development project, this gearbox was co-produced by Chevrolet and Germany's Zandfabrik Freidrichshafen (ZF). It aided the Corvette in reaching necessary fuel economy numbers because it forced a shift from first gear to fourth under normal driving conditions.

No matter how good, how exciting, how well built or how well it performs, people will always find something in a new car to criticize. With the ZR1, it was the appearance. Some said it was too tame and too similar to the regular production versions.

the ignition except for the one coded to the car would fail to start and would disable the ignition for any attempt for three minutes. Performance improved once again with Z51-equipped coupes turning 0-to-60 times in 5.8 seconds and registering top speeds of 154 miles per hour. The convertibles were capable of nearly 140 miles per hour with the top down. For the 1986 model year, Chevrolet dealers produced 7,315 convertibles and 27,794 coupes.

For 1987, Engineering managed to boost the engine another 10 horsepower to 240, largely through the use of roller-bearing hydraulic valve lifters that lessened power lost to friction. In addition, the heads were redesigned to improve burn efficiency by centering the spark plugs in the combustion chamber. In an interesting twist of fate, Engineering adopted the same measures that stiffened the convertible up to Corvette standards for 1986 and applied them to the coupes. The Z51 suspension continued to be offered for the coupe (with manual transmissions) but not for the convertible, which carried over its own Z52 version. The convertible, in magazines tests, scored an impressive 0.87G lateral acceleration (the Z51 pulled 0.91G around the 216-foot diameter circle).

Straight-line acceleration continued to impress, with 6.3 seconds required to 60 miles per hour. Top speed for the ragtop was a theoretical 150 miles per hour. There was nothing theoretical about the sales increase for the convertible to 10,625 (at $33,647) while coupes slipped to 20,007, for a total of 30,632, down nearly 5,000 cars from 1986.

A new camshaft and cylinder heads added 5 horsepower to the output, up to 245 horsepower. Engineers mounted new lower-profile Goodyear Z-rated P275/40ZR-17 tires

(for speeds above 149 miles per hour) on 17-inch "Cuisinart" wheels, nicknamed for their resemblance to food processor blades. Handling wizards added rebound travel in the rear suspension, and they reconfigured front suspension geometry to improve directional control in severe braking conditions. Engineering changed front disc brake calipers to dual-piston versions that they wrapped around thicker rotors for more braking power and better brake cooling.

Because 1988 was the 35th anniversary, Design and product planners created a commemorative edition of 2,000 coupes, painted white with a white leather interior. Badges and medallions further identified the car.

The process of getting it nearly right at introduction and then getting it right and then more right and still more right after that, played out again with the 1988 and the 1989 models, as well. Production for 1988 dipped despite the steady improvement. Only 7,407 convertibles sold and barely twice that many coupes, 15,382; this brought the total to only 22,789 cars. The coupe base price crept up to $29,955, while the convertible sat at $35,295.

The ZR1, scheduled for 1989 wasn't quite ready, but Chevrolet did introduce two elements of the long-rumored car. One was a new six-speed manual transmission, built in collaboration with Germany's highly regarded Zandfabrik Friedrichshafen (ZF) that was operated, or more accurately overruled, by its own computer, the Computer Aided Gear Selection (CAGS). This was another Engineering effort to satisfy the EPA and the well-heeled performance enthusiast. A driver, accelerating at one-third throttle or less at speeds below 20 miles per hour with a fully warmed engine would find the CAGS restricted shifting by requiring the driver to

go straight from first to fourth gear. At 20 miles per hour in fourth, the engine idled along at 1,050 rpm. Simpler than the previous much-maligned and mostly misunderstood Doug Nash–designed 4+3 manual, it accomplished the same kind EPA numbers and, ultimately, the same kind of enthusiast disrespect. It did, however, make very clear the quality and quantity of torque that the 350-cubic-inch L98 engine produced. While zipping along at 65 miles per hour in sixth gear, the engine loafed at barely 1,600 rpm. Buyers who ordered the six-speed gearbox also got the engine oil cooler, heavy-duty radiator, and electric radiator cooling fan that were part of the Z51 package.

The other feature introduced for 1989 was the FX3 Selective Ride Control Delco-Bilstein electronic suspension. Chevrolet offered this only on Z51-equipped six-speed coupes. The four gas-filled Bilstein shock absorbers could be changed by a cockpit control that adjusted shock valving from "Touring" to "Sport" to "Performance" settings that would also vary within themselves based on the car's speed at the moment.

If those weren't enough technical marvels, the wheels of vehicles with RPO UJ6 now contained tire air pressure monitors that transmitted signals to warning lights on the instrument panel. If pressure fell below desired levels, the driver was warned. This system was intended for 1988 introduction, but last minute problems delayed it to 1989.

Base Corvette price, including the Z52 suspension/handling package, was $32,045 for the coupe. Sales reached 26,412 of the coupes and rose again to 9,749 convertibles. These were offered at $37,285 and a new $1,995 option RPO CC2, a removable hard top, reminded its 1,573 buyers of the best of the old days.

The very best of the good old days was delayed a year, postponed due to a slow start getting engine production up to speed. Option code ZR1 was first introduced in 1970 to designate a very finely done LT1 350-cubic-inch solid-lifter "racing" package. It was coming back, and it would represent an exceptional refinement of the sports car builder's art.

Those who had heard of options ZR1 and ZR2 would wonder why this was not ZR3? They would ask, as many did in 1970, if the initials meant "Zora's Racer?" because Duntov always preferred the small block in *his* sports car. But that was then; this was now. What it meant this time was "King of the Hill."

The new LT5 engine was part of the reason for the delay in introducing the ZR1 until the 1990 model year. The 350ci 90-degree V-8 had dual overhead camshafts and four valves per cylinder. It was jointly invented and developed by Chevrolet and Lotus Cars of England. The engines were assembled by Mercury Marine in Stillwater, Oklahoma.

167

chapter 14

Ferrari at a Fraction of the Price: 1990–1996

In late spring 1986, Don Runkle, then Chevrolet's 40-years-young chief engineer, met with *Road & Track* editors and talked about the future. He spent a long dinner laying out the future of Corvette. Not only as he hoped it would be, but largely as it eventually became.

"If you look at Chevy's heritage, in 1929 its ad, 'The six for the price of a four' was famous. The competition, which was only Ford, had a four-cylinder, while Olds, Cadillac or Buick had sixes or straight-eights. The Ford customer couldn't buy them. He didn't have enough money. Chevrolet brought the Buick, Cadillac and Olds stuff to the Ford customers," the GM exec said.

"We could obviously build a $100,000 Corvette and blow away the [Ferrari] Testarossa, but I'm not sure what the point of that exercise is. That just shows that you can do it. Our goal is to do it at 25-percent of the price."

Runkle described the battles that ensue within GM over the character of the Corvette. Half the decision makers see Chevrolet Division as GM's sales volume leader, and every Chevy product must carry that forward. The others argue that the Corvette is very profitable and it contributes much more than its share to the publicity and prestige not only of Chevrolet but of the corporation. Any high-tech development—engine, chassis, suspension—further reinforces Chevrolet's technological stature in the car world. Then Runkle told the editors of a project involving engineering expertise from Lotus and Chevrolet, an engine producing perhaps 400 brake horsepower.

"It is so expensive. Some people at Chevrolet don't think the additional volume it would generate would be worth the investment. My position is that this project has nothing to do with volume. This is a different thing. This is

to get the Corvette to be an unquestioned leader."

Within weeks of that dinner Runkle's prediction came closer to reality. On May 1, 1986, at about 2:30 A.M. in Norwich, England, engineers at Lotus fired up the V-8 engine known internally as the LT5—Chevrolet's brand new dual-overhead camshaft, four-valve per cylinder small block—for the very first time. They ran it up to 3,000 rpm, held it for 30 minutes, and then uncorked the champagne. It resulted from 18 months of discussion, design, and development. It was Chevrolet's first new V-8 in 21 years, since the Mark IV was introduced in 1965.

Getting it done took some unusual alliances, the recognition of values beyond costs, and the identification of who Corvette's next generation of competitors would be and what they would be doing.

The Corvette, as it moved up-market with the C4, attracted attention from German and Japanese car builders who believed that they could build a better Corvette. Porsche already used the Corvette as its benchmark for engineering the 944. Nissan, producing the fabled Z-cars, used Corvettes as CAD-CAM computer screen savers. Honda let it be known that its high-tech, midengined Acura NSX was meant not to show how dumb Detroit was but how smart Japanese technology had become.

Russ Gee, a director of powertrain engineering at Chevrolet-Pontiac-Canada (CPC), had investigated alternate powerplants for the Corvette. Everyone knew the engine was Corvette's only shortcoming. The small block V-8 had evolved steadily but undramatically since its introduction in 1955. Gee turbocharged V-6 engines, with an eye to midengine installations. There were problems with vibration and problems with Corvette owners' perceptions of any

The Callaway Twin Turbo bears a Corvette Regular Production Option code, B2K. These were first offered through a limited number of dealers in 1987. Fully assembled production cars were completed and shipped from Bowling Green to Callaway's shops in Old Lyme, Connecticut, for extensive modification underhood. Callaway's arrangement was founded on a handshake agreement with chief engineer Dave McLellan.

engine less than eight cylinders being un-Corvettelike. Early experiments with turbocharging Chevy V-8 engines yielded unacceptable fuel economy. (Those problems would be worked out later by Reeves Callaway.)

Lloyd Reuss directed development of the Cosworth four-valve head for the Vega while he was chief engineer. It wasn't too far a leap to consider similar heads for the V-8. Russ Gee began working on them in October 1984. A month later, Tony Rudd, managing director of Lotus, owned by GM at the time, came calling to offer his firm's engineering services; a plan was hatched to create four-valve, dual-overhead camshaft heads to fit Chevrolet's small block.

Production realities from the Bowling Green assembly line affected the design. The L98 engines were installed into the Corvettes from the bottom. The absolute maximum width of any engine had to fit within the frame rails. By April 1985, it was apparent that an L98 with taller, wider heads would not fit. Changing the assembly line was enormously expensive; changing the frame rails was worse. Engineers and project managers began to figure numbers in their heads. The most reasonable solution came down to creating an entire new engine, even with the add-on costs of re-engineering intakes, and every other piece that bolts onto the block.

Lloyd Reuss loaded his guns and went before GM Chairman Roger Smith, according to Anthony Young. Young, a thorough historian on the development of

The first Callaways were available only with manual transmissions and were not legal in California. For 1988, an automatic was offered and cars could be delivered in all 50 states. Just 184 cars sold in 1987, another 124 in 1988, only 69 in 1989, and just 58 in 1990.

When Chevy introduced Callaway's Twin-Turbo to dealers, the product planners already knew the ZR1 was coming. Callaway's acceleration to 60 miles per hour was only 4.6 seconds, to a quarter mile was 13.2 seconds, crossing the line at 109. Top speed was 175 miles per hour. By 1990, that was improved. Top end was up to 191 miles per hour, and 0-to-60 took only 5.1 seconds.

The 390-horsepower Twin Turbo went out of most dealerships at about $65,000. Just 58 sold in 1990. Before the 380-horsepower ZR1 arrived at about $59,000, Callaway owned the niche. However, similar to Chevrolet's direction with the ZR1, the Connecticut cars looked only subtly different from Corvette's regular production.

high-performance engines, reported on this project and the results in his 1994 book, *The Heart of the Beast: History of the LT5 V8 and ZR1 Corvette.* He learned that Reuss sold Smith on the benefits that this engineering would offer to other products over time throughout the entire corporate product line. He emphasized the growing Japanese threat. The Corvette meant as much to them as it did to GM; to the Japanese it was a target, not the technological and performance benchmark.

Smith understood and agreed. Engine development at GM took as long as six years. With the economy and GM's own financial condition threatening projects every day, Reuss, Gee, and Roy Midgley, chief engineer of the 90-degree V-type engines at CPC understood that all days off were canceled. Smith's funding could end at any moment; the further the project had gone the tougher it might be to turn off the cash flow. The project was designated the LT5; Runkle called it the King of the Hill.

Dave McLellan studied the performance characteristics of each exotic car Corvette owners would consider if they won the lottery. The new Corvette must hit 60 miles per hour in four to five seconds. The engineering managers knew that, with a 350-cubic-inch V-8, that would require at least 360 horsepower, 400 would be better—it would have a better ring to it. This new engine could not be a gas guzzler. It would be an engine designed from scratch, carrying over no parts from any existing GM engine. Then the tough part: He wanted a prototype engine running by May 1986, one in a car three months later. CPC made it clear to Lotus that this engine, which may only have a total production run of 6,000, would be treated the same as any engine expected to go into six million automobiles.

Once the LT5 project was approved, Chevrolet had to find a plant to manufacture it. It was too small a run for any GM facility, which meant outside vendors. Roy Midgley selected Mercury Marine in Stillwater, Oklahoma, because it had sophisticated computer-controlled manufacturing technology and it could engineer aluminum castings. After months of meetings and proposals, Mercury learned in mid-March 1986, that it was the supplier.

At this same time in 1986, Lotus began gathering parts with which to build the prototype from suppliers throughout Europe and the United States. Jerry Palmer's staff in Chevrolet 3 made sure that when owners opened John Cafaro's large hood, what they saw looked like an engine that produced nearly 400 horsepower. Some features should be apparent. Lotus engineers concluded that dual injection intake ports per cylinder were the best way to ensure optimum fuel mixing for performance and economy. On partial throttle, below 3,000 rpm, each cylinder used one inlet runner, one injector, and one inlet valve. The cam lobe for that valve provided mild timing with little overlap. A heavier foot signaled the

Performance statistics were all anyone needed to hear in order to lust after a ZR1. Racing from a standstill to 100 miles per hour and back took 14 seconds, barely longer than the standard L98-engined Corvette took to get to 100. Chevrolet hoped to sell 4,000 per year.

The LT5 aluminum block V-8 boasts dual overhead camshafts, four valves per cylinder and smooth, even, tractable torque and power. The engine is so strong that the six-speed ZF transmission mated to it is programmed to jump from first to fourth upshifting under routine driving conditions without any noticeable hesitation or balkiness. This allowed fuel economy of as much as 26 miles per hour on the highway.

Electronic Control Module (ECM) to open the butterflies in the second runners and turn on their injectors. Cam timing for the second intake valves was wilder. Palmer's designers created 16 distinct tubes running from the injection system's main plenum to the cylinders below. The dual-overhead camshafts were clearly outlined in sculpted cam covers.

By early 1987, Lotus was subjecting development engines to brutal tests. One durability test ran the engine alternately at peak horsepower speed for five minutes and then at peak torque speed for five minutes, alternating continuously for 200 hours. Cracks appeared in the cast crankshaft resulting in an expensive specification change to nitrided forged steel. Once that and other changes were made, the LT5 ran the test flawlessly; however, there were other problems threatening the LT5. Engineers fretted while Reuss fought hard for its very existence. GM was cutting budgets throughout CPC. Yet Roger Smith let it slip through unmolested. Months later, on Christmas Eve 1987, the first Mercury Marine preproduction prototype LT5 ran on MerCruiser's own dynamometer.

Starting in January 1988, Lotus was ready to assemble an engine out of production parts. There was still testing to do. It was clear the LT5 would not make a September 1988 introduction. Chevrolet management wanted to offer a warranty on the engine that necessitated it be right before it was

produced. GM would fully warrant the engine against any mechanical failure. If it broke, GM would replace the engine. That kind of reliability required some 2,000 design changes. Every moving part within the engine was balanced to tolerances common to Formula One racing engines capable of 14,000 rpm, not just the LT5's 7,000. At a press demonstration, Terry Stinson, LT5 project engineer at Mercury Marine, balanced a nickel on its edge on the engine plenum in a completed running car. It remained there, on edge, until he retrieved it.

The worldwide introduction took place in Geneva, Switzerland, in March 1989. It was a gratifying event for the crews at Lotus, Mercury Marine, and Corvette. But it was humdrum compared to the press launch at Riverside Raceway in September 1988, described by Anthony Young. While the project managers spoke during the media introduction, two Mercury engineers, Chris Allen and Ron Opszynski, starting with a short block, completely assembled an LT5, finished by the time Roy Midgley wrapped up the presentation.

"They had been rehearsing this for weeks," Young wrote, "performing like a two-man pit crew. They put their tools down just as Midgley finished his last sentence. Midgley asked Allen and Opszynski if the engine would start. Both gave a thumbs up. Midgley said, 'Gentlemen, start your engine,' Allen recalled vividly.

"Ron flipped the switch, and the engine turned over. I pulled the throttle linkage and when those throttle plates opened and everyone heard the engine roar to life, that was the moment. In that dark amphitheater camera flashes started going off, people started clapping and whistling—it was amazing."

Before the car was displayed in Geneva, Roy Midgley, chief engineer of V-8 passenger engines, had, by himself, built an engine too. First production engines built by Mercury employees came off their line on July 13, 1989. The engines produced 380 horsepower. Installed in the Corvettes, they propelled the cars to 60 miles per hour in 4.2 seconds and up to a top speed of 172 miles per hour. No one was disappointed.

Midgley and his crew started immediately to squeak more power out of it. Very subtle air intake modifications and improvements, revising cam timing, and reducing exhaust back pressure helped them get 405 horsepower for 1993. Even more impressively, they still cleared the EPA gas guzzler mark of 22.5 miles per gallon. With 405 horsepower and 180 miles per hour capability, it still measured 23.1 miles per gallon on the test cycle.

A car capable of 170 to 180 miles per hour needed brakes capable of hauling down this 3,000-pound-plus missile. Braking from 150 miles per hour was one thing. Coming down from nearly 200 was much more difficult. During early days of development before engines were ready, development mules were still narrow body Corvettes, not wide versions needed to accommodate Goodyear's new tires. Engineering built a 400-horsepower V-8 with nitrous oxide injection. This would get the car to top speed in the least distance to allow more runoff in case the brakes failed. Corvette racers Kim Baker and John Powell were hired to do handling and brake testing. In Powell's very first test, he had wanted to do a 0.50G deceleration test from maximum speed to get a feel for the car. Yet the calibration was incorrect and when Powell got on the brakes, he hauled the car down to a standstill at nearly 1.0G without any problem.

One of the biggest questions about this new LT5 King of the Hill package was if the body should look special. Should it have wings, spoilers, and scoops? Reuss wanted visual significance; Palmer argued for the opposite, telling Anthony Young, "The differences should be subtle. The only ones who really care are the Corvette people. They'll know." Palmer's staff built a mockup following Reuss' ideas; they incorporated many of them in the whole Corvette line-up for 1991. Only Palmer's understated widening of the rear of the car and squared-off taillights marked the LT5. The back end enlargement, 1.5 inches on each side, started with new outer door panels feathering in the additional size. It accommodated Goodyear's first 35 series Eagle road tire, ZR315/35-17 rears, mounted on 11-inch-wide wheels.

The final decision was what to call the car. "King of the Hill" was what it was, although a name such as this made people inside Chevrolet very nervous. It invited challengers to depose the King. There were other considerations, though. When Doug Robinson, the development manager of Corvette reexamined his target vehicles, he found Porsche's 928, 968, and 959, Ferrari's Testarossa and F40, and Lamborghini's Countach. Chevrolet hoped to sell this car to Europeans—it needed a name easily translatable. The heritage of the small block racing package introduced in 1970, the ZR1, had a nice ring to it.

Following Geneva's introduction and a wildly enjoyable media introduction through Switzerland and France afterward, Lloyd Reuss and his colleagues had to face another production reality. Only 84 preproduction prototypes, for engineering, media preview, and photography, were built but not sold as 1989s. On April 19, 1989, Chevrolet division notified all its dealers that the ZR1 option would not be available until model year 1990.

U.S. buyers had to be content with normal production Corvettes for 1989. This was no slouch, but by midmodel year, the enthusiast magazines had characterized the coming ZR1 as the second coming.

The 1989 models introduced the six-speed manual transmission and the FX3 adjustable suspension (a $1,695 option) developed for the ZR1. Dealers sold 16,663 of the

In celebration of his fifth year producing Twin-Turbo Corvettes, Reeves Callaway created a limited edition (no more than 50) Speedster. This was a car that gave everyone who wanted more flash and dazzle something to dream about. Callaway's staff designer Paul Deutschman created the sleek, startling appearance.

With twin Garrett Rotomaster Compact turbochargers at maximum boost of 12.3 psi, Callaway and his engineers pulled 450 horsepower out of Chevrolet's pushrod 350-ci V-8. Starting with the stock engine management system, Callaway's computer wizards worked with his engineers managing air flow to make this engine legal in all 50 states and the most powerful U.S. production powerplant.

coupes, base priced at $31,545, and another 9,749 convertibles at $36,785 base price. Total production reached 26,412.

Model year 1990 finally introduced the ZR1, a $27,016 *option* on top of the price of the $31,979 coupe. Some 3,049 buyers couldn't resist and paid $58,995 for the King of the Hill. At this price, it came in not at 25 percent of the price of Ferrari's Testarossa but at 33 percent and at 80 percent of the Porsche 928GT. The ZR1 beat both to 60 miles per hour by 1.5 seconds as well, making it an extraordinary value for its price. Due to gas-guzzler burdens, CAFE requirements, and EPA mandates, the LT5 was rated at 375 horsepower, down 10 from the prototype. Even so, Chevrolet engineers created another protection for ZR1 owners. This was the so-called "valet" switch. A key-operated limiter overrode the ECM; no matter what throttle position the parking attendant (or the neighbor or teenage offspring) might try, only the milder injection tube operated.

Still again, the base Corvette was quite a car. Engine management and breathing improvements increased L98 output to 245 horsepower; optional sport exhaust brought about another 5 horsepower, bringing the total to 250. Sound power of the Delco/Bose sound system, now with a compact disc player, doubled to 200 watts. Bosch introduced its ABS-II antilock braking system, which sensed the car's lateral acceleration and merged that sideways movement data to straight line braking information to determine how much tire slip to tolerate.

Design redid the interior for 1990, replacing the instrument panel (still, now a combination of LCDs, light shows, and analog dials) with a new console, door panels, and a driver's side air bag. A real, working glove compartment replaced the too-long-lived and seldom-loved breadbox.

Production in 1990 amounted to 16,016 coupes, including the 3,049 ZR1 buyers, and 7,630 convertibles (at $37,264), for a total of 23,646. Production in 1991 decreased to 14,967 coupes at a base price of $32,455. Convertible sales also slipped to 5,672 as prices jumped to $38,770. Among the coupes, 2,044 were ZR1s for which the price also increased by a substantial $4,676 to $31,683, or $64,138 for the second edition of the limited production coupes. Externally, Chevrolet made what many thought was a mistake in 1991 when the company changed the rear body panel of all standard coupes and convertibles to the squared taillights introduced on ZR1s in 1990. While the hotter car still wore the wider bodywork, 1990 owners had expressed pleasure when the subtle distinction was made and 1991 buyers made their discontent known when that uniqueness was taken away. Palmer's subtlety required a more critical eye in 1991.

Model year 1992 brought a number of changes, including a new LT1 small block powerplant, an electronic traction control system to more successfully get the car's power to the ground and keep it there, and a new Goodyear tire, the Eagle GS-C, to further aid in that task. The LT1

Rarity, especially at this level, breeds costs equally rare. The fully-optioned Callaway Twin Turbo coupe sold for slightly more than $81,000. The styling and engineering improvements to create the Speedster lifted the Speedster up to just about $150,000.

Dick Guldstrand, a racer with a longtime relationship with Corvettes, wanted to pay homage to the legendary Grand Sports of the 1960s. He did this first with a car he called the GS-80, a 375-horsepower Traco-engined car he produced from 1985 through 1990. When the Corvette ZR1 arrived, Guldstrand decided to go farther.

resurrected the legendary designation of the 370-gross horsepower small blocks from the early 1970s. Those engines ran on leaded premium to operate in 11.0:1 compression ratio environments. But the EPA changed all that. When the new engine arrived in showrooms, 20 years after the end of the first LT1, it produced 300 *net* horsepower and did that with high-octane unleaded fuel at 10.2:1 compression. On the street that meant 0-to-60-mile-per-hour times of 4.0 seconds—0.6 seconds off the ZR1 pace and three full seconds better than the 1972 pace. While the old LT1 probably would eke out 11 or 12 miles per gallon, the new engine, with 50 horsepower more than the L98, returned 17 miles per gallon city and 25 highway.

The Bosch Acceleration Slip Regulation (ASR) performed like its ABS (antilock braking system) in reverse, controlling wheel spin under acceleration, not braking. Meant to limit those "OhmyGod" moments, the ASR

worked like an instantaneously reactive, very intelligent limited slip differential. Coupled with Goodyear's new directional, asymmetrical P275/40ZR17 Eagle GS-C tires front and rear, Formula One and Indy racing car technology for wet as well as dry racing came to the street.

On July 2, 1992, many of the principals responsible for making the Corvette into what it became, gathered in Bowling Green for a celebration: The one millionth Corvette, a white convertible, drove off the line. It went a few blocks to its new home in the National Corvette Museum, less than 1 mile from the end of the Bowling Green assembly line.

The big news for 1993 was Corvette's achievement under the hood of the ZR1. Midgley's and McLellan's goal of 400-plus horsepower got to the dealerships. The intake valve head shape and the valve seat were subtly changed to improve fuel flow and overall breathing. The result of this microtinkering was a huge jump to 405 horsepower. With

The LT1 engine incorporated a new camshaft, cylinder heads, a higher compression ratio, and multiport fuel injection to achieve 300 horsepower compared to the previous 250 horsepower L98. The standing start quarter-mile required 13.6 seconds to reach 102.6 miles per hour. Top speed of the 3,223-pound coupes was reported to be 160.

Guldstrand replaced the standard Corvette transverse plastic springs with coil-over units to more easily adjust ride height. He replaced the ZR1 17-inch wheels with his own 18s, 10-inch wide in front, wearing Goodyear Eagle P285/35s, and 12 inches at the rear with 335/35R-18s in back. This provided him with nearly neutral handling and 0.95G lateral acceleration on a skid pad.

the replacement of Goodyear's Gatorbacks with its asymmetrical GS-Cs as introduced on the 1992 LT1, wet weather maneuverability improved at the modest cost of dry-pavement pure-brute acceleration. So 0-to-60-mile-per-hour times slipped 0.2 to 4.49 seconds.

Outside and inside the car, Chevrolet Division celebrated the 40th anniversary with an appearance option; RPO Z25 for $1,455 provided ruby red exterior paint and interior leather but had no effect on performance. Some 6,749 were produced. Total production crept up slightly to 21,590, in 5,692 convertibles (at $41,195 base) and 15,898 coupes (at $34,595). Only 448 were ZR1-equipped, still at $31,683 extra despite the improved engine.

The PASS key system introduced in 1986, was upgraded with the addition of a new Passive Keyless Entry (PKE). A tiny transmitter in the key fob signaled one of two receivers in the car body to open one or both doors and light the interior. Walking away with the keys in pocket or purse automatically locked the car and set the alarm, confirmed by a brief sound of the horn. With the key fob still in the car while walking away, nothing happens. No horn sounding is a reminder to return for the keys.

For 1994, Chevrolet and Corvette engineers continued their efforts at improvement. A safety-related change replaced the recently reintroduced glove compartment (with

Bosch's traction control system, Acceleration Slip Regulation (ASR) was introduced as standard equipment on all 1992 Corvettes. The ASR could retard engine ignition, apply brakes, or decrease throttle—all done electronically—to avert wheel spin. The system had a manual over-ride for those times when the driver desired shrieking noise and smoking tires.

The big improvement for 1992 was under the hood. The new LT1 engine produced 300 horsepower. With true dual exhausts (and catalytic converters), acceleration from 0-to-60 miles per hour took only 5.3 seconds.

its ill-fitting door) with a passenger-side air bag, and this provided the opportunity for an interior makeover. The interior studio redesigned the seats making them more comfortable to a wider variety of bodies. Goodyear introduced "Extended Mobility Tires" (EMTs), essentially run-flat rubber useful at 0 air pressure for up to 200 miles as fast as 55 miles per hour. A monitor on the instrument panel alerts the driver of low, or no, pressure. For a driver alone at night or in foul weather on a freeway in rush hour, there is no longer any risk. Corvettes still carried spare tires, jacks, and tire irons, and the EMT was available only on about 5,000 of the 1994 model year cars with either the FX3 option (with slightly softer springs) or the base suspension, but not the Z01 or ZR1.

Engineering and electronics engineers replaced the Engine Control Module (ECM) with a new Powertrain Control Module (PCM) to control not only the engine's new sequential port fuel injection, but the transmission as well. The new SPFI system instructed the injectors to work simultaneously with the engine firing order. This provided smoother idle, quicker throttle response, and it reduced exhaust emissions.

Production numbers for 1994 inched up again: Total Bowling Green output was 23,330 cars, of which 17,984 were coupes (base price $36,185) and 5,346 convertibles ($42,960, including the new glass back window with electric defogger). Only 448 ZR1s were sold, although the price of $67,443 was slightly less than previous years because more equipment was standard on the base car. The bleed-

through of engineering from the ZR1 to the LT1 had produced so good a car that with a few options (the G92 performance axle at only $50 and the FX3 electronic ride and handling option at $1,695) a buyer had as close to a ZR1 as most customers could measure. The extra 105 horsepower made the biggest difference in speed ranges very few owners ever saw, and insurance companies began to react to the ZR1 alpha-numeric the same way they had to muscle cars in the late 1960s and early 1970s.

For 1995, Corvette was once again the Indy 500 Pace Car. A wild dark-purple-and-white scheme was chosen and replicas were available to the public. The two-tone combination put off more people than it attracted; only 527 were produced. In total, 4,971 convertibles sold, at $43,665 base price (plus $2,816 for the pace car replica option). Only 448 ZR1s were delivered in 1995, as in 1994, adding to the total 1995 coupe sales of 15,771. The ZR1 price held while the coupe went up by a minimal $600 to $36,785. In anticipation of the next-generation Corvette's introduction, earlier scheduled for 1996, Chevrolet discontinued the ZR1 package at the end of 1995 model production. Even when management acknowledged that C5 would not be available until 1997, they held to the decision to drop the ZR1. Mercury Marine built the last LT5 engine in November 1993. The total ZR1 count was 6,939 from 1990 through 1995.

Cars fitted with Goodyear's EMT tire package had no need for a spare tire, jack, and lug wrench. For the 3,783 customers who ordered the $70 option, WY5, another $100 credit was available for taking the N84, a delete code that provided extra storage room and saved some weight.

Spy photos confirmed that C5, the code name for the next-generation Corvette, was coming and that 1996 was the final year for the C4. Customers wrestled with waiting for the new car, not yet completely known or buying the familiar. To make matters more difficult, Chevy released its new 330-horsepower LT4. Engineering used a new aluminum head design, new camshaft, and Crane roller bearing rocker arms, among other parts, to increase power output.

Externally, Designers and product planners created two packages with visual appeal. The first was a silver painted Collector's Edition, Z15, for $1,250. Besides color and special trim, it used the recently retired ZR1 wheels (but not the tires), also painted silver. More exciting visually was the Grand Sport package, RPO Z16. Only 1,000 of these were produced in either coupe or convertible form ($2,880 for the convertible option, $3,250 for the coupe). Coupes made use of the full ZR1 wheel and tire option, including the fat, squat P315/35ZR-17 rears, barely contained by add-on fender flares (not, however, by body panels as with the ZR1). Convertible Grand Sports took advantage of the tire package for the Commemorative Edition. Cars were painted Admiral Blue with twin white racing stripes centered on the car and bright red slashes across the left front fender,

Exterior appearance between 1991, 1992 (yellow coupe), and 1993 (aqua convertible) was virtually unchanged. These were body designs carried over into 1994 without noticeable modification. Chevrolet continued the practice of stretching Corvette body life out over a longer period while continuing to make improvements beneath the surface.

Production reached 21,590 cars in 1993. Base price on the 5,692 convertibles produced rose to $41,195. A total of 15,898 coupes were sold, starting at $34,595. Model year 1993 marked the 40th anniversary of Corvette, and 6,749 of the total production were delivered in Ruby Red.

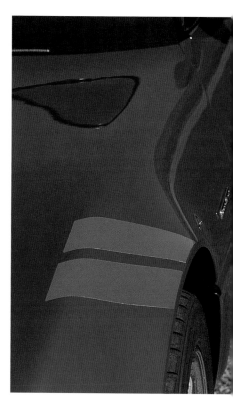

Only 17,167 coupes were produced during model year 1996. Chevrolet did as much as it could to maintain interest in the Corvette body style that every enthusiast knew was slated for replacement at year end. The Z15 Collectors Edition and Z16 Grand Sport Package, in both coupe and convertible models, were part of this effort.

Thirty years after Zora Duntov's racing Grand Sports were conceived as open roadsters for events such as Sebring, Chevrolet Division brought the designation back for a limited series of commemoratives. Called RPO Z16, only 1,000 were produced as convertibles or as coupes.

181

reminiscent of the identification slashes pit crews would mark on race cars to recognize one team driver from another.

The F45, "Selective Real Time Damping" replaced the previous FX3 with a new system that took road surface and suspension load inputs 60 times a second, altering shock characteristics with equal frequency.

The final C4 coupes sold for $37,225 base price, and Chevrolet built 17,167 of them while 4,369 convertibles moved out of showrooms, starting at $45,060 each. Total production was 21,536, including the Grand Sports and 5,412 Collector Editions. The new $1,695 LT4 engine option went into nearly a third of all the cars.

The fourth edition Corvette carried on for 13 years, another long run for a popular car. Chevrolet sold 368,180 of them, turning nearly $100 million in profit to General Motors. The car entered the era with few equals. It withstood attacks from Nissan's stylish front-engined 300ZX, from Acura's technological midengined NSX, from Mitsubishi's whiz-bang all-wheel-drive 3000GT VR-4, from Porsche's precise 959, 944, and 968, and from Detroit neighbor Dodge with its entertaining, Neanderthal 10-cylinder Viper. Lamborghini replaced its Countach with its Diablo, which for all its bravado represented only a slight advancement of the benchmark. Only Ferrari, with its race car-like F40 and F50, moved off into such rare space that few could come close. England's Gordon Murray with his $1 million McLaren three-seater F1 paid attention, but very few paid him.

Corvette's competitors came and went. And they kept on coming. And, probably to their chagrin, so would Corvette.

The Grand Sport took advantage of a new engine offered for 1996, the LT4. This was a 330 horsepower V-8 with new aluminum heads, Crane roller rocker arms and a different cam. It would be a one-year engine, optional throughout the Corvette lineup with manual gearboxes only, for $1,450. Another 6,359 of these engines were ordered beyond those fitted in the Grand Sports.

Grand Sport coupes, the RPO Z16 option, cost an additional $3,250 over the base coupe price. This was $370 more than convertibles, the difference being the addition of rear fender flares and wider, more expensive ZR1 rubber available for the coupes.

chapter 15

Like Seeing a Ghost: 1997

It first fluttered in the hearts of a few dedicated men in August 1988. At that time, it was meant to be released four years later, as a 1993 model, the 40th Anniversary Corvette. Between then and its eventual introduction, the next-generation Corvette, the C5, was slipped and picked up, blindsided and preserved by a cast of characters that ranged from some of the most brilliant and dedicated in modern auto making history to some whose motivations make some observers wonder whose side they really were on. The saviors broke rules or performed end runs to get money, find engineers, approve designs, build prototypes, and run development cars until they broke or froze or boiled. Then they found more resources to fix them and run them more. They produced this car despite the hard-fought efforts of others who seemed bent on making new rules, challenging and obstructing the car building process, stopping the car every chance they found.

Author James Schefter recorded the conception, birth, infancy, and battles that produced the new Corvette in his book, *All Corvettes Are Red*. The title comes from a quote from John Heinricy, Corvette racer, endurance record holder, and supervisor of C4 to the end of the program. Heinricy maintains that all other colors are just mistakes. Schefter's history offers a deep, dark view into GM and how the C5 struggled to life.

There were Titanic egos involved, an adjective that correctly described their size and, in some cases, their end. But they weren't the only ones that ended careers at GM; during what would finally be eight years to bring the new Corvette to market, thousands of employees left in the darkest days of the industry's economy. GM hemorrhaged people, engineers especially. So many left that at some critical periods, there were not enough to do the work. Engineering staffs at Ford and Chrysler swelled at this time; they had their pick of hundreds of experienced, qualified individuals bought out of their jobs at GM when it worried about impending bankruptcy. In the course of reinventing the Corvette, General Motors, which already had reorganized before C5 started, would reorganize itself again and again.

By 1988, Corvette's competition had changed. Porsche's cars started at $45,000, priced beyond consideration for Corvette buyers and those "affordable" front-engine cars had four-cylinder engines, capable of producing Corvette-like top speeds but not the sound nor the grunt-like acceleration. Japan was the biggest competition, producing cars whose prices were right in Corvette's ball park. Mazda's RX-7, Nissan's 300ZX, the Mitsubishi 3000, and the Dodge Stealth were on the horizon; Toyota had a new Supra coming. Acura's NS-X, while wildly different from the street-fighter-in-a-suit image of the ZR1, was sold for $10,000 less. General Motors gave Chevrolet Division $250 million to spend to develop a car that would take on all comers until at least the year 2000. Lloyd Reuss, GM executive vice president, shared with Corvette chief engineer Dave McLellan and Chevrolet Design studio chief Dave Palmer the goal of making a car that would *beat* all comers. Whatever had been good in 1988 must be great in 1993. There would be no back pedaling, only improving: performance, handling, body design, interior comfort, and baggage space would all be better. In 1989, Jim Perkins was in place as GM vice president and Chevrolet general manager. There were few men in his business more enthusiastic about automobiles.

In late spring 1989, however, the ground beneath GM began to shake. It was a financial earthquake and it was big.

The new car is referred to as the Fifth Generation Corvette, C5. This designation confused loyal enthusiasts at first who believed it was number six. For purposes of labeling, Chevrolet incorporated the 1953-through-1962 production cars under the group of the first-generation Corvettes.

Washington legislators and insurance industry lobbyists wrestled with automotive engineers and performance enthusiasts during the decades following the first gas crisis. Enthusiasts have won: the new aluminum block, LS1 350-ci V-8 engine produced 345 horsepower, the highest "net" rating ever from a Corvette engine. It is sufficient to get the car from 0-to-60 miles per hour in 4.7 seconds.

coupes, and 9,749 convertibles beyond break-even. Still, when the GM financial picture came clear before management's startled eyes in late fall, it looked like the Chevrolet-Pontiac-Canada (CPC) group, home of the Corvette, might lose $2.6 billion in 1990. At that point, the new Corvette was not just slipped. It was derailed, put on indefinite delay.

The Engineering buildings were located on the opposite side of the Warren campus from the design department. Corvette Engineering was led—*inspired*—by Dave McLellan, an innovative, imaginative creator who frequently left his staff alone to make his ideas happen. Roger Smith's off-hand remark in the Design auditorium not only resurrected midengines but also the all-wheel-drive ideas that dated back as far as XP-882. Nevertheless, expensive engineering had not proven beneficial to Chevrolet, as the ZR1 program had shown. Four-wheel drive was something Corvette would leave to car makers content to sell a few thousand cars a year, at prices and production levels not in Corvette's league.

But the C4 chassis was a problem that did need attention. Buyers complained about the high, broad door threshold they had to hurdle to enter the car. Corvettes, even the $60,000 ZR1, still rattled and squeaked; its competitors did not.

Advanced Vehicle Engineering was kicking around the idea of a "backbone" frame, a variation of a ladder-frame with main rails passing along the outside of the car, crossmembers tying one side to the other, and all of these pieces nailed into place by the central backbone, the tunnel that took the drive shaft from the engine to the rear axle. Forsaking the C4's modified unibody, if Engineering attached the body directly to the frame it could eliminate the bird cage, taking with it the high doorsill and all the body attachment points that eventually began to wiggle. Thin-walled steel, formed under high pressure, would have the strength of the old frame and much less weight.

Engineering liked the idea of hydroforming. The major frame rails for C5, one on each side, would be made from a single piece of rolled, welded steel. C4s were collections involving more than 20 separate pieces welded one to another. The slightest error in measurement, alignment, or welding would be magnified by the time the bird cage was added and the body attached. The new rails started out as 14-foot-long sheets 2 millimeters thick that were first rolled into a 6-inch-diameter tube and laser welded. The tubes were placed into a 200-ton press and filled with water at 7,000 psi. The water pressure would expand the tube like a sausage within the press, shaping and conforming the steel to the bends and rectangular channels of the mold. It would come out of the press 13 feet long and perfect. At the rate of 15 an hour, they'd also be identical.

While $250 million is a sizable sum, it is not enough to allow too many false starts or mistakes. Chuck Jordan's designers were headed in one direction, following Roger

Profit statements still looked rosy in press releases while the inside story was very black, or more accurately, very red ink. Yet, an off-hand remark by GM Chairman Roger Smith during a body design review of Corvette ideas sent the Design development and experimentation skewing off course toward midengine/transaxle configurations. It wasted a year.

Smith's message to the board would cost Corvette another year, moving the 1993 launch back to 1994, to contain costs, and Chevrolet would build a traditional Corvette, with engine in front, drive in rear. By midyear, more bad financial news slipped C5 again, to 1995.

Each reschedule resulted in new design directives. Chuck Jordan, GM's vice president of design since 1986, delivered the messages to an increasingly impatient design staff. John Cafaro, after his substantial contributions to C4 (its basic shape and its clamshell hood), was rewarded with the primary design authority for C5. As each quarter's financial statements brought another year's delay to introduction, however, he reminded anyone who'd listen that the Japanese, Corvette's target competitors, were not standing still and they could bring out the 300ZX in three years. This Corvette was on the way to being a six-year car.

Bean counters, of course, saw it differently. The division sold every Corvette it produced, unlike anything else it made. A 1986 tax law had ended the car loan interest deduction, effective 1989. All U.S. car makers felt it, except Corvette. The sports car continued to pump in $100 million in profit, something like $4,000 per car, each year after the initial investment was paid off. Production was paid for at 16,500 cars; in 1989 Chevy sold 16,663 coupes, 163

Smith's expedition into front cockpit, midengines, and rear drive, while Dave McLellan's engineers were strong advocates of front engine, midcockpit, rear drive. The delays forced the two sides to come together, to work side by side for the first time, to meet their goal.

When this remarkable collaboration was completed, it produced a car with resistance to twisting and flexing nearly *five times* as great as the C4. There was another benefit to this working arrangement and the adoption of the hydroformed chassis.

It produced a compromise that made everyone happy. The midengine Corvette idea died hard. Midengines offered the designers unparalleled opportunities to produce a car so different from anything before that Jerry Palmer and his staff fought hard to keep it alive. McLellan also liked pie-in-the-sky engineering projects. But Perkins and Reuss could not afford it. This backbone chassis, however, encouraged the idea of a transaxle, a one-piece transmission/differential mounted at the rear. The less costly variation moved the transmission to the back of the car and bolted it directly to the rear axle. This moved weight rearward, allowing a nearly 50/50 front-to-rear weight balance that midengines were all about anyway. The rear transaxle also removed the transmission bulk from the cockpit footwell, which allowed the entire compartment to move forward slightly, offering further design options. Relocating the cockpit opened up rear space for a real luggage compartment. Golf was the game of business. Japanese cars accommodated two golf bags. So would the Corvette. And all of this was very affordable. It was a compromise that left no losers.

In summer 1990, Bob Stempel, a former engineer and Chevy general manager, became GM chairman and Lloyd Reuss was to be president. They were friends of Corvette, supporters, but their hands were tied. They inherited a corporation on the ropes. Corvette took another hit, and it was a big one.

James Schefter reported that instead of the C5 for 1995, the board offered a thorough reskin for C4. C5 was slipped far back to 1998. But this presented other problems. For 1997, all passenger cars sold in the United States were to have side-impact protection, structure that could not be incorporated into the C4. This led to near battles within GM's boardroom. Some felt the Corvette was superfluous these days; no other American car maker had such a car and GM could no longer afford the luxury of this exclusive product. Others thought that Chevrolet, GM's car maker for the masses, was the wrong parent for such exclusivity—GM definitely needed it but felt the car should be its own marque altogether. Jim Perkins fought like his life depended on it, arguing that making the car its own product line would confuse and destroy customer loyalty. Killing off the showcase product would damage GM's image irrevocably. Corvettes were the source of more than half the stories originating

from GM except for financial analyses at that time; if it was killed, writers would look more deeply into how GM was so shaky it would kill its golden goose.

Perkins got a small budget to reskin C4. C5 stayed a 1998 introduction. Then Lloyd Reuss spoke; recognizing the side-impact requirements, he reinstated the budget for the C5, for a new body, backbone chassis, and now for a 1996 launch. C5 would be introduced first as a Targa-roof coupe. Then in 1997, a full convertible with trunk and an entry-level, fixed-roof coupe—a $25,000 to $30,000 concept close to Perkins' heart, a "boy-racer" he nicknamed "Billy Bob"—would arrive.

But first new profit and loss statements for the corporation arrived. CPC lost $3.3 billion, not the $2.6 billion predicted. Numbers for 1991 were revised to suggest, at least in whispers, that GM could be bankrupt sometime in 1991. Roger Smith's reliance on separate plants for separate vehicles and high-tech robots to replace low-tech people made GM vulnerable when sales dropped. Investments in expensive equipment and factories dedicated to only one car model could not quickly be refitted to produce others. GM's profitable lines suffered from lack of capacity while others just suffered. Corvette's budget was cut, the car was slipped once more. In 1991, GM lost $4.5 billion; Lloyd Reuss was relieved of duty by new President John Smith. Bob Stempel, paralyzed by the scope of the disaster he inherited, resigned in October 1992, and John Smale replaced him as board chairman. Corvette's budget was cut, and the car slipped once more. The proposed 40th Anniversary 1993 C5 would

Designers started with clean paper. Wheelbase was stretched 8.3 inches to 104.5, but overall length grew just 1.1 inches to 179.6. This provided a more comfortable ride, more stable handling, and more interior space. Yet overall weight dropped by 69 pounds. Tires were narrowed to accommodate improved Cd goals. The C5's 0.29 is the lowest of any gas-powered car available in the United States.

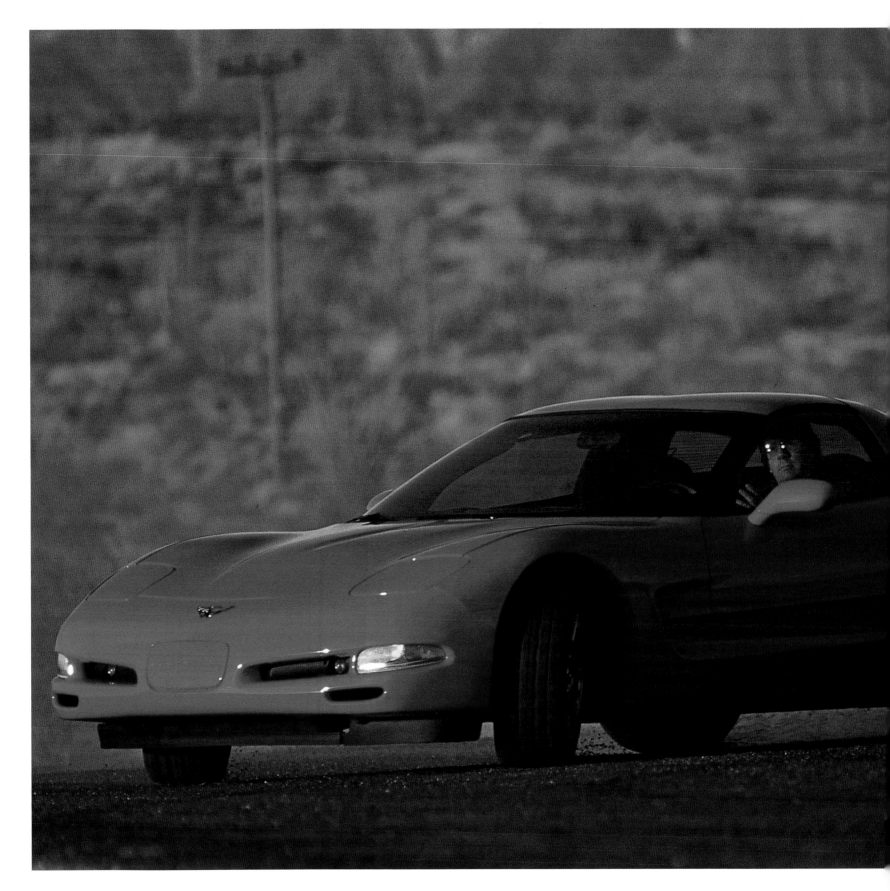

now appear in 1997. Engineers were told to find a way to retrofit 1997 side impact to the C4 as a worst case scenario.

Following Stempel and Reuss out the door, Dave McLellan retired in August, replaced by Cadillac's chief engineer, Dave Hill, an engineer with McLellan's brilliance but with far greater management and performance skills. Chuck Jordan retired in October, replaced by European design boss Wayne Cherry as administrative boss and by Chevy design chief Jerry Palmer as director of design for North American Operations (incorporating CPC as well as Oldsmobile, Buick and Cadillac divisions).

According to Schefter, the first driveable C5 test vehicle was a $1.2 million mule called CERV-4. Soon after, there was a half-price copy, CERV-4b. These 1993 C4 bodies were set on C5 rails and ran around Milford or GM's Desert Proving Ground in Mesa, Arizona. They were indistinguishable except that they had a trunk. There was scarcely any money to create these most necessary first cars, so Jim Perkins discretely funneled Chevrolet money into the sports car program he'd fought so hard to preserve.

Following the CERVs would come "alpha" and then "beta" test cars, each series with close-to-correct C5 bodies, all heavily disguised. These were each built more closely to production specifications. Then came prototypes, nearly perfect from an engineering and design point of view, fabricated from preproduction versions of production parts. Once those had been devoured by testing, the next step was prepilot cars, the first ones actually assembled in Bowling Green, starting in August 1996. "Pilot" cars, the very first salable production vehicles, were begun a month later.

The two CERVs used C4 engines and existed primarily to examine the chassis. They got cobbled-together interiors to test heating, ventilation, and air conditioning. The new powerplant for C5, known as the Gen III, was an all-new adaptation, the third generation of the decades-old Chevy small block. Responses from thousands of owner—and customer—surveys reinforced another lesson from the ZR1: Corvette owners wanted torque, not turbos or superchargers. They saw no need to pay for four-valve heads with dual-overhead camshafts. Engineer Dave Hill liked the ZR1's LT5, and he also liked his former division's 32-valve Northstar; but he was a realist. He knew pushrod engines were not as tall as multiple overhead-valve and cam engines. A low hood improved forward visibility, long a complaint, and it was essential to achieve their aerodynamic drag coefficient targets, crucial to meeting its fuel consumption goals.

The Gen III engine would be cast in aluminum to save weight. Engineering set a target weight of less than 3,500 pounds for the car with full tanks, two passengers, and luggage. Every pound of weight affected consumption, tire, brake, and engine wear, shortened shock absorber life, and put additional strain on chassis and driveline components.

Adoption of a rear-mounted transmission, coupled to the differential, settled weight balance at 51.4 percent front, 48.6 percent rear. Chevrolet claims lateral acceleration of 0.93G, the benefit of a new Short-Long Arm (SLA) rear suspension and better balance. Tires are P245/45ZR17s front and P275/40ZR18s rear.

This car was introduced on January 3, 1997, following a seven-year-long secret development program. In the process, designers and stylists looked at every piece and part of the existing cars and found ways to eliminate nearly 1,500 of them. For model year 1998, Corvette will introduce a full convertible model to supplement the first-year C5 coupe with its removable roof panel.

Worse than that, it slowed performance. Engineering developed research figures equating improved acceleration time with increased sales. Weight became an obsession.

When it all came together, despite the enormous obstacles in budgeting and financing, the monumental upheavals in management that interrupted thought processes and concept consistency, it worked. The C5, wrapped in John Cafaro's slippery body, measured 0.293cd in the wind tunnel, the lowest of any production vehicle made anywhere except for GM's own electric vehicle, the EV1. With its twin gas tanks straddling the rear axle and new Goodyear run-flat Extended Mobility Tires requiring no spare (the rears 1 inch wider than those of the 1996 C4's), the C5 offered 25 cubic feet of cargo space. This was larger than Cadillac's largest full-size sedans. Because of the central tunnel and rigid side rails, Engineering developed the lightweight floor pan of composite material sandwiching balsa wood in the center between plastic layers. This resisted temperature intrusion and vibration better than previously selected foam core. Balsa cost more, but Hill had decided early on that there was money to spend to make the car lighter or better. Something that did both offered a bonus.

A rigid parts sourcing and pricing system was invented by Jose Ignacio Lopez (who would later be accused of taking his innovations to Volkswagen, initiating a huge scandal). Hill's engineers looked at every single part in the C4 and went after anything better, lighter, or simpler. Through Lopez' system they had not only all GM parts to shop from but every auto part from any maker of any car in the world. Engineering found ways to eliminate more than 1,400 separate parts, each piece costing from fractions of a cent to many dollars. Eliminating these parts also cut 69 pounds from the 1996 C4 weight. John Cafaro's body, formed in plastic not fiberglass, saved weight as well. C5 uses sheet molded compound (SMC) and reaction injection molded plastic (RIM). These technologies produced lighter, stronger, and more rigid panels. Cafaro's giant clamshell hood from the C4 was abandoned for 1997; in creating the C5, Engineering examined not only the cost to buy the car but also the ongoing costs of ownership. Insurance companies factored in replacement parts and labor charges when establishing premium rates. The large hood with bonded fenders made the C4 expensive to repair. The C5 fenders are bolted onto the frame.

The rear suspension no longer relied on the half-shafts to perform suspension functions because new upper control arms locked the rear wheels into place much more accurately. The transverse fiberglass springs on C5 were softened compared to those on the C4, a byproduct of the stiffer backbone frame. This allowed a better ride plus improved tire contact with the road despite surface changes.

The LS1 GEN III engine produced 345 horsepower, 15 more than the 1996 C4's top-option LT4. This moved the car from 0 to 60 miles per hour in 4.7 seconds with the six-speed manual gearbox. Yet EPA fuel economy numbers were published as 18 city/29 highway miles per gallon. Chevy quoted a top speed of 172 miles per hour.

When the car was introduced to enthusiast magazine writers at Road Atlanta in November 1996, it was a universal love fest. Writers long critical of Corvette and those forever in love agreed that it was a great car to drive, an immense improvement over its predecessor, and it had, in every measure, moved the benchmark for sports cars far along the bench. Its projected price in the area of $40,000 set it in competition with BMW's six-cylinder 189-horsepower Z3 roadster, Mercedes-Benz's long-awaited 185-horsepower supercharged four-cylinder SLK, and Porsche's much anticipated 201-horsepower flat six-cylinder Boxster. The new Corvette matched them in style, yet it outhandled them on the skid pad, outaccelerated them to 60 miles per hour and beyond, matched them in braking, and outdistanced them in the driving range. It provoked admiring prose.

Kevin A. Wilson, writing in the January 6, 1997, *Auto Week*, said, "Forget understatement. This car is a blast to drive! That is a judgment shared by both acknowledged Corvette-o-philes and hard critics of earlier Corvettes." *Automobile* magazine's David E. Davis—who had been a Campbell-Ewald agency writer and penned the great ad that read: "Twice A Day He Takes A Vacation," referring to the commuter who accomplished those miles in a Corvette—wrote about this new Corvette, "We have driven the Ferrari 456GT and 550 Maranello, the Dodge Viper GTS, all the Porsches, the Jaguar XK8, and the Aston Martin DB7, and the 1997 Corvette C5 is a legitimate contender in their league. We particularly admire the fact that Chevrolet has developed this car for useful performance on real roads, rather than skidpads. . . . The '97 Corvette C5 is a home run in every way."

Road & Track's Ken Zino used a word rarely associated with Corvettes before the C5 when he wrote: "The Corvette has been reborn with poise, while still advancing its sharp performance characteristics that have kept true believers happy for so many years."

Great prose generally is inspired by strong emotions, clear thoughts, or idyllic visions. Car enthusiasts know that sometimes, too, it has been motivated by great automobiles.

In the November 1955 issue of *Esquire* magazine, Barney Clark published great prose, writing about a car current at that moment. His words were timeless. That they fit more contemporary emotions—or automobiles—is evidence of Clark's skill. He wrote, "Years ago this land

knew cars that were fabricated out of sheer excitement. Magnificent cars that uttered flame and rolling thunder from exhaust pipes as big as your forearm, and came towering down through the white summer dust of American roads like the Day of Judgment.

"They have been ghosts for 40 years, but their magic has never died. And so, today they have an inheritor—for the Chevrolet Corvette reflects, in modern guise, the splendor of their breed.

"It is what they were: a vehicle designed for the pure pleasure of road travel."

Some things never change.

Index